AFTER THE FAMINE

The Irish Family Farm in Eastern Ontario, 1851–1881

The Irish Famine saw hapless Irish citizens starve to death and die of disease, while the population of its neighbour, England, lived in relative bounty and apparent apathy. *After the Famine* investigates the subsequent emigration of many surviving Irish to Eastern Ontario and tells the story of how, despite hardships, the Irish in Canada managed to survive and prosper after fleeing tragedy. The author explains how the Irish adapted to their new land, and how we might account for their triumph as farmers under somewhat less than favourable environmental conditions.

Examining their successful farming life in rural Ontario through their agricultural performance, changing family structures, and farming adaptations, this book is a must-read for anyone interested in the fate of the Irish after their greatest calamity.

EDWARD J. HEDICAN is a professor emeritus at the University of Guelph.

After the Famine

The Irish Family Farm in Eastern Ontario, 1851–1881

EDWARD J. HEDICAN

UNIVERSITY OF TORONTO PRESS
Toronto Buffalo London

© University of Toronto Press 2020
Toronto Buffalo London
utorontopress.com

ISBN 978-1-4875-0555-4 (cloth)
ISBN 978-1-4875-2384-8 (paper)
ISBN 978-1-4875-3230-7 (EPUB)
ISBN 978-1-4875-3229-1 (PDF)

Library and Archives Canada Cataloguing in Publication

Title: After the famine : the Irish family farm in eastern Ontario, 1851–1881 / Edward J. Hedican.
Names: Hedican, Edward J., author.
Description: Includes bibliographical references and index.
Identifiers: Canadiana (print) 20190216042 | Canadiana (ebook) 20190216190 | ISBN 9781487505554 (hardcover) | ISBN 9781487523848 (softcover) | ISBN 9781487532291 (PDF) | ISBN 9781487532307 (EPUB)
Subjects: LCSH: Irish – Ontario – Admaston (Township) – History – 19th century. | LCSH: Immigrants – Ontario – Admaston (Township) – History – 19th century. | LCSH: Farmers – Ontario – Admaston (Township) – History – 19th century. | LCSH: Irish – Ontario – Admaston (Township) – Social conditions – 19th century. | LCSH: Immigrants – Ontario – Admaston (Township) – Social conditions – 19th century. | LCSH: Farmers – Ontario – Admaston (Township) – Social conditions – 19th century. | LCSH: Admaston (Ont. : Township) – History – 19th century. | LCSH: Ireland – History – Famine, 1845–1852.
Classification: LCC FC3100.I6 H43 2020 | DDC 971.3/810049162009034–dc23

University of Toronto Press acknowledges the financial assistance to its publishing program of the Canada Council for the Arts and the Ontario Arts Council, an agency of the Government of Ontario.

Canada Council for the Arts
Conseil des Arts du Canada

ONTARIO ARTS COUNCIL
CONSEIL DES ARTS DE L'ONTARIO
an Ontario government agency
un organisme du gouvernement de l'Ontario

Funded by the Government of Canada
Financé par le gouvernement du Canada
Canada

And as I was green and carefree, famous among the barns
About the happy yard and singing as the farm was home ...
Oh, as I was young and easy in the mercy of his means,
Time held me green and dying
Dylan Thomas, *Fern Hill* (1945)

During that baleful year, 1847, there poured into Canada the most polluted as well as relatively the most swollen stream of immigration in the history of the country.
Gilbert Russell, *American Historical Review* (1937)

From famine and death, the most exalted object which we are capable of conceiving, namely, the production of the higher animals, directly follows.
Charles Darwin, *On the Origin of Species* (1859)

Famine seems to be the last, the most dreadful resource of nature.
Thomas Malthus, *An Essay on the Principle of Population* (1798)

Sleep now, O sleep now,
O you unquiet heart!
James Joyce, *Chamber Music* (1907)

Contents

List of Maps, Figures, and Tables   ix
Preface   xi
Acknowledgments   xiii

1 Introduction   3
2 Theoretical Perspectives on Farm and Family   35
3 The Agricultural Conditions of Renfrew County   62
4 Land Use and the Allocation of Resources   77
5 Measuring Agricultural Performance   107
6 Population and Family in Transition   128
7 The Irish Family and Household   159
8 Conclusion   176

Notes   199
References   209
Index   225

Maps, Figures, and Tables

Maps

1 Location of Renfrew County, Eastern Ontario   xv
2 Map of Renfrew County, 1888   xvi
3 Map of Admaston Township, 1879   xvii

Figures

1 Land use in Admaston Township, 1851   81
2 Land use in Admaston Township, 1861   82
3 Land use in Admaston Township, 1871   83
4 Household variation in labour intensity, Admaston Township, 1851   120
5 Household variation in labour intensity, Admaston Township, 1861   121
6 Household variation in labour intensity, Admaston Township, 1871   122
7 Irish population pyramid, Admaston, 1851   130
8 Irish population pyramid, Admaston, 1861   131
9 Irish population pyramid, Admaston, 1871   132

Tables

1 Length of growing season, Southern Ontario   71
2 Wheat production, Admaston Township, 1851–71   86
3 Oat production, Admaston Township, 1851–71   88
4 Potato production, Admaston Township, 1851–71   90

5 Other crops grown, Admaston Township, 1851–71 91
6 Livestock production, Admaston Township, 1851–71 96
7 Crop production, Admaston and All-Ontario, 1851–71 99
8 Livestock production, Admaston and All-Ontario, 1851–71 101
9 O'Hare household, Admaston Township, 1851 112
10 Average household variation in workers' productive intensity, 1851–71 113
11 Household variation in labour intensity, Admaston Township, 1851 117
12 Household variation in labour intensity, Admaston Township, 1861 118
13 Household variation in labour intensity, Admaston Township, 1871 119
14 Household surplus labour capacity above Chayanov norms, 1851–71 124
15 Irish population by age and sex, Admaston, 1851 130
16 Irish population by age and sex, Admaston, 1861 131
17 Irish population by age and sex, Admaston, 1871 132
18 Age categories, percentage of population, Cavan (1841) and Admaston (1851–71) 134
19 Mean marriage age, Cavan (1841) and Admaston (1851), by farm size 137
20 Ratio of children to adults, Cavan (1841) and Admaston Township (1851–71) 139
21 Composition of Irish households, Admaston Township, 1851–81 144
22 Mean family and household size: Cavan, Ireland, and Admaston, Ontario, 1821–71 167
23 Farm size compared to mean household size: Admaston, Ontario, 1851–71 170

Preface

The Irish Famine of the late nineteenth century is one of those unprecedented events in human history that seems to defy comprehension and description. Australian author Thomas Keneally (1998) called it *The Great Shame*. Keneally meant more than the imponderable figures of death and disease – between 1841 and 1922 Ireland's population dropped in half from almost nine million – but also the whole history of suppression, the pernicious Penal Laws, the rise of the Irish Brotherhood, the failed uprising of the Young Irelanders, and so on, into more modern history with the IRA bombings, the "Troubles," and further suffering. Cecil Woodham-Smith's (1962) *The Great Hunger* popularized the plight of the Irish in the 1840s to a wide audience. Thomas Gallagher's (1989) dramatic account of the Great Famine and the subsequent Irish diaspora touches on similar themes of protest, famine, and uprising in the subtitle to *Paddy's Lament*: "Prelude to Hatred."

The Irish Famine and its aftermath continue to generate interest among scholars and popular writers from many points of view. This book is the result of my own personal processes of discovery as much as it has been a consequence of intellectual curiosity. I've always wanted to find out more about my Irish roots, but my parents could not tell me much, probably because they did not know much themselves. We had this family myth about "two brothers coming over from Ireland. One was born on the boat or shortly after. One brother went to America and the other stayed in Canada." Admittedly, this story is not much to go on.

It all began by accident when I was searching through our university library for material on a topic quite different than that which eventually took hold of my scholarly imagination. My hand chanced to fall upon an old leather-bound tome entitled *An Index to the Act or Grant Books and Original Wills of the Diocese of Dublin from 1800 to 1858*, published in 1899. I quickly leafed through the index to find the following entry:

"Hedican, Bernard, pensioner, Chelsea Hospital and Quebec, Canada, 1835, W[ill]."

From that point on I was hooked. Before long I had booked a flight to Ireland, where I searched through archives, library holdings, headstones in graveyards; interviewed local historians; and visited genealogy centres, mainly in Counties Clare, Kerry, and Limerick. I was never able to find out about the fate of my namesake Bernard. At the National Archives in Dublin I was told that most of the historical records had been destroyed during the Irish Civil War of 1921–2. The archivist told me, rather sardonically, that many people in Ireland would rather have a free country than an archive.

Upon my return from Ireland, I was approached by the usual number of upper-level undergraduate students wishing to do what are colloquially called "reading courses." There were too many students to accommodate on an individual basis so I held a meeting to discuss a program of action. I told them about my trip to Ireland, and they indicated that they wanted to "do real research," not just read books. These meetings evolved into what we began to call "the Irish Study Group."

At about this time I had discovered that a relative of mine had settled in Admaston Township, Renfrew County, just after the Great Famine. A plan of action was developed. Some students would start with the 1851 census of Admaston, listing the names of the various families and their land holdings on their laptops, which would make placing the names in alphabetical order possible. Next, they would proceed to the other censuses of 1861 to 1881. In the meantime, other students searched for journal articles, books, and other publications relating to Irish immigration to Canada, itemizing each piece of research with a brief abstract. Remaining students did some brainstorming, devising clever ways that the incoming data could be organized into theoretical arguments. Each week we met in a round table fashion, with each group reporting on their findings to the other students.

Eventually there was enough data gathered from 1861 to 1871 to formulate an academic paper, which was eventually published in the prominent anthropology journal *Ethnology*. The name of each student was duly recorded as making a significant contribution to the research underpinning the article and each student received a copy of the paper. I told the contributors that in twenty or thirty years from now they could show their children their names in a publication in a university library. Needless to say, they were all pleased. So far as I was concerned, the students could collect far more data than I would able to do in one academic career, but most of all we were having fun "doing real research."

Acknowledgments

I wish first to acknowledge the contributions of those University of Guelph students who contributed in such a significant manner to the present study: namely, Shannon Clay, Sonya Djurakov, Tara Hedican, Brigette Marcotte, Sarah Van Norman, Emma Norton, and Rowena Ridder. A special thanks to Janice Hicks, our departmental computer specialist, who completed the various figures for this book. In addition, as I have also indicated at various places in the footnotes, I am indebted to the many contributions, insights, conversations, and documents made available by Carol McCuaig, the eminent author and Renfrew County historian.

I also wish to express my appreciation to the many helpful people who provided information for this study from the National Archives of Ireland, the National Library of Ireland (especially the Genealogy Service Room, which houses the Tithe Applotment Books, 1823–38, and the Primary Valuation of Ireland, commonly referred to as Griffith's Valuation, 1848–64 and the many parish registers), and the Registry of Deeds, all of which are situated in Dublin. There are also many heritage centres situated across Ireland. The one most useful for my purposes was the Clare Heritage and Genealogical Centre, Church Street, Corofin, Co. Clare. The County Clare Roman Catholic Church Records are available on LDS microfilm. The records most useful for this study were those from Clonloghan (1828–86), Kilmihil (1849–80), and Kilmurry (1839–80). *The Clare Champion* (www.clarechampion.ie) was also useful for our search. Similar records can also be found for Counties Kerry and Limerick and, for that matter, for most of Ireland.

In Ontario, particularly useful was the Ontario Land Registry Office, Renfrew Division #49, situated in Pembroke. In addition, records can be purchased for a nominal fee from the Upper Ottawa Valley Genealogical Group, also in Pembroke. Especially important for the present research has been the information housed in the Heritage Renfrew Archives, Renfrew, Ontario (email: renarch@renc.igs.net). Of course, not to be overlooked are the various genealogical sites, such as Ancestry.com, Rootsweb.com, wikitree.com, familytreemaker.com. The National Library and Archives of Canada (www.collectionscanada.gc.ca/databases) was also consulted. I am particularly indebted to the helpful staff of the National Archives for their patience in searching through the Canada West Census data, especially as this pertains to the agricultural census of Renfrew County, for the time periods discussed in this book.

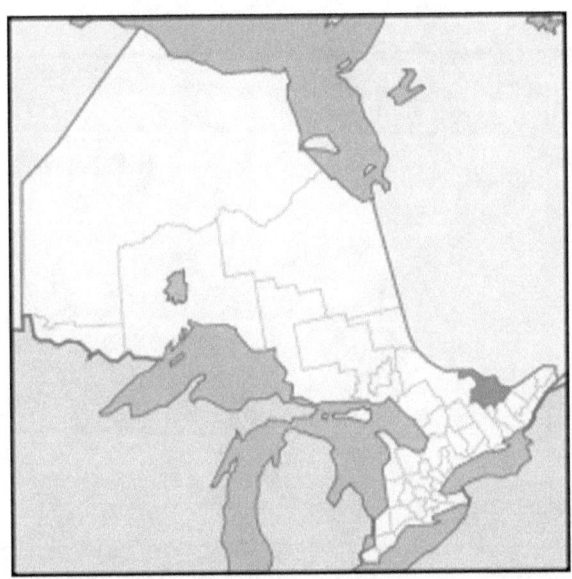

Map 1 Location of Renfrew County, Eastern Ontario

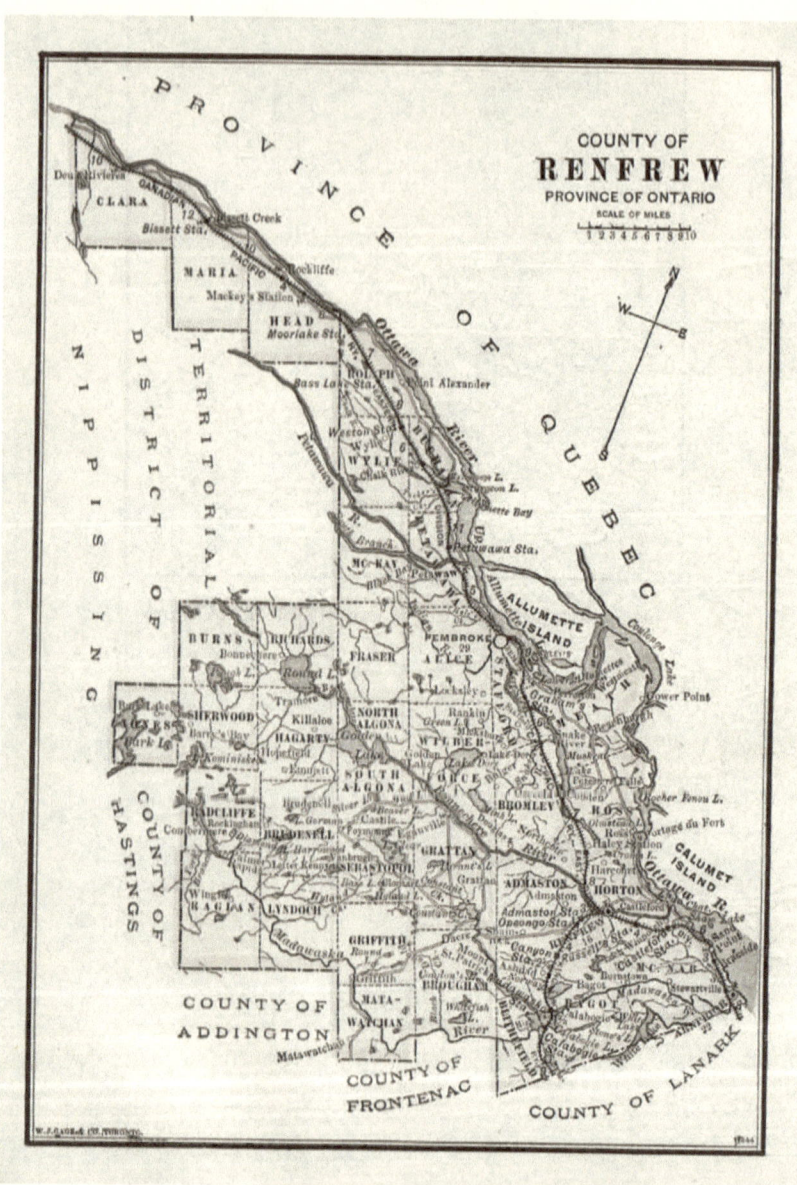

Map 2 Renfrew County, 1888

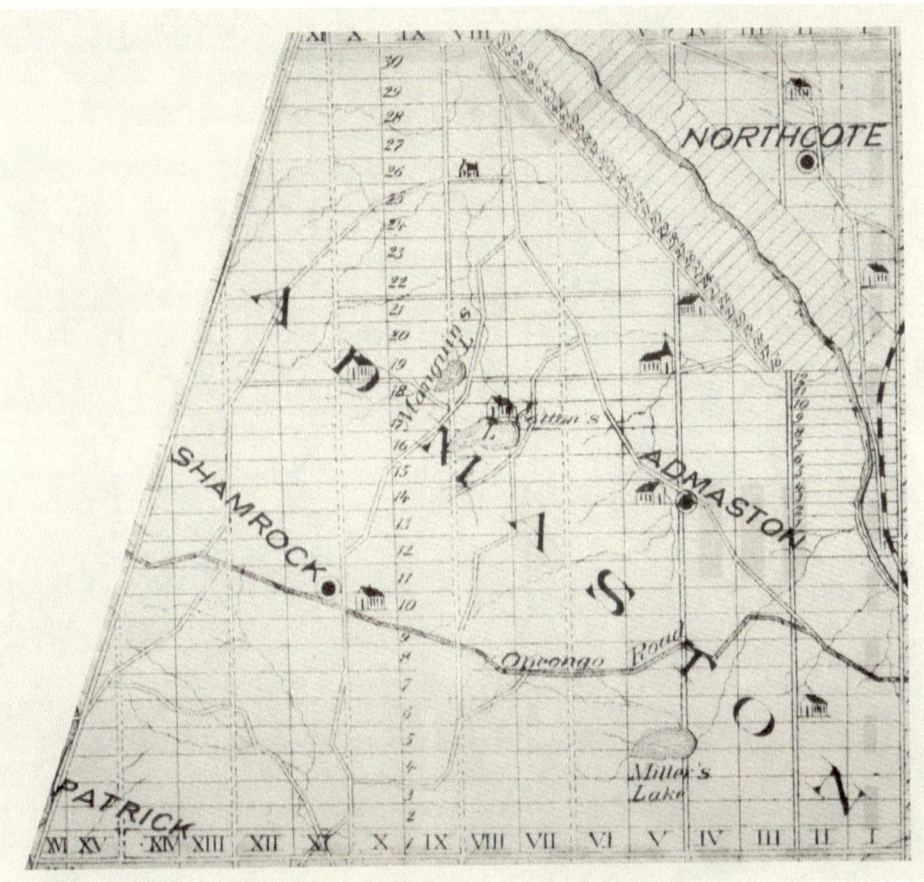

Map 3 Admaston Township, 1879

AFTER THE FAMINE

The Irish Family Farm in Eastern Ontario, 1851–1881

Chapter One

Introduction

This book examines the history of the Irish farming community of Admaston Township, situated in Renfrew County in the Ottawa Valley, over several decades in the period following the Great Famine in Ireland. Between 1845 and 1849, due to the failure of the potato crop, Ireland suffered one of the greatest tragedies that could befall a nation: millions of its citizens starved to death or were displaced. Meanwhile in neighbouring Britain, itself largely complicit in this disaster through centuries of social, economic, and political domination, many lived in relative bounty and showed remarkable indifference to the fate of the hapless Irish people. The English overlords enjoyed the fruits of Ireland's agricultural production, and then mostly turned a blind eye to the misfortune of their neighbours.

The research that is discussed here illustrates how the Irish managed to adapt to their new land, despite the many hardships that most other settlers no doubt also had to cope with, and how we might account for their success as farmers under less than propitious environmental conditions. Surely one of the most horrific narratives of European history concerns the Irish Famine, the unimaginable loss of life from starvation and disease, and the subsequent emigration to many parts of the world. The question that this research asks is, How did the Irish in Canada manage to survive after fleeing such a tragedy?

The aim of this book, then, is to attempt to explain how the Irish immigrants not only endured but also managed to flourish in the aftermath of the Famine once arriving in Ontario, then called Canada West. The Irish immigration to Canada has been well covered by historians. One can hardly begin reading about this history without becoming familiar with the names of Donald Akenson (*The Irish in Ontario*, 1984), Catherine Wilson (*A New Lease on Life*, 1994; *Tenants in Time*, 2009), Bruce Elliot (*Irish Migrants in the Canadas*, 2004), John Mannion

(*Irish Settlements in Eastern Canada*, 1974), Don Mackay (*Flight from Famine*, 1990), and Cecil Houston and William Smyth (*Irish Emigration and Canadian Settlement*, 1990), to name a few of the more outstanding scholars in this field. I find no fault with the work of these eminent specialists and in fact would highly recommend them. However, with such a complex phenomenon as the post-Famine settlement of the Irish in Canada, many more perspectives are surely welcome.

As an anthropologist I find that the Irish settlement in Canada is a particularly intriguing area of research, but most of my colleagues have avoided this subject for whatever reason. It would be hard to envision that this is the result of those in another discipline regarding this conceptual territory as their private preserve. And it cannot be because anthropologists are latecomers to the study of history, since, as I amply demonstrate later on, there are over a century's worth of historical studies in the discipline.

In terms of Irish studies by anthropologists, the names of Marilyn Silverman and Philip Gulliver are prominent through their historical anthropology of Thomastown in County Kilkenny, *Merchants and Shopkeepers* (Gulliver and Silverman 1995), and their collection of essays entitled *Approaching the Past* (Silverman and Gulliver 1992). In addition, Thomas Wilson and Hastings Donnan's *The Anthropology of Ireland* (2006) contains a comprehensive overview of anthropological research conducted in Ireland. These anthropological studies are progenitors of two classic works on Ireland, *The Irish Countrymen* (Arensberg 1968 [1937]) and *Family and Community in Ireland* (Arensberg and Kimball 1940). All in all, there have been many anthropological studies of the Irish in Ireland, as the extensive references to the voluminous research discussed in Wilson and Donnan's *The Anthropology of Ireland* (2006) aptly illustrates, but unfortunately comparable anthropological research on the Irish adaptation to Canada is noticeably absent from the academic record.

As far as Irish immigration to Canada is concerned, most scholars have concentrated on the virtual exponential population growth in the country as the most significant causal factor of the exodus from Ireland. As such, Ireland's rapid population growth is usually cited as the root cause of the eventual catastrophe, such that "the factor which gave greatest cause of concern was the rapid rise in population from the mid-century. From about two and half million in 1767 the population of Ireland had risen to over four million by 1781 and twenty years later it was close to five million" (O'Tuathaigh 1972: 5). However, demographers were never able to agree on the *primum mobile* responsible for this rapid acceleration in growth. Whatever the cause, however, in a very short period, by the early 1850s the Irish countryside was virtually depleted of its human population, leaving a demoralized and grief-stricken populace to mourn the loss. Yet, despite this calamity, the Irish people managed to rebuild their lives in new lands, and in many cases to prosper, finding opportunity where others might have found only despair.

Upper Canada circa 1850

Upper Canada (later becoming Canada West in 1841, and now called southern Ontario) was populated in the early 1700s by Algonquian-speaking peoples, such as the Anishinaabe (Ojibwa), who relied on a mixed economy of hunting, fishing, and limited horticulture (cultivation of crops mostly in a forested environment). Previously, the Wendat (Huron), Petun (Tabacco people), and Neutral-Erie were dispersed by the Iroquois (Haudenosaunee) in 1649–50 (Labelle 2013). In 1764, the British made their initial purchase of land in Ontario. Called the Niagara Purchase, and also known as the Treaty of Fort Niagara, it was signed by Sir William Johnson for the Crown and Twenty-Four Nations from the Six Nations, Menominee, Nipissing, and Mississauga, among others. Twenty years later, in 1784, Chief Joseph Brant led nearly 2,000 Iroquois Loyalists from New York state to southern Ontario. The Iroquois, or Haudenosaunee, were then granted a large tract of land along the shores of the Grant River, called the Haldimand Grant, as compensation for their losses during the American Revolution. Almost from the beginning of this land settlement, controversy erupted over the extent and exact location of the Haldimand Grant. Further issues revolved around the selling of land by Brant; he claimed that the grant had been conveyed to the Haudenosaunee with a title that was "an estate in fee simple," thus giving his people the right to sell the land at their option. This claim was disputed in 1793 by the lieutenant governor of Upper Canada, John Graves Simcoe, leading to a protracted disagreement, which was not resolved until the late 1840s (Hedican 2017: 61–91; Munson and Jamieson 2013: 49–76).

The first settlers in southern Ontario were, therefore, political refugees seeking a new home after the American Revolution. British settlers soon followed, seeking relatively inexpensive land away from the industrialization and population growth of their home country. Agriculture supported a burgeoning population. At the time of the War of 1812, Ontario's population was a meagre 75,000; in 1851 about 950,000 lived in Upper Canada, and by 1860 the population, which had been doubling every twelve years, reached 1.4 million. The population densities were highest around Lake Ontario and west to the Grand River. York (renamed Toronto in 1834) had a population of about 30,000 residents and was the largest city in Upper Canada, although this amounted to only 3 per cent of the total population (McCallum 1980: 3–22; Harris 2008: 342–3; Russell 2012: 82–95).

In 1851, Hamilton, with a population of about 14,000 inhabitants, nearly rivalled Toronto for the value of its exports. The Irish were the largest of the various ethnic groups in the city, but they were also the poorest overall and apparently the most disadvantaged. As Russell (2012: 347) explains, "The poor did not vote and had no voice. Many families lived on the edge of absolute destitution; some immigrant Catholic Irish were transported in wagonloads to country towns and dumped there." No doubt word of this sort of treatment of Irish immigrants in the urban centres and country towns would have compelled them to eschew a life in the larger population centres in favour of a rural lifestyle, earning a living through agriculture.

During the 1850s Ontario was fortunate to have some of the best grain-growing territory in North America; wheat was the staple product of most Ontario farmers. Exports of Ontario wheat rose by 500 per cent during the 1840s, which reached a peak in the early 1860s, after which it fell off rapidly. With the failure of the wheat market just before the time of Confederation, agriculture in Upper Canada fell into a state of crisis, as there was no commercial substitute. As Russell (2012: 3) explains, "Both Lower Canada and Upper Canada ... experienced agricultural crises that profoundly shaped British North America." These crises were precipitated by the limit of good farmland within the St. Lawrence lowlands and the consequent need to find ways to make farming sustainable on a relatively fixed land base. The various phases of immigration into Upper and Lower Canada caused farm families to search for ever more lands on which to settle and thus provide for generations to follow. As a result of this expansionism the St Lawrence lowlands could no longer contain the need for additional farmland.

In some areas crop failures caused by soil exhaustion and diminishing markets led to hunger and malnutrition, as farmers could not produce enough wheat even for their own consumption. The building of railways in the 1850s helped to ameliorate food shortages by opening markets for agricultural goods; it also stimulated the export of dairy products to Britain and the United States. However, high immigration in the mid-nineteenth century, and the sudden collapse of the wheat market in 1857, had dire economic consequences. Land prices began to drop precipitously; many farmers, in an attempt to take advantage of the wheat boom, became over-extended financially and were unable to pay off mortgages on properties. At the time of Canadian Confederation many farmers' sons were no doubt eyeing a move to the northwest where agricultural lands were less expensive.

By the early 1860s in Ontario there was an agricultural shift away from wheat as a stimulus for economic growth to more diversified farm products and animal domestication. Agricultural production moved away from export markets and towards domestic markets, to feed the growing urban populations of Ontario. In turn, industrial growth in the urban centres supplied manufactured goods to the farm population. It can be concluded, then, that the two decades between 1850 and 1870 was a period of agricultural transformation. The monoculture of the wheat economy in Ontario gave way to a more diversified pattern of agricultural production. Hay and oats were grown to feed farmers' livestock, especially horses and cattle; barley replaced wheat as an export product in the 1850s. General commodity production for sale outside Ontario declined somewhat in favour of production for local consumption, which provided a measure of stability to regional producers.

This trend was especially true for the raising of sheep for wool and hogs for fresh pork, hams, and bacon as a dependable home market became more attractive to farmers than the volatile export market. In fact, local farmers had difficulty keeping up with the regional demand for agricultural products, such that "a large portion of the growth in domestic demand was met by a dramatic rise in imports" (McCallum 1980: 51). As Ontario farmers shifted agricultural production away from the export market to meet local demand, capital gained from this successful diversification was then used to purchase livestock and improve their buildings. In turn, the growing population expansion of Upper Canada provided a new source of revenue, thus giving Ontario farmers access to "relatively large amounts of capital needed for commercial production of cattle, wool, meat, butter, and cheese" (ibid.: 52).

This, then, was the state of agricultural development in Ontario during the late 1840s and early 1850s, when large numbers of Irish immigrants arrived. Available agricultural land, even at reasonable prices with the short-lived decline in prices, was mostly beyond the reach of many immigrants. Even so, a rise in immigration meant that the availability of fertile agricultural land became virtually non-existent in the province by the mid-1850s. What was left was land with uncertain soil fertility and, forested areas comprising swamps and rocky outcrops, much of it situated in regions with adverse climatic conditions. By the time of the Irish Famine, Ontario was already undergoing a demographic crisis precipitated by settlers' attempts to glean a living from ever more marginal lands, a process compounded by large-scale immigration. In Ontario, a process that Russell (2012: 7) describes as "infilling" began to take place. This process was a part of a larger movement which encouraged young families to start new farms in the Ottawa Valley region.

Irish immigrants during this period of the early 1850s were comprised mainly of single persons, young married couples, or small incipient families trying to make the best of a rural farming life and shunning the squalor, poverty, and disease of the urban environments. Of course, good agricultural land would always be for sale in southern Ontario but few of the Famine Irish would have the financial resources to avail themselves of this option. This book, then, is the story of how the Irish who fled the Great Famine managed to cope in their new country, feeding their families and making a new life for themselves under mostly harsh and marginal conditions. Somehow, many of the Irish immigrants managed to flourish through hard work and the help of their neighbours, and eventually established farms which were larger and more prosperous than they would ever have dreamed of back in their home country of Ireland.

Irish Emigration to Canada

Canadians of Irish descent claim forebears who were immigrants from the land mass comprising the present-day Republic of Ireland and Northern Ireland. All together, between 1825 and 1970, about 1.2 million Irish arrived in Canada with more than half of these arriving from the period between 1831 and 1850. Before the Great Famine of the late 1840s, most of the Irish immigrants were Protestant, probably because they had greater economic means to travel than their Catholic counterparts. In all, more than half of all British immigrants to Canada were Irish; however, during the Famine migration of 1847 when more than 100,000 Irish immigrants landed at Quebec, they were mostly impoverished Catholics – a situation that was atypical of Irish immigration to North America during the first half of the nineteenth century. In Upper Canada by 1850, during the heaviest period of Irish immigration due to the Famine, there was little suitable farmland left that had not been claimed. While the Irish were found in many areas of the province, they were particularly prevalent in the Ottawa Valley, probably because it had the least propitious soil and climatic conditions for agricultural success in the northeastern part of Upper Canada.

Ulster was a source of many Irish immigrants. There the rural population had reached unsustainable densities of 750 people per square mile; in Armagh more than half of the Irish farms were under five acres. In central Ireland, in the area around Tipperary, which was also a source of many Irish Immigrants to Upper Canada, emigration was stimulated by the actions of landlords who kept raising rents and evicting tenants. Such landlords were more interested in expanding grazing on their lands rather than preserving tillage, thus creating conditions which further displaced tenants.It was not just the potato famine that pushed Irish tenants from the rural landscape of Ireland, but the economic conditions that favoured a massive shift in the Irish agricultural economy from tillage to pasturage for domesticated animals.

Most of the immigrants who arrived with little or no capital hoped to secure land as free grants to settlers, or under a pre-emption program which required little or no down payment. (This program was initiated to settle underpopulated areas or those with poor agricultural potential.) Later the purchase price was paid usually at a minimal rate once fields were cleared and buildings erected. For example, many families started out with a forested lot, simple tools, and not much relevant experience. Everyone in the family old enough had to work, as the tasks were numerous: clearing fields; building a house, sheds, and barns; planting and tending crops; and often contributing to the needs of neighbours as well. Needless to say, for some families the pioneering life became too much for them to bear. Wives died in childbirth, men from farm accidents, particularly those caused by falling trees. As Cole Harris describes in *The Reluctant Land*, the struggles of the pioneering life could be devastating for some:

> Everywhere there was work; every able member of the family worked. For some, pioneering became overwhelming. The rate of insanity in pioneer societies was high, and there are instances in the records of people who gave up and walked away – a man, for example, who set off for the local gristmill with a little grain, sold it, and carried on. The woman and children [were] left behind. (2008: 326–7)

At the time of Canadian Confederation, in 1867, the Irish comprised the third-largest ethnic group in the country (after the English and French), amounting to nearly one-quarter of Canada's population. Many of the Irish during this period found work on construction projects, which included the building of railroads, canals, or roads, or in the lumber industry. The Irish were particularly involved in the building of the Rideau Canal, and could therefore be considered instrumental in building Ontario's early transportation infrastructure. Various settlement schemes, such as Peter Robinson's organized land settlement program of Catholic farmers in the 1820s in eastern Ontario, also attracted large numbers of farming families from Ireland, particularly from Tipperary and Cork (Bennett 2011; Mannion 1974; Ryan 1991; Wilson 1989).

According to the 1931 census of Canada, the total population of Irish ancestry amounted to about 1.3 million people, one-half of these living in Ontario. Two-thirds of these were Protestants, while the remaining one-third were Catholics (Akenson 1982: 221, 1991). By 2006 Statistics Canada reports that people of Irish ancestry (either full or partial Irish descent) amounted to about 4.3 million Canadians and were then the fourth-largest ethnic group. Ontario has the largest number of people of Irish ancestry; almost two million Ontarians are of Irish descent. British Columbia, with 600,000 people of Irish ancestry, has the second-highest number (Canada 2008). In 2004 the Ontario legislature proclaimed March 17th to be "Irish Heritage Day" in recognition of the enormous Irish contribution to the province's history and development. After 2010 the Irish are once again immigrating to Canada after the slump in the Irish economy and a slowdown in the economic surge known as the "Celtic Tiger."

The history of the Irish in present-day Canada can be traced back to the mid-1500s, when fisherman travelled to Newfoundland from the port cities of Cork and Waterford (Power 1991). After the War of 1812, Irish immigration to Canada increased dramatically; between 1825 and 1845 the Irish comprised 60 per cent of all immigrants to Canada. However, just in terms of overall numbers, about 624,000 Irish arrived in Canada in the two decades between the years 1830 and 1850, averaging near 31,000 persons per year over this period. The Irish arriving in Canada during the several decades before the Famine were mainly the most destitute Catholics, many of whom had been landless tenants evicted from estates owned by absentee English landlords (Clark and Donnelly 1983: 390–6 in passim; Maltby and Maltby 1979: 32–76; O'Driscoll and Reynolds 1988: 711).

Hence, the availability of land at relatively low cost was an important factor in attracting Irish immigrants to Ontario. Many of the nearly one million migrants who arrived in Canada during the nineteenth century, Redclift (2003) suggests, were also attracted by the relative absence of social barriers to upward mobility in their new country. The rigid social divisions in their home country tended to keep the lower classes in a permanent state of poverty and servitude. In Ireland there was simply not enough land to feed all who were trying to eke a living from it. The scarcity of land tended to drive rents up, which depleted the resources of the poor tenant farmers even further. There was little security of tenure for most Irish farmers, and if they tried to improve their holdings, the landlords were likely to raise rents even higher. So, as far as the tenant farmer in Ireland was concerned, rigidity in the existing class structure between landowner and tenant farmer created a social barrier that was virtually insurmountable.

The availability of land in Canada may have been an attraction for Irish immigrants, but this inducement did not necessarily lead to long-term or permanent settlement. Irish immigration to North Hastings County can be used as an example of the consequences of various circumstances that were unpredictable to the new settlers. Free land grants were offered in North Hastings beginning in 1856, which led to the establishment of three Irish settlements: Umfraville, Doyle's Corner, and O'Brien Settlement. However, a crop failure in 1867 caused a cessation of further road construction in the area near the Irish settlements and led to settlers moving out of the area. By 1870, about the only successful farmers remaining in these three settlements were those raising grazing animals rather than those engaged in crop production (Ryan 1991).

The Irish Diaspora

To begin with, here are some disconcerting facts concerning Irish history of the nineteenth century. In 1800 it is estimated that there were five million people living in Ireland, and by the 1840s this figure had grown to over eight million. In terms of farm holdings, one historian relates that "the figures of the 1841 census reveal the appalling insecurity of Ireland's vast population. Only seven per cent of holdings were over thirty acres in size; 45 per cent were under five. In Connacht the holdings under five acres went as high as 64 per cent. Over two-thirds of the Irish people were dependent on agriculture for a livelihood in 1841" (Green 2001: 220).

According to O' Tuathaigh's (1972: 129) estimates of the population density in rural Ireland, the census of 1841 suggests that the average density per square mile of arable land (that is, excluding towns) was about 335 people, though there were marked regional variations. In general terms, population densities increased in Ireland as one travelled from east to west. Rising population densities in Ireland, which made life increasingly difficult for rural farming people, were no doubt a primary cause of emigration from the island. The result was that, between 1820 and 1920, 4.7 million Irish people immigrated to America. By 2001 the population of Ireland reached 3.8 million, a 120-year high, a level which has been attributed to immigration and birth rate increases (Moody and Martin 2001: 437; Coogan 2002).

Despite the overall magnitude of the Irish Famine (1845–9), current research has shown that it was nonetheless regionally experienced, with certain locales being harder hit than others (Crawford 1989, 1997; Donnelly 2001; Gallagher 1982; 2001). One apt summary of this period stated that the "intensity, duration and the timing have given to the Great Famine a notoriety unsurpassed in Irish history" (Crawford 1989: v). One prominent result of this calamity was that nearly three million people disappeared from the Irish countryside by 1855 because of emigration and excess mortality. Ireland's population dropped from about 8.5 million in the mid-1840s to between 4.2 and 4.4 million by the first decade of the twentieth century (see Vaughn 1989). Although possibly as high as 10 per cent of the Irish population died from starvation and malnutrition-related diseases between 1845 and 1851, many more died at sea en route to North America or Australia. The Canadian quarantine station at Grosse Îsle kept records of those who died there, but they were often inadequate because, in many cases, the victims could not be identified.

Prior to the Great Famine in Ireland, emigration to Canada varied considerably from one decade to another (Elliot 2004; Houston and Smyth 1990; MacKay 1990; Mannion 1974; and Moran 1994). Migration from Irish ports to British North America (Canada) between 1825 and 1945 reached a high of 40,977 individuals in 1831, and a low of 2,228 in 1838. Curiously, and for reasons that are not well understood, corresponding figures for Irish emigration to the United States for this period are much lower, reaching a high for example of only 6,199 persons in 1842, and a low of 1,169 in 1838. Of course, there is no reason to conclude that sailing from an Irish port necessarily meant that the individual migrant was an Irish person. In addition, these figures should only be tempered by the fact that many Irish people sailed from ports in Great Britain, children were frequently not counted, and many of the Irish people who initially migrated to Canada eventually found their way to the United States later (see Akenson 1984: 12–20).

A factor contributing to the higher immigration rates to Canada, aside from the reduced fares, was the role of the transatlantic timber trade, as it was upon returning timber ships that Irish passengers were carried to Saint John and Quebec City. Thus, in the mid-nineteenth century, it was primarily the logistics of the new staple trade in timber that bound the Irish to Canada. As Houston and Smyth (1988: 32) indicate, "the large number of cargo ships coming and going offered would-be immigrants an opportunity for cheap and ready transportation." After 1848, fares to the United States dropped, making it easier to get there quickly. Most of those who went to Canada before 1848, it should be noted, quickly crossed the border to the United States.

The "Appalling" Figures

For the two-year period of 1846–7 the number of Irish migrants to Canada soared to 145,185. Writing in the autumn of 1847, the chief emigration agent for Canada West (Ontario) noted that three-quarters of the immigrants in that year were Irish. He described in rather graphic terms that "during that baleful year, 1847, there poured into Canada the most polluted as well as relatively the most swollen stream of immigration in the history of that country" (Tucker 1931: 537). And these were the fortunate ones, as many more died at sea, or shortly after at the quarantine station at Grosse Îsle in Quebec, and more in and above Montreal. This amounted to an "appalling figure of 20,365 recorded deaths out of a total of 98,105 emigrants to Canada in 1847 [and] does not consider those whose early deaths in the hinterlands were either never recorded or not included in the emigrant death toll" (Gallagher 1982: 211; cf. also Duncan 1965: 22–3).

"Already by the end of May 1847," Donnelly (2001: 180) notes, "there were forty vessels in the vicinity of Grosse Île, with as many as 13,000 emigrants under quarantine, stretching in an unbroken line two miles down the St. Lawrence." A week after the number of refugees on the island was reported to be about 21,000, and, by early September, no fewer than 14,000 emigrants were still held in quarantine aboard ships in the river. The death toll at sea had been extremely high, yet at Grosse Île shortly after the arrival of the first ship, deaths numbered 50 a day, with as many as 150 people buried on 5 June alone. An expert on the Irish Famine, Kerby Miller, in *Emigrants and Exiles*, calculated that the death toll among the almost 100,000 immigrants to British North America in 1847 reached at least 30 per cent of the total. This means about 30,000 Irish people died en route to Canada, or in Canada itself. To this could be added, according to Miller (1985: 292), another 10,500 who perished on their way to the United States. The combined mortality of Famine emigrants was therefore about 50,000 persons, an appalling figure to contemplate indeed.

Notwithstanding these formidable setbacks, most of the Irish immigrants made a successful adaptation to their new home. Most of the Irish arrivals bypassed the Atlantic provinces in favour of Quebec and, especially, Ontario (see Houston and Smyth 1988: 30–2, 1990). Unlike their American counterparts to the south, Irish settlers in Canada tended to eschew an urban environment, preferring instead the farming life of the rural areas. Data from recent historical research have challenged a commonly held assumption that the Irish in Canada were primarily a city people, a view promoted by sociologist Ken Duncan (1965), but fervently opposed by historian Donald Akenson (1984, 1988).[1]

Irish Catholics tended to settle in rural areas in Ontario, largely to avoid dominance of the Protestants, who were more numerous in the urban centres, and, especially, harassment by their old enemies in the Orange Order (see Akenson 1991; Currie 1995; Houston and Smyth 1980; McGowan 1999; Nicholson 1985; Scott 2000). Conflicts stemmed from the Orange Order's two main tenets of anti-Catholicism and loyalty to Britain, which were pitted against the largely Catholic goals of forming a Republic of Ireland independent of British control (Houston and Smyth 1978; Keogh 2009; Scott 2000; Wilson 2007). These old country enmities appeared to have followed the Irish settlers even into the rural areas, as the murder of five members of the Donnelly clan and the continuation of ancient feuds in Lucan, near London in southwestern Ontario, in the 1880s would attest (Miller 1962). However, by 1900 these conflicts had largely subsided, as succeeding generations of Irish Canadians became more concerned with local, contemporary matters than with the religious tensions and conflicts of previous centuries.

Notwithstanding these "appalling figures," there were apparently many Irish emigrants with sufficient means to begin life anew, or who were healthy enough to work in Montreal or elsewhere in eastern Canada to secure enough money to purchase land for a family farm. As Akenson (1984: 34) noted, "The Irish migrant to Ontario arrived in terrible physical condition, but his body emaciation should not be equated with cultural impoverishment or with technological ignorance ... in Ontario he passed through the cities on the way to settling successfully in the commercial farm country of small towns and isolated farmsteads."

In time, many of the Irish who had arrived with little means in the nineteenth century were able to pull themselves out of poverty. DiMatteo (1996), for example, has examined probate records from this period to show that many Irish, both those born in Ireland and Canadian-born, were successful in accumulating wealth. The Irish settlers in earlier decades may have experienced many economic hardships but by the 1890s the Irish in general attained a level of wealth comparable to that of the rest of the Canadian population.[2] In fact, even as early as 1861, the Irish (both Catholics and Protestants) of Leeds township in Akenson's (1984: 247) study owned farms whose average cash value ($1,428) was significantly higher than both the value of farms ($1,119) owned by the Native-born Canadians or other foreign-born farmers ($1,026). Among the Irish themselves in 1861, the Catholics possessed farms that were more highly valued ($1,476) than those of their Protestant counterparts ($1,381), suggesting that the commonly made distinction between the poor Catholic and the wealthy Protestant farmers may not be an entirely accurate assumption to make.

By twenty years after the Great Famine, the Census of Canada for 1871 revealed that 66.1 per cent of persons of Irish ethnicity lived in Ontario, and in the province of Ontario, 48.1 per cent of the Catholics of Irish descent and 59.4 per cent of the Protestants of Irish descent were farmers. Only 6.9 per cent of the Irish lived in cities (Darroch and Ornstein 1980: 326–7; Akenson 1984: 46–7). Another common belief, oft-repeated but not born out by the facts, is that the Irish Catholics became an urban proletariat; in reality, 77.5 per cent of those of Irish descent lived in rural areas (Akenson 1984: 41).

Another point of contention about Irish adaptation in North America is the view held by some that the Irish were too technologically unsophisticated to be good farmers, or that Irish rural people did not have the necessary skills to farm in the New World. To contradict – or at least revise – this view, Akenson (1988: 22) has referred to its promoters as engaging in "deplorable works of ethnic piety," and suggests furthermore that "the common cultural assumptions about nineteenth-century Irish immigrants are wildly inaccurate and indeed virtually racist in the assumption of Irish cultural backwardness" (ibid.: 22).

Before we leave the subject of the reception of the Irish in Canada, I turn to one of the iconic works of Canadian literature, Susanna Moodie's *Roughing It in the Bush*. Many Canadian historians and literary scholars (although probably few anthropologists) are no doubt familiar with Moodie's works and her virulently anti-Irish diatribes. Her observations at Gross Îsle, scornful as they may be, reflected not uncommon sentiments of the English towards the Irish at this period:

> A crowd of many hundred Irish emigrants had been landed during the present and former day and all this motley crew – men, women, and children, who were not confined by sickness to the sheds (which greatly resembled cattle-pens) – were employed in washing clothes or spreading them out on the rocks or bushes to dry. The men and boys were *in* the water, while the women, with their scanty garments tucked above their knees, were tramping their bedding ... each shouting and yelling in their uncouth dialect ... vicious, uneducated barbarians, who form the surplus of over populous European countries ... you would think they were incarnate devils, singing, drinking, dancing, shouting, and cutting antics that would surprise the leader of a circus ... Forcing our way once more through the still squabbling crowd, [which was] just landing a fresh cargo of emigrants from the Emerald Isle. One fellow, of gigantic proportions, whose long, tattered great-coat just reached below the middle of his bare

red legs, hid the defects of his other garments ... bounded and capered like a wild goat from his native mountains. "Whurrah! My boys" he cried. "Shure we'll all be jintlemen!" (Moodie [1852] 1913: 30–4)

As for these tirades, Akenson (2005: 296) satirically comments, "For the Moodies the Great Famine coincided with their [meaning Susanna's] breakthrough into modest literary celebrity, and they forever after looked upon 1847 as a good year for the right sort of people."

In conclusion, most of the estimations based on extensive historical research have led to the belief that the Irish migrants to the New World were "much quicker, more technologically adaptive, more economically alert, and much less circumscribed by putative cultural limits inherited from the Old Country than is usually believed" (Akenson 1984: 353). The data presented in this book support this latter point of view, and are important to take into consideration in any assessment of the agrarian context of Irish Canadian family life.

The Irish of Renfrew County

Renfrew County is the largest county in Ontario encompassing an area from the west shore of the Ottawa River over to the northern tip of Algonquin Park. Today it consists of 17 municipalities, comprising 37 former townships. This area was historically an important fur-trading route linking Quebec City and Montreal to the Great Lakes and what is now the Northwest Territories. Later, in the 1800s, the timber industry was the economic mainstay of the area, leading to the construction of several railways between Ottawa and Georgian Bay and down to Lake Ontario, but these largely fell into disuse when the lumber trade went into decline. The first attempt at road construction was the Opeongo line, built in the 1850s using "corduroy" logs and other makeshift materials, which served to connect Farrell's Landing near Castleford on the Ottawa River with the interior wilderness.

The area between the Ottawa River and Opeongo Road was part of a vast territory, comprising nearly 57 million acres, that the commissioner of Crown Lands had reported in 1856 lay eastward from Lake Huron to the Ottawa Valley. The commissioner hoped to forestall the movement of the province's younger men to the western prairies and the United States by finding competitive agricultural land in Upper Canada. As an enticement to remain in the province, the commissioner began to lay out townships and offered free 50-acre land grants to settlers; in the process 800 miles of colonization roads were built, most of which were completed by the late 1860s. These free land grants were then laid out as lots along the Ottawa River and the Opeongo Road beginning in 1855; by the end of the 1850s more than 200 such lots were occupied. However, despite the early high expectations of the commissioner, many settlers were leaving the area. Immigrants complained of rocky conditions, blackflies, and early frost. Significantly, the few remaining settlers were the Irish and Germans. Likely these immigrants, the Irish in particular, felt that they had to succeed since returning to their home country was not an option (Harris 2008: 366–70; Russell 2012: 142–67, and R.E. Ankli and K.J. Duncan 1984: 33–9).

Renfrew County was officially founded in 1861 by an act of legislature. Settlement in Upper Canada during the early years was subject to numerous boundary changes due to adjustments in political and judicial divisions. Several Ottawa Valley townships, for example, were placed in the new district of Bathurst by legislation in 1823. During this time Renfrew was included in Lanark County, which was largely an area of non-surveyed land. The Municipal Institutions Act of 1849 later divided Lanark and Renfrew Counties into separate administrative jurisdictions.

A favourite destination of the Irish settlers to Canada was the sometimes fertile, but frequently rock-strewn and swampy country of the Ottawa Valley, especially Renfrew County, just west of Ottawa. In a curious way, Renfrew County resembled the farming conditions in many areas of Ireland itself, with bogs and hilly terrain, conditions which likely account for its being one of the last areas of southern Ontario to be put to the plough. These early Irish farmers were faced with the daunting task of clearing fields, planting crops, and erecting buildings for shelter and for storage of scarce equipment and machinery, all before the onslaught of winter. The farms, spread out over an extensive territory, were grouped together in local parishes and contiguous farms. The farmers no doubt survived such conditions by helping each other.

Admaston Township

The Township of Admaston, the site of this research, is situated near the town of Renfrew on the east, in the southern portion of Renfrew County. Its name is derived from that of a small village in Staffordshire, England. The first survey of Admaston commenced in 1838 and was completed in 1842. Noted as the first inhabitants were four Scottish families who settled the area even before the surveys were completed. However, by the late 1840s the major influx of settlers were Irish families; these Irish settlers were no doubt responsible for the naming of Mount St. Patrick and Shamrock (*Ottawa Citizen*, 30 October 1937).[3]

While many Irish counties are represented among the earliest families of Renfrew County, as far as Admaston Township is concerned, the majority came from Kerry and West Limerick, with a cluster of families from nearby Clare. Curtin's (2000) study of West Limerick in the 1845–9 years immediately after the Famine is particularly interesting because many of the people written about in this book immigrated to Admaston or contiguous townships. Curtin drew up a list of people who were shown in the 1841 Irish census but who were later missing from the Griffith's Valuation.[4] Many of the persons listed by Curtin as living in West Limerick in 1841 had names similar to those of the settlers who arrived in the Admaston district during the Famine period, but in the absence of immigration records such a conclusion cannot be entirely verified. However, since many local Admaston families are known to have originated from Curtin's district of West Limerick such a conclusion – that many of the post-Famine settlers to Admaston were from West Limerick – is a reasonable assumption to make.

Further evidence supporting the assumption that Famine immigration to Canada was largely from the counties in the west of Ireland, particularly Clare, Limerick, and Kerry, being also the greatest source of Irish settlers to Admaston, is provided by a study of Famine conditions in Ireland by O'Tualthaigh. For example, he indicates (1972: 204–5) that "the famine produced its highest quota of death, suffering and emigration in those counties where dependency on the potato was greatest, subdivision most acute, trade and communication least developed; in short, in the counties of the west and south-west." While many counties are mentioned, Clare, Limerick, and Kerry in particular "were the hardest hit."

In terms of the social groups who felt the Famine most severely, "Here the evidence is clear. The labourers and the cottier[5] classes were the chief victims of the famine, and the small-farmer class scarcely fared much better" (ibid.: 205). The following list of comparative landholdings in Ireland between 1841 and 1851 is instructive, especially in relation to Irish landholdings in Renfrew County during about the same and later periods (ibid.: 206):

These figures demonstrate clearly that as far as the social structure of Ireland is concerned the number of cottiers and small farmers was substantially reduced, and that there occurred by 1851 a substantial consolidation of smaller holdings. As O'Tuathaigh (1972: 206) unequivocally indicates, "the cultivators ... had been, by one means or another, 'cleared.' A major social change had been effected." Not only had many small farmers died or emigrated, but landlords, who were having financial trouble of their own, tended to use the vacant land for pasturing livestock.

Holdings	1841 (in '000s)	Per cent	1851	Per cent
1–5 acres	310	44.9	88	15.5
5–15 acres	253	36.6	192	33.6
15–30 acres	79	11.5	141	24.8
Above 30 acres	49	7.0	149	26.1

Under such conditions in Ireland, one can only imagine the delight among the surviving cottiers and small-farmers upon arriving in Admaston, despite its somewhat unfavourable agricultural conditions, in which a farm of 50 acres was considered on the small side. A cautionary note must be made here in any discussion of farm size, especially in comparing the size of a farming operation from one country to another. In Ireland, for example, a farm comprising 10 acres may have 9 acres of this under cultivation. Correspondingly, a 50-acre farm in Renfrew County may well comprise 50 acres overall but have only a few of these acres under cultivation.

A typical farm comprised not only acreage devoted to the cultivation of crops, but probably also acreage devoted to pasture or other uses. One farmer may specialize in crop production and another in raising sheep, horses, or dairy cows, such that the requirements are going to be different depending upon the choices an individual farmer makes in terms of the allocation of resources. In Renfrew County, each farm would also probably have had a sizeable area devoted to a woodlot used for the provision of firewood and lumber for building materials such as posts for fences and corrals. All in all, then, comparing farms just in terms of size can lead to false conclusions. In historical terms, we will also need to be cognizant of the changing patterns of farm use since the available territory devoted to farming is ultimately a limited resource – there are only so many ways of dividing up the farm area, but its overall size is not going to change regardless of the farmer's allocation decisions.

Real People, Individual Lives

Most of the discussions in this book are based on various statistical materials gleaned from censuses and other related data. A few notes are added here on various Renfrew families to remind the reader that behind the statistics are the lives of real people who put down roots, worked, raised families, and otherwise dealt with the difficulties and revelled in the joys of life much as we do today.[6]

John McMahon: Landlord-Assisted Emigration

John McMahon (1822–1896) and his wife, Ann Madigan, came to Canada at the time of the Famine. A large group of McMahons settled in Renfrew County, in many cases coming here directly from County Limerick (McCuaig 2003: 119–22). Many of the families in County Limerick who came to Admaston and nearby townships had their origins on either the Monteagle Estates or the adjoining district of Glin, although it is not entirely clear how much monetary or other assistance was extended to them. In any event, the whole matter of assisted emigration has been a controversial topic in the literature on Irish emigration during the Famine years.

The first Baron Monteagle, Thomas Spring Rice, was not the typical absentee landlord reviled as the cause of suffering of the poor on their estates. In fact, he is quoted in 1852 as saying, "I believe that ... we are entrusted with the wealth and intelligence exceeding those of our tenants, in order that we may assist them in their difficulties, provide for them the means of education, encourage and direct their efforts as cultivators, and promote their physical, moral and intellectual improvement" (O'Mahoney and Thompson 1994: 5).

At the height of the Famine, Baron Monteagle expended large amounts of his own money to sponsor public works programs to help avert starvation on his estate. Although he was reluctant to evict his tenants, some of whom had been in arrears of their rent for three years or more, he nonetheless presented them with the option of having their assets sold as partial payment of their debt, or to be used as a means of buying tickets, costing between two and a half to three pounds (which most tenant farmers could not afford), so that they might emigrate. Apparently if it were not for the assets of his second wife, Baron Monteagle would have gone bankrupt because of his assistance to tenant farmers.

There are some researchers, however, who have a less than complimentary view of Baron Monteagle's apparent self-sacrifice. Gerard Moran, for example, in his study of assisted emigration entitled *Sending Out Ireland's Poor* suggests that the motivation was primarily to clear the baron's land of its tenant population (2004: 30). A study of land-assisted emigration conducted by Desmond Norton (2005) finds a wide range of differences in the forms of assistance during different time periods and locales in Ireland. For example, Norton notes that "humanitarian feelings aside, landlord-assisted emigration during the famine years was an important aspect of programmes of estate improvement ...[which] was probably on a larger scale than modern historians have hitherto assumed" (24–5). In terms of emigration assistance programs during different time periods, he notes that "the pre-famine years reflected a concern for tenant welfare," but during the 1847–8 period the welfare of "landlords became prominent ... through substantive programmes of estate clearance" (40).[7] As an example, the Limerick landlord Francis Spraight sent over two thousand former tenants to Canada, and readily admitted, "I could not have got rid of them by any means, if it had not been for the failure of the potato crop" (qtd in Miller 1985: 304). Surely, though, not all Irish landlords felt this way about their Famine-stricken tenants.

In the end it matters little if John McMahon was assisted in his emigration to Canada by Baron Monteagle, and it does not matter at all whether the baron's motive for assisting Irish immigrants was a humanitarian gesture or one motivated by self-serving economic preservation. What matters is that John McMahon and his wife Ann would almost certainly have lived a life of poverty if they had remained in Ireland, and possibly died of starvation as was the plight of so many of their countrymen.

In Canada, the McMahon family prospered. By 1900 one could count as many as eleven McMahon families living in the Admaston-Renfrew area. One couple, Simon McMahon (1825–1901) and his wife Catherine Doyle (1838–1887) of Admaston Township, had 18 children, with Catherine tragically dying while giving birth to their last child when she was age 49.

Thomas Enright: Chain Migration

Thomas Enright was born at Ballylongford, northern Kerry, about 1803, and came to Canada with his wife, Bridget Holly, settling in Admaston Township prior to the Famine. Between 1840 and 1855 they had seven children, who for the most part appeared to marry other descendants from the Ballylongford area in Kerry and settle near each other in Admaston. As a matter of fact, a map prepared from the 1841–51 census lists the farms of Pat Enright, Daniel Enright, and John Enright all contiguous to each other in Admaston Township on the 10th and 11th concessions (Bennett 1992: Appendix, Township of Admaston, Early Settlement). Patrick Enright (1812–1864) and Anne McMahon (1812–1898) came from the Glin parish with their children to settle in Admaston during the Famine. Similarly, James Enright (1816–1895) and his wife Honora Scollard (1822–1899) also came from Glin at the time of the Famine, bringing with them two children, having had ten children altogether.

This concentration of Enright families became known as the "Enright Settlement." All of these Enrights came from within a radius of just a few miles in Ireland, such as from the parish of Glin, County Limerick, and from neighbouring parishes such as Ballylongford, over the border in County Kerry. As the family history relates, at least seven members of the Enright family came out together with some of these families, which were previously connected by marriage in Ireland. Four Enright brothers took up a block of land in a section of Admaston Township, where they all spent the first winter together on one of the properties before building houses on the other farms. Their mother and some other grown children joined the brothers later, and a remaining brother, Michael, apparently arrived in 1856 (Bennett 1992: 29–32; McCuaig 2003: 14, 32–3).

The pattern of immigration exemplified by the Enright families of Admaston has been term "chain migration." A chain migration has been defined by Ottawa Valley historian Bruce Elliott as following a pattern in which "one emigrant is followed by another, who is followed by others in turn, draws upon kin groups, the members of which need not necessarily have lived close together before the move" (2004: 4). And, as Carol McCuaig asserts, "numerous examples of chain migration between families can be seen among the people who settled in Admaston Township because of the Great Famine. Two examples are the Carmody and Enright families from Ballylongford" (2003: 13).[8]

The Enright family histories illustrate that the flight from the Famine-stricken areas of Ireland was not necessarily a haphazard exodus. It is no doubt true that those fleeing their country would take whatever means were available, but it is also no doubt accurate that many of the migrants worked out an exit strategy whereby existing family and friendship connections were utilized to facilitate their adaptation to their new country of arrival in a pattern of chain migration, all of which probably facilitated their survival.

John Windle: Adaptation and Perseverance

For those who would cast the Irish as a shiftless lot, hardly capable of looking after themselves, the case of John Windle (1811–1894) belies that common stereotype. Windle had been a labourer in West Limerick when he was forced out of Ireland in 1847 because of the Famine, arriving in Renfrew County in 1848. Although Windle left home with nothing more than the clothes he wore, within five years of leaving home he owned 200 acres of land and 18 head of livestock. However, it appears that Mr Windle faced his share of tragedy. His wife, Mary Walsh, whom he married shortly after his arrival in Canada in 1848, died in childbirth the following year; their son John died three days after her death.

John Windle, who was 35 years old at the time, did not spend his time mourning his misfortune. A year after his first wife's death, he married Bridget Kiely, a woman 20 years his junior who had come from County Limerick in the 1830s. Altogether John and Bridget had eight children between 1851 and 1871, although their first born, Johanna, died in infancy. According to the inscription on their tombstones, Bridget died on 1 September 1894, and John one day later, on 2 September 1894, an unusual coincidence.

What is noteworthy about the lives of John and Bridget Windle, although probably not unusual for the time, was their perseverance in making a productive life for themselves and their children. The 1851 census, for example, indicates that the Windles farmed 100 acres of land, comprising 19 acres of crops, one acre of pasture, and 80 acres of woods. From this land he harvested 75 bushels of wheat, 390 bushels of oats, and 100 bushels of potatoes. The family also owned a span of oxen, one cow and three pigs. Bridget made 50 pounds of butter and salted down a barrel of pork.

The census of 1861 illustrates the continued prosperity of the Windle family. John at that time owned 200 acres of land valued at 1,000 dollars, which was a considerable sum at this time. That year the family produced 300 bushels of potatoes and 200 pounds of maple sugar. Over the intervening decade their livestock increased to a total of four oxen, five cows, nine pigs, and enough sheep to produce 30 pounds of wool.

It is important to note that this was not cleared land that Windle purchased, as would be the case with farms back in Ireland. The land was heavily forested; trees had to be cleared before any crops could be grown. Of course, the wood that was harvested was an important economic asset, as it was used for fuel and to build houses, farm buildings, and fence rails. In the first year, crops of potatoes were simply planted among the tree stumps until the farmer had time to remove them.

The census information that was collected in those early years provides a valuable account, in terms of specific facts and figures, of the precise mode of adaptation of the Irish settlers after they left Ireland. In the case of John Windle and his wife Bridget, we are able to see how hard they must have worked, the manner in which they adapted to their new life in Canada, and how, through perseverance, they were able to live a life of relative prosperity, one that would not have been possible back in their Famine-stricken homeland. It was through the efforts of such Irish immigrants as John and Bridget Windle that much of Canada was settled in the nineteenth century (Census, Renfrew County, 1851, 1861; McCuaig 2003: 145–9, 2006).

Timothy Lynch: Family Connections

The Famine years saw the migration of several of the children of Timothy Lynch and Eliza McCarthy of Kilrush, County Clare. Their son, Thomas Lynch, left Ireland in 1846 with his wife, Catherine Daley, and infant son. They managed to survive their stay at the Grosse Îsle quarantine station and stayed for a while in the Pakenham District, before eventually arriving in 1852 at Admaston, where he took up farming. Thomas's 19-year-old brother, Timothy, followed them to Ontario in 1847, also trying to escape the Famine. The Lynch family managed to stay in touch with their relatives back in Ireland even though they were dispersed over a large area, as the following letter illustrates. The letter gives some interesting insights into the thoughts of the Irish settlers of the time, after their life in Ireland and their struggles to live and adapt to life in North America.

From Daniel Lynch to his brother Timothy in Admaston[9]

March 12th, 1882

Dear Brother:
   Received your letter of the 11th which gave us great pleasure to hear from you once more for I did not Expect to Ever hear from you or anyone in Canada. I wrote several letters and got no answer. I did not have the right direction but Thanks be to God that you are well and doing well as this date leave me and my wife and family present thanks be to God for his mercy to us all.
   Dear Brother I mean to let you know that there is a son of Brother Patrick comes out, him and his sister in August 1880, the girl is in Boffolo and he is in Chicago a very good boy and doing well. He has sent Home £12 since he came out and his sister sent some from Boffolo he tells me that they are doing well at Home. He has a large family there ten more at home as yet so you may think we are pretty well made for breeding. We had fifteen children, nine boys and six girls. We have buried six boys and two girls, one of the girls was married she died one year ago last May. The oldest of mine got married last June. I have three boys and three girls yet.
   Dear Brother I am in the police force in Chicago for the last fifteen years, good wages but Dangerous work for they don't think much about shooting a police man. The times are pretty dull in Chicago and provisions very

dear. Butter from 45 cents to 55 cents per pound; potatoes one dollar and 25 cents per bushel, and everything else according.

There are a great many people from Killimer and Kilrush and neighbourhood in Chicago. I am very glad you have lived in the farm with your boys for City Life for youngsters is a bad place, too much drinking and night walking and Bad Company. But you nor anyone in the Country don't know anything about such as I do.

Dear Brother let me know if you have heard from Martin or where he is he wrote home some time ago and sent money home but left out where he was and Daniel did not have his address, Let me know if you write home and if there's any of the old neighbours there around you. I hope you will not get too tired of writing since you know where to write again.

You must Excuse this writing for I am getting too old to write and Espesily I wrote this in a hurry so now I must Conclude by sending you and your wife and boys and girls my Best Love and Compliments and also to Mrs Thomas Lynch and family. I will send you all particulars in my next letter so I wish you good By and good Luck to all. I wrote this in five minutes as I had to go on duty.

When You write direct your letters to Daniel Lynch, 2847 Hickory Street, Chicago, Illinois.

Write soon. I will send you some papers weekly so that you will see what Crime there is committed in Chicago. So no more at present good By.

The particulars of the Lynch family history illustrate the difficulties of maintaining family connections after migrating to North America. In Ireland family farms were passed down through the generations and many people lived fairly close to relatives. Upon arriving in their new country families frequently dispersed over great distances. It was difficult for immigrant family members to stay connected with one another in their new locations; it was even more difficult to maintain ties with relatives back in Ireland. After a generation or two these close family connections, maintained in Ireland for perhaps hundreds of years, tended to quickly dissolve in North America.

James Sullivan: Inheritance Issues

If it were at all possible Irish farmers would attempt to give a portion of their land to their sons when they married. The idea behind this practice was that a married son could make better use of a father's land while the son was still young enough to raise a family. If he was forced to wait until the aged father passed away to inherit property, the son might well be past middle age himself. In most cases impartible inheritance of a farmer's land, in that only one son, usually the eldest, would stand to inherit the farm property, was restricted. Most landholdings were subject to subdivision. For example, Curtin (2000: 31) reports on a 671-acre townland east of Ballyhahill. At one time, in 1833, this land contained 43 holdings, but by 1846 this number had risen to 91, of which 76 were less than 3 acres.

The case of James Sullivan of West Limerick illustrates the difficulties of farm sub-division. In 1823 he left his 23 acres of Lisready Cripps and travelled to Canada with his wife and sons (Curtin 2000: 7). They first settled in Lanark County, which at this time included what was to later become Renfrew County. Afterwards he obtained land in Admaston Township, which he willed to his sons, Andrew and James. In the 1861 Census of Canada West, Andrew is seen to occupy this land. James Sullivan's last will and testament gives interesting insights into the terms of property allocations during this period before Canadian Confederation.

> I, James Sullivan, of the Township of Lanark and the District of Bathurst and Province of Canada, Yeoman, being week in body but sound in mind thanks be to God Almighty for His mercy – I do make this Will and Testament.
>
> First, I will my body to the earth and my soul to the Almighty God that gave it. And second that all my lawful debts be paid out of my property and Thirdly I will my beloved wife Ann Lot 3, East half in the eight Concession of the Township of Lanark during the time of her natural life and all my moveable property. And to my sons Timothy and Morris I will the aforesaid lot number three in the eight concession of the Township of Lanark after the demise of my wife Ann; and I will to my son Edward £25 to be paid out of my property in Cash, Cattle or Grain when he is twenty six years of age provided that the property is at that time able to pay it; And to my sons Andrew and James I will my farm in the Township of Admaston, but they are to assist to pay my lawful debts; And to my daughter Ann I will bed and bedding and two cows and four sheep, pots, kettle, knives and forks and spoons at the time of her marriage.
>
> And I appoint Patrick O'Connor, Timothy Ryan and Thomas Radwell to be my lawful executors. As witness and seal this 6th day of May 1844.[10]

James Sullivan and his wife had five sons and one daughter. His problem was how to provide for these family members after his death. Difficult decisions needed to be made because there was only so much property to go around. Two of the sons, Timothy and Morris, were to inherit property that their mother was to live on, but they were not allowed to assume ownership until their mother passed away, which could be decades after James's death. How would these two brothers have managed dual ownership of a single property? Would they have attempted a subdivision, which may not have been allowed by local laws, or would they have sold the property and split the proceeds? In any event, what would they have done in the meantime while their mother was still alive and they themselves had families to feed?

There is also the situation with another son, Edward, who was willed cash from the property inherited by Timothy and Morris. There was the stipulation, "if the property is able to pay it." Who would decide this matter? The remaining sons, Andrew and James, were given another portion of James's property, but it was stipulated that they would need to pay off some of James's debts. The daughter, Ann, was to inherit various cows, sheep, and household utensils, but where were they to be stored and cared for until she was married? Whatever the outcome, family friction around these issues of inheritance was a distinct possibility.

Edward Hedican: Settle and Disperse

Edward Hedican was born in County Kerry, in southwest Ireland, in either 1823 or 1825, depending on which census report one might believe.[11] In the 1851 census of Canada West he is listed as living in Horton Township, which is immediately adjacent to Admaston on the west, working on the farm of the widow Margaret McGregor. On 2 January 1855, Edward married Catherine Enright, a member of one of the large Enright families of Admaston township; their first child, Michael, was born the following September. The 1861 census indicates that Edward was the owner of 100 acres of property in Admaston (lot 18, concession 7), which he farmed. The Walling's Map of 1863[12] indicated that he was living on the French Lake Road, located on this plot of land.

By 1871, according to the Admaston census, Edward Hedican was the owner of an additional 200 acres (lot 11, concessions 9 and 10), only one lot over from his existing 100 acres of 1861, and that he was the father of 11 children. According to the 1881 census Edward and his family had moved up to the northern end of Renfrew County (Clara, Head, and Maria Townships), where he purchased a new farm. However, this was only a temporary arrangement, as one of Edward's elder sons, John, entered the United States at Port Huron in May 1882, while the eldest son, Michael, had taken over the property at Head Township.

At this point there was a general dispersal of the family, with sons Thomas, Edward, and daughter Bridget moving to Ashland, Wisconsin. Meanwhile Edward followed John to North Dakota in 1885, a short time after the American wars with the Dakota Sioux; they both purchased property there and built separate, but adjoining, farms under the existing pre-emption process.[13] Edward and John did not farm their land in North Dakota for very long. Edward purchased his property in Ramsey County in April 1887 for $200 and sold it the same year for $550, a handsome profit indeed.

Meanwhile Thomas purchased a tavern and Edward became a police officer in Ashland; Edward was shot on 30 March 1893 while engaged in a gunfight with William Martin, also known as the "New Orleans Kid," outside the Blue Light Saloon. The details of this tragic incident were graphically portrayed in the *Ashland Daily Press* under the headline "Ed Hedican Shot."

The article detailed the incident by indicating that "Stalwart Ed Hedican, one of the bravest and most efficient officers of the police force of Ashland lies dead from the effects of a bullet. A half hour before his death he was in the prime of life [and] was stricken down suddenly while doing his duty as an officer of the law." After describing more of the gruesome details of Edward's death, the article then goes on to indicate that his remaining brothers were living in Texas, Michigan, and Ontario, as well as in Ashland. Not mentioned were brothers living in Seattle, Washington, and Grand Forks, North Dakota. Apparently, the old adage about apples not falling far from the tree did not apply to this Irish family; they instead appeared to scatter like chaff before the wind.

The history of males in the Hedican family illustrates a three-part adaption process of Irish immigration to Canada. First, a young man worked on an established farm for three or four years, learning the art of farming in Ontario, while at the same time saving money for the eventual purchase of land of his own. Second, he married a local woman familiar with farm life, and used his savings to purchase as much land as he could manage under an existing pre-emption program. Third, he raised his family, while securing additional land if possible. As the family matured and the children began to reach adulthood, he would sell his farm holdings and use some of the funds to buy a farm for the eldest son (Michael in this case).

The next step was to help the second son become established (in this case John, who moved with his father and remaining family to North Dakota), again buying land under a pre-emption program, through which large amounts of land became available for settlement after the defeat of the Sioux in the uprising of the mid-1880s. Other grown children moved to various areas to take advantage of economic opportunities. For instance, Thomas and Edward moved to Ashland, Wisconsin, during a boom in iron mining in the states bordering the upper Great Lakes.

Preliminary Definitions

Farming, as a form of economic activity, involves the allocation of limited resources to competing ends. In general, the economic dimension of society involves aspects of social behaviour devoted to the *production, exchange,* and *consumption* of goods. Goods can be defined as anything of value, either material, such as crops or labour, or social, such as a fulfilment of an obligation of some sort. Every decision that a farmer makes regarding the ends to which resources are to be directed involves certain costs.

The choices that a farmer makes, such as which fields to plow or which crops to plant, are often referred to as *opportunity costs*, meaning that for each decision that is made one thereby forgoes all the other alternative decisions that could have been made in any one particular circumstance. For example, once a farmer decides to grow wheat on a plot of land, he obviously cannot also grow barley in the same space. Thus, in an "analysis of production possibilities, where attention is paid to what to produce, opportunity cost takes cognizance of the fact that as resources are shifted to producing something else the efficiency of the resources ... declines and costs rise" (Schneider 1974: 246).

Resources could be the factors of production such as land, labour, and capital, whereas *means* are the "resources that may be used to obtain some valued goal" (ibid.: 244). Economics is therefore regarded as the study of how people relate means to ends, in which the means are insufficient to obtain all desired ends. *Production* is any act of transforming materials. In anthropology, the *consumer unit* is generally considered to be equivalent to the *household*, i.e., the decision-making unit for consumption.

A *household* refers to people who may or may not be related by ties of kinship; however, these individuals share a common living space, which most likely includes common food preparation and consumption, and budgetary items such as food and rent. A variation of this unit, the *stem household* contains two (and only two) married couples related through the males. In Japan and China, for example, only one son remains in the household, who brings in a wife who is expected to perform the role of the caretaker of her husband's parents. This arrangement is called a *patrilineal stem household*, which would be the most common stem household form because it is unlikely, though theoretically possible, for a *matrilineal stem household* to exist if a husband moved into his wife's household while her parents were still alive (Skinner 1993; Bachnik 1983).

The household economy is also referred to as the *domestic mode of production*. As Robert Netting explains, there are over one billion people, or about one-fourth of the world's population, belonging to households involved in family farming. On the family farm people "produce much of their own subsistence as well as some food or fibre to sell, supplying labor largely from their own households, and possessing continuing, heritable rights to their own resources" (Netting 1989: 221). Much of the labour on the family farm is devoted to such tasks as planting seeds and cuttings, ploughing fields, weeding, caring for irrigation systems, fencing fields, and harvesting and processing of farm produce.

The term *subsistence economy* is one which has caused a degree of confusion in anthropology. A simple definition would be that such an economy involves "production and exchange intended for local consumption," whereby *subsistence* is "the means of procuring food/making a living" (Sidky 2004: 440). Schneider (1974: 252) recognizes that "subsistence economy" is "a poorly defined term which seems to mean a production situation in which producers are barely turning out enough to eat or do not choose to produce more than they can eat, so that no economy in the sense of markets and exchange, is possible."

It is important to distinguish between *capitalist production* and *simple commodity production*. The former term refers to production of commodities for their exchange value and for the generation of profit. The latter term refers to the production of commodities for their *use value*, which is the benefit one derives from using a product. In this instance a commodity can be sold, and the funds derived from its sale can be used for the purchase of another use value commodity that the producer requires, rather than for the sole purpose of accumulating capital.

This distinction between capitalist and simple commodity production is an essential one as far as the present discussion of nineteenth-century Irish farmers is concerned; these farmers produced goods beyond what their household required, but the goods in turn were used to purchase or trade for other needed goods, such a farm machinery or livestock. Thus, one may argue, the fact that a farmer produces goods beyond the household's requirements does not necessarily disqualify the use of such an example in an analysis of Chayanov's theory (defined and discussed below), if such production is for its use value, rather than to generate capital.

Since anthropologists usually conduct fieldwork among people whose economies are mostly designed to meet their immediate needs for food and shelter, as opposed to making a profit in a capitalist exchange system, two opposing schools of thought have developed in the discipline. *Substantive economics* is based on the principle that models of capitalist economic systems are unsuitable for the analysis of capitalist societies. It advocates for analysis of the culturally distinct ways in which the production, distribution, and consumption of goods and services take place in *each* society.

Formalist economics is based on the principle that all societies possess common abstract properties and, as such, the capitalist principles of Western market economies are also pertinent to non-Western economic systems. The argument that the *formalists* make is that people in non-Western societies may not orient their economies in pursuit of material gain, but they see profit in the social realm, as in the pursuit of prestige systems. The west coast potlatch is a prime example of this type of endeavour (Sidky 2004: 426; Schneider 1974: 2–14).

There is a purpose behind what may appear to the reader a belabouring of these various definitions and distinctions in economic anthropology. This somewhat protracted discussion of subsistence versus capitalist economies lays the foundation for what later in this book will become an important point about Chayanov's analysis of household economics. Chayanov's theory about agricultural production in terms of the consumer/producer ratio is based on the idea that farmers will only grow enough food as is necessary to meet the consumption needs of their dependants.

If a farmer is producing crops for a market economy, then there is an incentive to increase agricultural production beyond the specific needs of the household. A crucial theoretical argument of the present study is that the people living in the Irish farming households of Renfrew County should be regarded as practising a subsistence economy, rather than a capitalist one. It is no doubt the case that the Irish farmers at certain times would produce a surplus beyond their immediate needs, but that surplus would be traded for goods they lacked, as in the case of producing a few extra bushels of wheat in order to purchase the tea which they could not grow themselves.[14] Other goods needed on the farm, such as a team of horses, would require in exchange value a relatively heavy amount of agricultural production, yet I argue here that the principles are nonetheless the same, which is to say that the Irish farmers were engaging in a subsistence economy, rather than a capitalist one.

Irish Farmers as a Peasant Society?

The previous discussion concerning the difference between an economy primarily characterized by *commodity production*, whose purpose is the generation of profits, versus what has been termed *simple commodity production*, or production for a product's *use value*, reflects certain difficulties in anthropology in terms of how societies might be classified or categorized. For example, in Morton Fried's famous work *The Evolution of Political Society* (1967) the emphasis is on a continuum of increasing social and political complexity. According to this scheme, Fried classifies societies into four categories: "bands" (hunting and gathering), "tribes" (horticulture and herding), chiefdoms (advanced food production), and states (domestication of animals and diversified food production). These categories correspond to certain "levels" of socio-cultural evolution; based on measures of equality, designations such as "egalitarian," "ranked," "stratified," and "state" are applied to societies.

One of the problems with Fried's scheme is that it is based on political roles and exchange systems, and this has tended to obscure the economic processes that support each of these categories. Chiefdoms, for example, are relatively high up on the political scale, as the Indigenous people of the northwest Pacific coast illustrate, but maintain a hunting and gathering economic system not much different from that used by bands. An overall conceptual problem for anthropologists had been an inability to transcend a simple dichotomy between "traditional" and "state" level societies. However, it had become clear by the 1950s that there were societies with characteristics of both types, with a foot in both economic camps. Were these transitional types straddling traditional or state societies, or were they stable entities in their own right?

The first serious attempt to delineate an intermediate socio-economic type between the traditional and state was proposed by Eric Wolf in a 1955 article on "types of Latin American peasantry" and in a seminal book on the topic, simply entitled *Peasants* (1966). The term "peasant" has been defined as a person who works without the use of industrial technology (tractors, combines, etc.) to cultivate land in state societies. Peasants, unlike hunters and gatherers, can produce a modest surplus, a surplus that ultimately flows into the urban centres, either through taxes, rents in kind, or exchange through money or wage labour (Vincent 2012: 53–9). However, "typically they [peasant communities] remain geographically distinct from urban centers" (Perry 2003: 121).

Another important characteristic is that peasant communities are composed of people involved in family farming, and for this reason there has emerged a large body of literature which focuses on peasant societies as epitomizing what has been termed "the household mode of production" (see Shanin 1990). This type of agriculture is highly pervasive worldwide. For example, it has been estimated that over one billion people belong to households involved in family farming, suggesting that these are stable entities and not merely transitional types (see Harris and Johnson 2000: 198; Miller, Van Esterik, and Van Esterik 2001: 70). In family farming, farmers "produce much of their own subsistence as well as some food or fibre to sell, supplying labor largely from their own households, and [possess] continuing, heritable rights to their own resources" (Netting 1989: 221). Family farming is always part of a larger market economic system (Wolf 1966: 8). Thus, farmers in peasant communities rely primarily on their own subsistence activities to produce their own food, but also participate in larger market systems.

This participation in wider markets suggests that peasants may increase their agricultural production beyond their own subsistence needs in terms of cash crops or other forms of agricultural surplus, but usually the cash derived from the sale of this surplus is used to purchase additional land to provide for the increased subsistence needs of a growing family, to purchase goods that the family cannot produce itself, or to increase their agricultural efficiency, for instance in purchasing horses instead of oxen to plough their fields. This increased production, however, remains in the realm of production for *use value* as opposed to an engagement in capitalist production for the sake of earning a profit only.

In describing the role of peasant farmers – especially those emigrating from Europe – in the history of Canadian agriculture, historian Peter Russell (2012: 15–17, 99–100, and *passim*) has adopted Max Weber's concept of ideal types. In this approach there are three ideal types of farmers: peasant, pioneer, and profit maximizer. As Russell (2012: 15) further explains:

> The peasant farm family's goal was to achieve the highest possible degree of autonomy from external circumstances, in order to avoid starvation and make provisions for the next generation. The usual means of attaining this autonomy was through the highest possible degree of self-sufficiency ... *the peasant family household was geared not to profit maximization* but to risk avoidance. (emphasis mine)

Thus, Russell's definition is in complete accord with that derived from anthropology in that the main characteristic of the peasant economy is to maintain a viable subsistence economy to avoid starvation. The peasant's goal was autonomy, as opposed to the farmer's goal of producing a profit.

Russell further explains that the sole motive for increasing agricultural output or increasing the farm's assets, as achieved, for instance, by clearing additional land for crop production or pasturage for domesticated animals, was to ensure that the peasant family would never starve, despite crop failures or other calamities. This is not to say that peasant farmers did not participate in labour exchanges with other farmers on a seasonal basis, or that certain crops might be sold at a local market to purchase other crops that the family might need, but, as Russell (2012: 16) maintains, "distant markets dealing in money were marginal to it." In addition, a bumper crop coinciding with higher than normal prices would lead to the peasant farmer selling crops that were surplus to the family's needs. In this way the peasant farmer would be able to acquire sufficient cash to purchase goods that could not be produced by the farm household itself. (See also Rudolph [1992: 119–38] for a more extended dialogue on the economic strategies of the European peasant farm family.)

This foregoing discussion is meant to lay the basis for my argument in this book that the Irish farmers of Admaston Township in the mid nineteenth century could be regarded as comprising a "peasant" society. This is an important point in a theoretical sense because regarding Irish farmers of eastern Ontario during this time as relying primarily on subsistence produce, albeit while also engaging in a market economy, allows me to analyse Irish agricultural production using the model proposed by the Russian economist Alexander Chayanov. My argument is supported by two prominent Irish historians, Samuel Clark and James Donnelly, in their book on Irish political unrest (during the 1780–1914 period) entitled *Irish Peasants* (1983). Their work builds on the earlier studies of Eric Wolf and others cited above. Wolf, for instance, characterizes the Irish peasant as an individual belonging to a small family farm that combines subsistence tillage with some commercial production and that employs little or no wage labour (1983: 12). Clark and Donnelly (1983: 12) confirm that "the peasantry in Ireland serves as a good illustration" of the characteristics of peasant family farming widely discussed in the literature. Thus, since it has been successfully argued that peasant farming existed in Ireland itself during the time period of the present study, I feel confident in utilizing the term "peasant" to characterize the Irish farmers of Renfrew County in eastern Ontario and, furthermore, to use this concept in conjunction with the theoretical approach used in the Chayanov model of agricultural production.

Chapter Two

Theoretical Perspectives on Farm and Family

In the field of what has been termed "Irish diaspora studies," it has been noted that "no one academic discipline is going to tell us everything we want to know about the Irish Diaspora. The study of migration, emigration, immigration, population movements, flight, scattering networks, transnational communities, diaspora – this study demands an interdisciplinary approach" (O'Sullivan 2003: 131). These areas of interest cut across not only the disciplinary lines of history and anthropology, but also those of economics, political science, sociology, and geography, among other areas of study (Coogan 2002). It is therefore important to examine the nature of this nexus between history and anthropology.

History and Anthropology

Attempts to combine the disciplines of history and social or cultural anthropology have long had currency. In fact, the relationship between history and anthropology has been a matter of intellectual interest and controversy for at least the last century. F.W. Maitland, for example, wrote in 1899 that "anthropology must choose between being history and being nothing" (qtd in Mair 1965: 36).

Alfred Kroeber, an influential American anthropologist from the first half of the twentieth century, also understood anthropology as a historical discipline. He suggested that in order to understand human behaviour it was important for one to know the temporal and specific contexts in which such behaviour took place. His view contrasted with a more scientific perspective in which human behaviour is construed as a pattern of causal connections. Kroeber (1952: 5) described his historical perspective in the following manner:

> The essential quality of the historical approach as a method of science I see as its integration of phenomena into an ever widening phenomenal context ... The context includes the placing in space and time and therefore, when knowledge allows, in sequence.

Thus, Kroeber insisted that anthropology's subject matter was predicated upon a historical approach. As he explained concerning the historical growth of more general cultural patterns, eventually all of these patterns tend "to develop and progress, later to degenerate and die" (1963: 41). His mentor, Franz Boas, is commonly associated with the theoretical orientation of "historical particularism," even though the "historical" dimension of this paradigm would appear to be woefully underdeveloped. Yet, as Sidky (2004: 39) concludes, "The version of Historical Particularism expounded by Kroeber retained the idealist (culture as mental rules) antiscience, no-laws-and-causality-in-culture, interpretive, and particularistic thrust of the Boasian program."

George Stocking (1968, 1985) was another American anthropologist who promoted a research agenda employing historical and archival sources and methods. His view of the use of a historical perspective in anthropology is similar to that expressed by Kroeber in that Stocking refers to "an understanding of context and of change in time" as essential in comprehending cultural phenomena (1968: 109). However, Stocking also promoted the goals of "historicism," which he described as a "commitment to the understanding of the past for its own sake (ibid.: 4). He contrasted historicism with the idea of "presentism": "When the governing interpretive context is rather that of the *present-day* theoretical polemic, historical misinterpretation is the all too frequent result" (ibid.: 108). Misinterpretation, Stocking suggested, results from removing things from their historical context, and then judging them apart from this context, which is to say, "organizing the historical study by a system of direct reference to the present" (ibid.: 103).

In Britain, Evans-Pritchard (1961, 1981) was largely responsible for bringing historical perspectives into the field of social anthropology. He boldly declared that anthropology and history shared many aims and methodologies despite some of the apparent differences between the two disciplines in their particular perspectives and methodologies. He also reaffirmed Maitland's century-old assertion about the necessity of anthropology choosing between history and nothing (1961: 20).

Lucy Mair, another British social anthropologist, was led to ask the question, presumably based on Evans-Pritchard's foundational work, "What is anthropology if it is not history?" She notes that while "much has been written about the relation of history to anthropology ... contrasts and comparisons between the two studies have implied very different arguments at different times" (1965: 35). The application of history to anthropology can also result in meaningful synthesis: anthropologists can find out more about the past of the peoples that they study, or can learn from the writings of historians concerning social institutions that are no longer accessible to contemporary, first-hand study. A recurrent issue remains, as Mair notes (ibid.: 36), about whether the methodologies of historical research are amenable or appropriate for studying societies that interest anthropologists for which no written records exist.

The journal *History and Anthropology* has now been published for over thirty years, but in the initial issue of 1984 the editors felt the need to lay some groundwork in terms of the journal's scope and their views about the relationship between the two disciplines. The editors specify that the aim of the journal is not to explore the conditions that would help to bring the two disciplines together, or to retrace the historiography of a long debate caused by a mutual lack of understanding. Rather, the editors point out, the journal would explore

> two interesting movements [that] have developed within these two disciplines: an anthropologization of history, and, more recently, a historicization of anthropology ... Studied more closely, from the perspective of sociology of knowledge, these movements are complex and far from uniform. Each has its own chronology, and indeed, its own genealogy, according to disciplinary, institutional, and national traditions ... This journal would like to [propose that] anthropologists and historians come together on a project and pursue what then becomes common research, by confronting their material, and crossing their questionnaires, before publishing together the results of their inquiry. (Editorial Comment, *History and Anthropology* 1984: i)

In more recent times an emphasis on historical anthropology, especially in the context of Irish ethnographic studies, has been the focus of research by O'Neill (1984) on the parish of Killashandra in County Cavan, Gulliver and Silverman (1995) for Thomastown, County Killkenny, and an edited collection of Silverman and Gulliver (1992). Such studies of Irish historical anthropology, which have brought together historians, sociologists, and geographers, as well as anthropologists, demonstrate the commensurability that is possible between diverse disciplines in the pursuit of common goals and objectives. These works are of special interest because they explore the wider implications of specific Irish case studies as well as the interstitial areas between academic disciplines. Throughout they have emphasized an approach to historical anthropology through local-level research. As Silverman and Gulliver (2005: 163) explain, "local-level research allowed us to access conditions, events, actions, relationships, and meanings at ground level, to raise new questions, and to use the opportunity to search for answers."

Historical Anthropology

The lengthy introductory essay by Silverman and Gulliver (1992: 3–72) in *Approaching the Past: Historical Anthropology through Irish Case Studies* is particularly instructive in illustrating these possible commonalities of purpose. For example, an important distinction is made between *historical ethnography* and an *anthropology of history* or *historical anthropology*. A *historical ethnography*, for example, "provides a description and analysis of a past era of the people of some particular, identifiable locality, using archival sources and, if relevant, local oral history sources ... It was this kind of ethnography that at last brought anthropologists away from long-established, clumsy devices and assumptions such as the ethnographic present, autarchic 'communities,' and stable 'tradition'" (ibid.: 16). In other words, this perspective focuses on how the past leads to and functions to create the present, which would include both synchronic and diachronic studies of a past time. This approach could include a general viewpoint, covering many aspects of social life during an era, or it could concentrate on certain features, such as kinship relations, political movements, or religious phenomena.

A move away from a focus on the "autarchic community" has been a feature of social anthropology for at least the last generation or two of scholars. Yet, as Charles Tilley (1978: 213) observes, "the discipline of anthropology is far broader than ethnography." This points to a common misconception of anthropology among those in other disciplines who see it as relatively confined, in an intellectual sense, to matters of local interest, or to those of our "primitive contemporaries." The rejection of the idea of a closer relationship between anthropology and history, then, can be grounded in an objection of an epistemological nature. The objection of, say, historians to a closer working relationship with anthropologists might be based on grounds concerning the appropriateness of a focus on the European past which uses "theories, models, and methods which were developed by anthropologists in order to understand and interpret the non-European worlds" (Cohen 1987: 66).

Of course, there are anthropologists who dispute this characterization, especially if they have attempted to study European history using methods and theoretical approaches of a more up-to-date, innovative, and inclusive nature (see, for example, Wolf 1982: 1990). It should also be added, though, that anthropology has developed its own perspectives on viewing the past, a result of long-standing ferment in the discipline as a whole. From the historian's perspective the difference between history and anthropology is relatively clear; there exists a fundamental difference between what has been termed "narrative history and a history that uses social concepts around which to frame a study," as Silverman and Gulliver (1992: 52) suggest.

Historical anthropology, another approach to research, can be defined as a concern with recording and describing an insider's point of view, including their perceptions and assumptions of their own socio-cultural system in their terms (Silverman and Gulliver 1992: 19–21). The goal here is not to provide an analysis of history in an "objective" sense, which is to say, history external to the insider's perspective. The interest, rather, is in what people know about their place in life, and what they remember about their past, as they interpret or make sense of the interrelationships which connect the past to the present.

Historical anthropology, then, uses constructions of the past to explain the present. It also looks at the way traditions are invented, or the way in which the past is created in the present or, alternatively, how the past created and recreated the past (ibid.: 16). In this context of "invented" traditions, Cohen (2009) provides a relevant discussion of historical anthropology as "constructed" through narration, which he says has led to the "unsettled nature of the big story of historical anthropology ... [such that] the potential power of historical anthropology may lie in the *absence* of disciplinary configuration" (2009: 289).

Recent work continues to examine the interrelationships between history and anthropology. For example, in *Critical Junctions: Anthropology and History beyond the Cultural Turn*, Kalb and Tak discuss what they refer to as "a multiplicity of interlinked modernities" which provide the context, space, and place in which local and global histories interconnect (2005: 23). Also in this volume Handelman shares the view that the "relationship between anthropology and history is one of inequality ... History's capacity to deconstruct anthropology is unconditional, its rhetoric imperiously declarative; anthropology's capacity to deconstruct history is qualified, more possible than actual, and in any case, partial ... [anthropology's] epistemological status is in the historian's grip" (2005: 29–30).

Tagliacozzo and Willford (2009) refer to the academic disciplines of history and anthropology as "strange bedfellows." This relationship is also referred to as an "imbrication," implying regularly arranged, overlapping edges, as in the setting of roof tiles or fish scales, reminiscent of

Dirks's (2002: 59) allusion to an "ethnographic state" which "produces, adjudicates, organizes, and maintains the discourses that become available as the primary texts of history." Thus, historians and anthropologists find themselves as "strange bedfellows," a relationship which, given their coinciding interest in archival material, is probably not so "strange" after all.

Anthrohistory

The idea of blurred boundaries is the subject of a collection of essays entitled *Anthrohistory* (Murphy et al. 2011), which, as indicated in its preface, is the result of the work of scholars "who embrace this impulse to produce engaged and reflexive scholarship at the crossroads of anthropology and history ... [and] whose work seeks to produce knowledge between and beyond the two disciplines" (Bhimull, Murphy, and Patterson 2011: 4). Thus, the attempt by the scholars in this volume is to move beyond the frequently sterile intercalary or interstitial debate about what is historical, what is anthropological, and what is overlapping between the two modes of enquiry. More specifically, *Anthrohistory* is a volume which "searches for ways to produce ethically responsible knowledge in a world riven by violence and dominative forms of power" (ibid.).

A reasonable conclusion that could be drawn from the foregoing discussion of history and anthropology, whose literature extends for well over a century of debate and various forms of dialogue, is that both disciplines are identifiable in their own right by separate methodologies and epistemologies. Overall, it would not be accurate to characterize anthropology as another form of history, nor would the obverse of this be true. Instead, one could more accurately suggest that the disciplines share a conceptual territory, commonly referred to as "the past," although this terrain is viewed from different lenses.

Time, Place, and the Ethnographic Present

The concept of time in anthropology has always taken on a peculiar twist. The term "ethnographic present," as used in social anthropology, allows the researcher to describe past situations, places, and events as if they still exist, in their unaltered past state, in the present world. In other words, there is a certain "commingling" of tenses, of past and present, which could lead to confusion over this juxtaposition of "time then" with "time now."

There has been little discussion in the literature of anthropology pertaining to this temporal peculiarity, or as to the epistemological justification for it. Possibly the ethnographic present served a useful purpose in the past by allowing ethnographers time to analyse their field data at their leisure, unencumbered by undue pressure to publish their field results within a specific period of time. It is also entirely possible that several decades could have passed between the time that the original field data were collected and the time that the research results were eventually disseminated. The problem, of course, is that in the intervening years the society, community, or culture described in the original field enterprise might well have changed drastically, thus, at least partially, invalidating claims or generalizations that the ethnographer put forward.

Another, related, problem with the concept of the ethnographic present pertains to the perception of ethnographic research as a sort of timeless exercise, as if it is suspended in an ethnological vacuum, unaffected by the exigencies of the modern world. Certainly, Conrad Arensberg's classic study *Irish Countrymen* (1968 [1937]) could be seen to be faulty on this account. One cannot find any mention in his ethnography of current events in Ireland, such as the upheavals caused by tenant revolts. Arensberg evokes an air of bucolic bliss in the countryside of County Clare, while the country as a whole was bubbling with social and political ferment during the time of his fieldwork. The ethnographic record has no mention of these realities of time and place. If "the times" can be seen to be responsible in large part for the creation of local situations, then it can be suggested that the "ethnographic present" is an encumbrance on the road to achieving truth or validity, however that may be portrayed in social anthropology.

It has been pointed out, then, that an important aspect of historical anthropology is the analysis of conceptions of "pastness" (Humphries 2011: 254). This is particularly relevant because the "modern conception of time as linear implied that the past could no longer provide images of possible futures ... in which the classic and the sacred, culture, the nation, and evolution, in varying articulations, were the organizing concepts." In this sense the classical Greek and Roman philosophies were "positioned as ancestors of the modern West, and hence as progressive or timeless and as secular substitutes for religion" (ibid.). Hence, tensions were then created between traditional culture and modernization, especially given the general belief in progress in technology and science in the modern Western world; a belief not necessarily shared by other cultures, in which time may be cyclical, rather than linear, or in which temporal changes might not lead to progress, in the Western sense.

These difficulties of relating time and culture also play a significant role in attempts to study historical anthropology in relation to prevailing notions of place. The idea of place is firmly rooted in the local – the communities, towns, and villages that are the usual subject of anthropological enquiry. This focus on the "small-scale" has allowed research to be kept on a manageable scale. The conventional data-gathering techniques of participant observation, and loosely structured interviews, allow for the sort of face-to-face interaction that is one of the unique features of social anthropology. But what of historical anthropology, in which such close contact between informants and researchers is not possible, since they are separated by time and place?

Despite these spacial and temporal separations, the researcher nonetheless attempts to "get to know" the people, the research subjects, to become familiar with their living conditions, their habits, their social contacts and modes of interaction through whatever means available. Through census data the researcher learns about the household composition of a community, about its housing conditions, the age structure of the population, forms of schooling, and other important areas of local life such as agriculture and commerce.

Local church records are sources of information about marriages, births, and deaths. Records kept in regional centres can inform us about district divisions and administrative units, possibly for taxation or other purposes. Local libraries and museums can house personal diaries, recorded oral histories, first-hand accounts of early settlers, and many more such possible historical sources. It is evident that researchers are likely to have available for their purposes a surprisingly large store of data on past populations in any particular region where there exists a reasonably literate tradition.

Theoretical Goals and Objectives

It is, therefore, in the spirit of this interdisciplinary perspective that I explore in this study the Irish post-Famine experience in the Ottawa Valley region of eastern Ontario (see maps 1–3).

A township in Renfrew County, called Admaston, was chosen for my research purposes as a unit of analysis because of its high Irish population and the availability of records concerning such features as household composition, farm size, and agricultural productivity.

I have several theoretical objectives. A general goal concerns the epistemological endeavour of merging anthropology and history. While the field of historical anthropology is now well developed, this book represents, as far as I am aware, the first extended study in which an anthropological perspective is utilized to examine the adaptation of the Irish to farm life in Canada. Outlined below are three more specific research goals concerning the relationship between the Irish family in eastern Ontario and the exigencies of farm life that took place after the Famine.

In terms of theoretical perspectives, one of the primary goals focuses on certain analytical issues pertaining to the study of farm productivity in what are essentially pre-capitalist- or subsistence-level economies. For example, there is a debate in the literature of anthropology and several other disciplines concerning the applicability of the Russian economist Aleksander Chayanov's model of the "peasant economy," especially in its pre-capitalist form (see Hedican 2009). Essentially Chayanov (1966) proposed in *The Theory of Peasant Economy* that farm productivity was related to the internal composition of farm households, in terms of the relationship between the number of farm producers and the corresponding number of consumers that they support. In Chayanov's theory, increases in farm productivity in a pre-capitalist economy are inversely proportional to decreases in the producer/consumer ratio. In other words, at the basis of this theory is the proposition that farmers will only be compelled to work harder if they have more mouths to feed.

A second research goal of this study concerns an exploration of the internal composition of Irish households and a discussion of a long-standing debate in anthropology which has focused on a three-generational kinship unit that has been termed the "stem family." The data collected for this book on Irish Canadians provide a unique opportunity to shed light on this controversy. For example, discussions in the anthropological literature concerning the Irish stem family have been exclusively, as far as I can tell, restricted to Ireland itself. My research explores the stem family phenomenon among the Irish who immigrated to Canada, and examines if the move to a new geographical setting had altered in any way the frequency of this family form.

There are several alternative perspectives that could be explored here. One of these is the hypothesis that the Irish stem family is a "traditional" cultural phenomenon, in which case one would expect that it would be maintained in Canada, or elsewhere in countries where the Irish emigrated, at least for a generation or two, However, the stem family phenomenon might not be influenced by cultural factors at all. It could possibly be a result of other underlying factors, such as economic influences. If this were the case, we would expect that changing economic factors, such as an increase in farm size, or the availability of credit and capital, would provide the impetus for new family forms that were more adaptable to the new conditions of farm life: for instance, the three-generational form would give way to other configurations, such as the nuclear family. This research goal would furthermore serve to clarify the nature of the Irish adaptation, in both social and economic terms, to their new land, a land in which certain traditions were maintained and others changed.

A third theoretical goal centres on exploring the issue of the determinants of family size. The historical literature on the family has displayed an enduring interest in family size and the factors contributing to it. The historical data presented here afford an excellent opportunity to study the relationship between the size of Irish Canadian families and their agricultural settings, especially in terms of the size of the family's landholdings. Hence, this third research goal seeks answers to the question: What determines family size?

Theory as Problem-Solving

In many anthropology texts a discussion about history and anthropology is followed by a debate about whether anthropology is a science, or if it can be or indeed wants to be a science. Most of this discussion is based on the premise that the goals of anthropology extend beyond mere historical reconstruction and into the realms of theory and problem-solving. This discussion does not advocate an anti-historical approach, or deny the usefulness of a historical orientation; it simply makes the case for an alternative mode of knowledge acquisition.

The designations most often applied to a scientific orientation in anthropology are *empiricism* and *positivism*. Empiricism refers to the belief that one's scholarly work is grounded in certain facts or data; in other words, it is grounded in the concrete or "real" world. Positivism is a viewpoint based on the assumption that the social world is patterned in certain ways or that it has an orderly configuration. In addition, the term *nomothetic* is applied to forms of enquiry that search for social laws or regularities that are believed to exist in this concrete reality.[1]

It is beyond the scope of this book to lay out the history of scientific orientation in anthropology, but suffice to say that there has been as much ink expended on this form of enquiry as there has been on the relationship between history and anthropology. In any event, people obviously make choices which do not at times seem to make much sense from a scientific point of view, yet it could be argued nonetheless that aggregates of humans in the form of societies and cultures do have certain patterns in their movement through history that are knowable within certain parameters.[2]

If we take the development of agriculture, for example, there is little doubt about the major ramifications or consequences of a movement away from hunting and gathering, as has been persuasively argued in

Jared Diamond's (1999) Pulitzer Prize–winning book *Guns, Germs, and Steel*. While Diamond (1994 [1987]) has argued elsewhere that the adoption of agriculture was "the worst mistake in the history of the human race" (because of the consequent spread of disease, poverty, political subjugation, and so on) there are certain consequences of food production for which "scientific" explanations can be provided. This applies to population expansion, the development of social hierarchies, and other similar social processes.

Research Goal One: The Intensity of Domestic Production

Farmers' productivity can be explained in various ways. One could say that a farmer was a hard worker, or that he or she made effective choices in terms of crops sown. It might also be said that a farmer was lucky to have favourable weather conditions, or that there was a minimal loss of crops due to a low incidence of predatory insects or mammals.

Aside from explaining farm performance in terms of farmers' decisions, or the ecological situations in which they live their lives, one might also seek explanations in terms of the wider socio-economic sphere in which the farm life is situated. Farm performance, or what Marshal Sahlins (1971) once referred to as the intensity of domestic production, can also be compared across various similar situations in time and space. In terms of Irish farm households, Kane (1968), for example, drew comparisons between rural households in southwestern Donegal and those of an Irish American community in Ohio. Such comparative studies of are a valuable addition to the literature because they illuminate structural similarities and differences in Irish farming as related to different ecological and social settings. Thus, farm performance can be understood in a transitional sense, as an adaptive process. Differences between Irish American and Donegal households affecting farm performance include kinship structures that "serve as a central distributing point for services, minor economic aid, and the exchange of goods" (Kane 1968: 254).

Another example of these wider socio-economic trends is seen in ethnographic research in Ballyferriter in southwest Ireland. Based on his research in this area, Symes (1972: 25) noted that "the most important variable is the structure of the family unit itself [and these] variations occur both through time and through space." The sorts of variations that Symes discussed include such factors as decreases in household size owing to wider trends in depopulation; transitional or structural factors, such as those resulting in a change from "stem" to nuclear families; and a growing scarcity of farm labour. He concluded that, all in all, "with a fairly rapid decline of household size during dispersal [resulting from emigration and moves to urban centres] and the increasing age and diminishing aspirations of the farmer, the level of farm production may be expected to decline" (Symes 1972: 35).

Many previous Irish studies of the post-Famine period focus on the effects of depopulation. In contrast, the present study explores farm performance in the context of population expansion, rather than depopulation. From a theoretical perspective, the study of farming communities undergoing growth and expansion acts as a balance to those focusing on communities in decline. In addition, the longitudinal approach taken in the present study, extending over several decades in the same geographical area, can illuminate how variations in household size and composition may have affected farm performance and how other factors may have been responsible for farm performance.

Chayanov's Theory of Domestic Production

The theoretical perspective which informs the present study of Irish family farms in eastern Ontario is derived from the postulations of the Russian agricultural economist Alexander Chayanov. The purpose of applying Chayanov's theoretical suppositions to Irish farms is to test their validity in the case of worker/consumer ratios among the Irish, and then to further examine his approach in the case of Irish farms that were on the verge of entering a capitalist economy. Another goal here is to examine the wider theoretical implications of Chayanov's approach, especially as it has been used in anthropology. The study also aims to answer the following question: Is agricultural productivity primarily determined by the size and composition of farming households, or, alternatively, is such productivity the result of "external" factors, such as social organization, political structures, or religious ideology?

Alexander Chayanov (1888–1937) was a proponent of agricultural cooperation but was sceptical of the indiscriminate introduction of large-scale farms in Russia. Chayanov's scepticism was rooted in the idea that peasant households which practise subsistence farming will tend to produce only as much food as they need to survive. He believed that the Soviet government would find it difficult to force peasant households to cooperate and produce a surplus. Stalin criticized these views as a defence of the kulaks, although Chayanov was ultimately shown to be right concerning problems with Soviet agricultural planning. In 1930 Chayanov was arrested, spent five years in Kazakhstan labour camps, and was subsequently shot in 1937 (in the presence of his wife, who had arrived at the scene, expecting his release). Eventually, in 1987, he was exonerated of any wrongdoing by the Soviet courts (Bourgholtzer 1999; Durrenberger 1982; Harrison 1975, 1977; Hedican 2009; Sivakumar 2001).

Chayanov's views are presented in his treatise entitled *The Theory of Peasant Economy* (1966). In its most fundamental sense, Chayanov's theory states that productivity in pre-capitalist societies is directly related to the composition of the farming household. Thus, the amount of work done by the labouring members of a household will be inversely related to the number of dependent consumers that workers would have to support. Therefore, according to this supposition, the higher the ratio of non-working children or others not directly involved in agricultural production to workers in a household, the harder the other working members must labour to satisfy the consumptive needs of the whole (Durrenberger and Tannenbaum 1979, 1992; Lehmann 1986).

Chayanov's notion that family size and composition determine the level of productivity of economic activity appears to be a common-sense concept, but its apparent simplicity is deceptive; there are intricacies in Chayanov's concepts that are not always immediately evident. Chayanov's ideas have been the subject of an ongoing debate encompassing several academic disciplines. In anthropology, for example, Marshal Sahlins (1971) was initially responsible for demonstrating the relevance of Chayanov's approach to ethnological analysis. In this Sahlins utilized ethnographic data collected previously by Melanesian ethnographers during fieldwork in (mainly) Tonga and New Guinea. His attempts suffered from several difficulties, stemming from the fact that the original data had been collected for other purposes rather than for determining the intensity of domestic production in these societies. His main problem stemmed from the very small size of his samples; much of his analysis rested on a sample size of a dozen or so cases, a size which unduly accentuated certain trends, while minimizing others. An additional problem with Sahlin's analysis was the lack of a longitudinal or historical dimension that could illustrate how variations in household size could have led to a corresponding change in domestic production (Evans 1974; Smith 1979; Tannenbaum 1984a, 1984b).

Despite several shortcomings in Sahlin's attempt to apply Chayanov's theory of household production to the acephalous political organizations of Melanesia, he nonetheless was able to demonstrate the applicability of this theory to a range of ethnographic situations with diverse levels of domestic production. While Sahlins (1971: 49) acknowledged "the many evident defects of method implicit in the very imperfection of these techniques," he was nonetheless optimistic about the theory's potential utility, suggesting that the "the difficulties of this work are only exceeded by the promise of a new economics, distinctively anthropological." More recent ethnographic studies (Hedican 2003, 2009; Vanhaute 2004; Hammel 2005) continued to pursue this somewhat elusive goal of an economic approach to agricultural production that was, in Sahlin's terms "distinctly anthropological."

Research Goal Two: The Irish Stem Family

A second major theoretical goal of the present study concerns the nature of the Irish stem family and possible comparisons that could be drawn between Ireland and Canada in terms of the nature of changing family norms, types, and structures. As far as the literature on agrarian social organization is concerned, the Irish case has become epitomized as the classic example of the stem family system (see, for example, Birdwell-Pheasant 1992; Douglass 1988; Foster 1978; Goldschmidt and Kunkel 1971; Harris 1988; Verdon 1979).

Characteristics of the Stem Family

No standard definition has been proposed in the literature; the concept of the stem family can perhaps best be described by way of a set of descriptive categories. In terms of contrasting types, the stem family lies somewhere between the "nuclear family," which is usually characterized by a dispersal of all the children, and the "patriarchal family," in which all sons bring their wives into the household. The stem family shares with the patriarchal type a cross-generational continuity of households, and as is the case with the nuclear family, a dispersal of most children.

The stem family, in its most rudimentary form, consists of a three-generational household, usually associated with farming communities and the practice of impartible inheritance. Thus, one working definition of the stem family is that it is characterized by a "domestic group that gathered three generations under one roof: the father and mother, one of the married sons and his wife, and the couple's children" (Segalen 1968: 18). Laslett summarized the stem family as a social system wherein the "parents married off and kept within the group only one of their children whom they nominated successor" (1972: 160).

While Gibbon and Curtin emphasize the three-generational aspect, they also see inheritance as a primary factor responsible for the continuance of this organizational system: "the stem family was a three-generational structure which functioned to retain its original location (land and/or house) by means of dispersing most younger members, while preserving the main family stem by a principle of single inheritance. Parents married off and kept within the group only those nominated as successors" (1978: 429).[3] There is, then, a certain cyclical nature to such households. In the initial stage the elderly farmer and his wife retire from their active farming duties, settling into a small apartment or spare bedroom attached to the main household. At this point the eldest son takes over the farm work from his father, which effectively means that this first-born son inherits the family farm in its totality.

Demographic Factors and Internal Tension

If, as often was the case, the elderly parents did not retire entirely from active farm life until they were at least in their fifties or sixties, the eldest son would not be in a position to marry until he was in his forties or maybe even older. Under these circumstances the age difference between the eldest son and his potential bride was apt to be considerable, perhaps in excess of twenty years. Thus, considerable tension within the family might well have resulted from this lengthy delay in marriage due to the father's intransigence in passing the property to his son. Another source of tension could have been ambiguity or lack of strict rules when it cames to the issue of which son stood to inherit the family farm; this situation could result in charges of favouritism if the eldest was not the eventual inheritor. As a result, as Connell points out, there was "apt to be the bitterest trouble between young and old [with the result that] the situation might well be ugly" (1962: 517).

A tendency of delayed marriage would then serve to reduce the frequency of stem families even further, as the "window of opportunity" would shrink accordingly with the older age of the husband and the more imminent prospect of the death of his parents. Thus, Hannan (1982: 150) has noted that "most demographic analysts have concluded [by 1911] that ... a higher rate of celibacy and late age of marriage had become the main defining demographic feature of western Ireland."[4] This point has been supported by Guinnane's (1991) claim that high rates of non-marriage for Irish farmers, and a general high age at marriage, were factors tied to the accessibility of certain support mechanisms, such as continuing ties to one's siblings. Of course, another limiting factor of a demographic nature in the prevalence of stem families is that in a society of large families such as Ireland, parents could only reside with one of four or five sons; for the rest, the stem structure was not viable.

It was possible for the son to marry earlier, but this was not likely until the son could demonstrate to his potential wife's parents that he would definitely attain the economic means to support his wife and family. In fact, this usually resulted in close scrutiny of the son's assets during the marriage negotiations referred to as the "match." Sometimes a neighbouring farmer would be cajoled or bribed to pretend that the adjoining farm belonged to the eldest son, to make it appear that the son's farm was larger than it actually was,. Of course, once the wedding took place, and the ruse had been discovered, it was too late to turn back the clock, possibly resulting in longstanding bitter feelings between the families. Tensions were also apt to arise between the daughter-in-law and the rest of the family. The son's wife, as an outsider to the family unit, could soon resent being "lorded over" by her husband's family, especially by her mother-in-law, who may begrudge giving up control of the family's domestic duties.

The cycle of the stem family was completed when the eldest son had children of his own, and was finally broken at the passing of his parents. Therefore, there are certain demographic and developmental factors that affect the duration of the individual stem family. The result, then, is that even if the stem family was an optimally desired family form, it was probably only possible for about 15 per cent or less of all families. For example, in their study of 15 selected Irish townlands, Gibbon and Curtin (1978: 438) found 12.2 per cent of 295 households to be of the three-generation type. Similarly, Fitzpatrick's (1983: 361) study of three-generation households found that they comprised 13.8 per cent of farming households in one (1901) sample, and 14.1 per cent in another (1911). In two samples taken in Ballyduff, County Kerry, Birdwell-Pheasant found that three lineal generations were present in 14.3 per cent among "strong" farmers, whereas 12.6 per cent of households among farmers of more modest means were three-generational (1992: 219–20).[5]

Inheritance of the Family Farm

Impartible inheritance of the family farm is usually considered the end result of a partitioning process of the farmland until the point is reached in which to reduce its size further would mean that no one would be able to grow sufficient crops to survive. Of course, this partitioning was apt to have adverse results for the younger, non-inheriting siblings. Younger sons would be forced off the land, in most cases remaining as bachelors because of their lack of assets, or they would take up odd jobs as farm labourers, immigrate to countries where better economic opportunities might exist, or become priests. Likewise, the daughters would have to leave the farm as well. Some would marry the older sons who had inherited neighbouring farms, or the sons of shopkeepers in town. Other daughters might be hired on as farm helpers, barely earning their keep. In some cases, the daughters would remain on their natal farms as spinsters or aging aunts, or would join a nunnery.

As can be expected, this issue of succession, or what could be more accurately termed "postponed succession" in the Irish case, is likely to play an important role in discussions of the stem family. Succession has has been the subject of much debate. Varley (1983), for example, is critical of the notion that the stem family is explained in terms of its contribution to the farm's labour supply problem. In fact, he argues that this situation of postponed succession might not necessarily have the consequences intended, such as eliminating the need for paid labour. Indeed, the stem family could result in the heir remaining a bachelor, thus preventing family succession altogether.[6]

In any event, as Varley (1983: 386) argues, there is no evidence provided by Gibbon and Curtin (1978) that farmers planned a delayed succession of the family property in order to keep up the farm's labour supply. Gibbon and Curtin replied that while they agree that there was "no necessary connection between the stem family and the optimization of the on-farm labour supply," they postulate nevertheless that "there was an important connection between the two, even if it is not a necessary one," and also admit that "the exact relation between petty commodity production and the stem family remains to be specified" (1983: 394).

Stem families are therefore part of a long-term developmental cycle. Even in societies in which stem families are considered an ideal – or preferred – family type, they do not exist in a vacuum. One can see then that the stem family must be constrained mainly by its own "limits of growth," which is to say, that it is part of a system which is at least partly the result of certain economic factors. It would appear that Connell thought of the Irish stem family in a similar manner when he reiterated that, because of economic factors, eventually "subdivision must come to an end. The subdivision of holdings was slackening [even by the 1830s], simply because the farms, further divided, would give nobody a living" (1962: 52).

It is therefore evident that in the literature on the nature of human family types, the stem family has attracted considerable attention, especially among scholars interested in the sociology of the family, cooperative cultural studies, and the history and evolution of human social organization. Much of the interest in the development of stem families is related to the fact that they are found primarily in agricultural societies in which a growth in overall population size results in the diminishing availability of land (Segalen 1986; Douglass 1988; Guinnane 1991; Hedican 2005, 2009; Laslett 1972).

These sorts of economic rationales or arguments for aspects of human behaviour are compelling at a logical level. People undoubtedly see themselves as motivated by the exigencies of earning a living, securing food, and so on. However, as far as the existence of the stem family is concerned, there are possible explanations beyond the solely economic ones related to farm size or volume of produce that can be gleaned from this land. It is reasonable to assume that social and cultural factors are equally important in explanations of family structure and organization.

It is conceivable that people would desire to live in a three-generational family household in order that cultural norms, values, and practices could be passed down through the generations. On the social side, the members of the grandparental generation could help with household tasks, such as caring for children, which would enable their offspring to devote more time to farm labour, food preparation, and caring for animals, and to the innumerable other tasks requiring attention on the family farm.

The Irish Family Controversy

In anthropology, ethnographic studies of the Irish family began early in the first half of the twentieth century. Arensburg's study of County Clare in the west of Ireland in the 1930s, *Irish Countrymen* (1968 [1937]), and Arensberg and Kimball's *Family and Community in Ireland* (1940) have come to be seen as authoritative sources on traditional Irish family life. However, despite the pre-eminence of these studies, they have invited criticism because they appear to be anchored in a functionalist view of society. Indeed, as Birdwell-Pheasant (1992: 205) suggests, "the Ireland of Arensberg and Kimball often seems to float in a timeless void, isolated from the perturbations of modern history and disconnected from any meaningful cultural linkages with Ireland's Gaelic and British past."

In later years other critics, moving beyond the functionalist approach, have provided alternative views on the nature of Irish families. Connell (1962: 302), for instance, notes that "in the Irish experience the student of population finds exception to many generalizations." Connell sees the Irish family undergoing a process of "diffusion" after the Famine; marriage and its related traditions, such as the "match," often led to migration across Ireland. Brody's (1973) ethnography of "Inishkillane" (a pseudonym) in the west of Ireland saw changes in Irish social life in terms of a general process of decay, which he accounted for in terms of "demoralization." However, it is debatable if any of these later analyses are more concretely grounded in Irish history than was the case with Arensberg and Kimball (1940).

Comparative Approaches

In more recent decades, several fruitful approaches have appeared in the literature. Kane (1968), for example, discussed comparisons between rural Irish households in southwestern Donegal and those in an Irish American community in Ohio. These studies are useful because they illustrate similarities and differences of a structural nature in terms of Irish family adaptation to new social and geographical settings. Using a comparative case-study approach, elements of Irish family life can be understood in a transitional sense, or as an adaptive response, from one set of conditions to another.

In a similar vein, Syme's (1972) research, centred on farm performance in Ballyferriter in southwestern Ireland, linked various social and economic factors of farm life. His overall conclusion was that "the most important variable is the structure of the family unit itself, variations [of which] occur through time and space" (1972: 343). These variations are accounted for by such transitional factors as a change from stem to nuclear families, or a decrease in household size caused by depopulation. The massive decrease in Ireland's population as a result of the Famine made more land available (theoretically at least) for the remaining farmers, so that one possible result would be a decrease in impartible inheritance and possibly also three-generational households.

Historical Approaches

Over the following decade, the subject of Irish family structure continued to be a topic of theoretical interest. Fitzpatrick (1983: 343) noted, on the basis of historical research on Irish farming families before the First World War, that the family structure in Irish rural society was "strikingly uniform and distinctive" throughout the period between the Great Famine and the First World War, such that household size "remained strikingly stable over the era of the 'post-famine adjustment' between 1851 and 1881."

A contrary view is expressed by Gibbon and Curtin (1983: 380), who refer to Fitzpatrick's assessment as "extremely tenuous and unconvincing." Furthermore, they suggest that in Irish families "mean household size and number of resident kin have no necessary relation to household structure, and where continuity in household and number of resident kin do exist the fact is no justification for assuming continuity in household structure" (1983: 377–8). In other words, increases in household size are not necessarily linked to change in the structure of these families.

Another way to understand the organization of the Irish farming family is through what could be termed the "historical-demographic" approach. This line of thought is put forward by Breen, who points out that "it is well known nowadays that many of the most salient features of Irish rural life ... came to prominence as a response to the changed circumstances of the peasantry in the nineteenth century" (1984: 95). Then there is the suggestion by Harris (1988) that the Irish stem family controversy would benefit using empirical fieldwork data for theory testing. As an example, Harris uses data relating to a small group of farmers in the west of Ulster; she argues that many previous assessments in the literature "do not stand up to the test of detailed ethnography, and that ... ultimately the field data suggest that not only broad class categorization but detailed account of resources are necessary for a satisfactory analysis of the situation" (1988: 417).

A Gendered Approach

The kind of "detailed ethnography" that Harris suggests is presented in a study of the division of labour on Irish farms by Patricia O'Hara (1998). Contrary to Harris and her class approach, O'Hara suggests that Irish farms could be better understood in the context of a gendered discourse. As she explains, Irish farming "was very much a family operation in which all able-bodied members were involved ... Family work was structured around gender and age, a 'concerted effort' within which there was a rigid division of labor between women and men" (1998: 270–1).

A focus on gender relations and the Irish family farm is worthy of further consideration, especially since there is in the literature a perhaps undue focus on men as farmers/producers, and women as consumers/household members. This is apparently also the case with many census reports; they commonly list men as the "household head" and wives as simply "related" to their husbands, implying wives' secondary status within the farming family. In regard to the stem family dialogue, Harris comments that Gibbon and Curtin's (1983) study of Irish families ignored "what actually happens and ... how decisions are really made. The structural bias of their position is revealed by its assumption that all important decisions in relation to the family and farm succession are made by men. I do not accuse them of 'sexism'; I think they ignore women simply because to take them into account would involve a reconsideration of their structural-Marxist model of class relationships. However, the role of women is here important and has significant implications" (1998: 423). Similarly, Shortall's (1993) comparison of Irish and Canadian farm women makes similar points concerning the devaluation of women's contributions to farm life.

Research Goal Three: The Size of Irish Families

The third research goal of the present study is to utilize the information provided by the Admaston Township census files on Irish farm families in Canada to find out if there exists a correlation between the size of such families and the size of their farms. In other words, this data on Irish families in Canada could be used to address an ongoing debate in the comparative literature on the family on the the determinants of family size. There is also an opportunity here to compare Irish families in eastern Canada with their counterparts back in Ireland to find out if a change in family size has resulted from an adaptation to the Canadian setting, a setting in which farm holdings are apt to be larger than those in Ireland.

This comparative study of Irish families could then be seen as a theoretical contribution to the literature on the history of the family; there have been many competing ideas concerning the determinants of family size. The question about why families are the size that they are has not been adequately answered in the literature and is, therefore, from a historical perspective, an important question to ask.

As far as size of farming families is concerned, the conventional wisdom is that since farming is (or at least used to be before mechanization) a labour-intensive activity, large families, with more members can share the work load, are at a distinct advantage over smaller ones. Yet, in a logical sense, this may be putting cause and effect in reverse order, especially given the vagaries of "family planning" in the nineteenth century.

Yet, contrary to conventional wisdom on the subject, it is more likely that large farming families were a liability, especially when most of its members were younger than fourteen years. These dependent children needed to be fed and clothed, and were not capable of significantly contributing to the labour demands of the farm until they were at least in their teenage years, and then they were liable soon enough to get married and start their own families. The issue of family size is worth looking at, especially in the sense of Chayanov's consumer/worker ratio, to determine if large farm families were more or less productive than smaller ones. A beginning is to examine what various authors have had to say about the issue of family size.

The Determinants of Family Size

The literature on the family in historical perspective exemplifies a truly remarkable variety of explanations, without any single one being particularly dominant over another.

1. *Evolutionary* explanations, for example, maintain that families at particular points in time are seen as the result of earlier forms, and thus a "natural" sequence through time.
2. *Functional* explanations, which are concerned with the part each social unit within a culture plays in the total existence of a culture, often argue that families fulfil certain basic needs, in the Malinowskian sense, such as procreation or assisting in the integration of society, in the Durkheimian logistical scheme.
3. *Cultural* explanations propose that families persist because of the preferences and traditions of a particular society.
4. *Economic* explanations suggest that different family types are better suited to different productive tasks; for instance, the nuclear family is more compatible with urbanization and an industrial society.
5. *Biological-demographic* arguments are proposed by sociologists who suggest that families expand or contract as a result of population dynamics, densities, and distributions in certain areas, and that family size is also affected by variations in fertility and other biological factors.

This list could be expanded further, but suffice to say that there is an extensive literature that discusses the size, composition, and changing aspects of the human family, each with different explanations on these topics, without any one explanation being necessarily more persuasive than another. However, reading what individual authors on the subject have to say with regard to particular data sets, fieldwork settings, or comparative schemes is an interesting task in itself (Bongaarts 2001; Gagnon and Heyer 2001; Burch 1967, 1972; Kuznets 1978; Salazar 2003).

Biological Factors

Bongaarts, a proponent of the comparative approach, used data from household surveys conducted in 43 countries to isolate "the proximate determinants of household size [and] ... to identify the main demographic factors that account for variation in size" (2001: 264). He also conducted a historical study of several European countries as well as the United States and Canada, concluding that "the dominant trend is a steady decline in household size from around five members in the middle of the nineteenth century to between two and three in 1990" (ibid.). Unfortunately, despite a very substantial sample size which extended throughout a long period of time, Bongaarts was not able to offer a definitive conclusion regarding the question of family size except for the somewhat weak observation that an explanation lies in the "pervasive decline in fertility over the past century," which hardly seems plausible in light of the fact that the total global human population has recently surpassed the figure of eight billion.

Gagnon and Heyer's (2001) study of family size focused on early Quebec in the time period between 1608 and 1800. In this study the French Canadian population was examined in terms of the variations in fertility rates as a determinant of family size. The authors used a biological perspective to examine the hypothesis that "family size has a tendency to run in families. This phenomenon was first interpreted as evidence of the inheritance of fecundity" (2001: 645).[7] The authors used considerable data in support of their hypothesis that family size is the result of biologically inherited factors, yet they were nonetheless led to conclude that "family size does not run in families in the early French-Canadian population" (ibid.: 656). Well, if biology is not the answer to the question about what determines family size, how about other logically viable alternatives?

Cultural Factors

As an alternative to the biological approach, in a study of Irish marital patterns, Salazar (2003) used what he referred to as the "cultural factor" to examine the issue of family size. After a lengthy discourse on the history of such demographic factors as nuptial rates and marital fertility, as well as on topics such as family systems, land tenure, emigration, and religion, he concluded that "Irish marital fertility was high ... simply because the Irish wished to have large families" (ibid.: 276). So, the conclusion here is that family size, among the Irish at least, was simply a matter of choice.

In another study of Irish families, O'Grada and Walsh (1995) shared a similar "cultural" explanation for the size of families in Ireland. The focus of their study was on the differences between fertility patterns among Protestant and Catholics. As a result of their investigation,

O'Grada and Walsh offer the opinion that the Catholics had developed a different set of cultural values concerning family size than that of their Protestant counterparts. Their conclusion is that "Catholic religiosity or 'culture' remains the best explanation for the gap" (1995: 278).[8]

Economic Factors

There are a number of studies that present empirical data in support of economic conditions as a causal factor in family size. Clay and Johnson (1992), for example, pose the question about which comes first; size of farm or size of family? While this is not a purely chicken-and-egg sort of situation, we are nonetheless left to ponder whether the answer to a question of this type lies in ultimate causes or factors of origin. In this case the researchers present data derived from a survey of 42 countries in sub-Saharan Africa which was designed to determine the effects of farm size on the size of families. Ultimately the authors were not able to find a conclusive relationship between the amount of land managed by farm households and their cumulative birthrate. However, as Clay and Johnson (1992: 504) conclude:

> The results suggest that farm size does increase the marital fertility of farm couples but the possibility of a reciprocal effect [i.e., that increases in family size result in increased farm size] is rejected. Moreover, the mechanism by which a large-sized farm results in a larger number of surviving offspring born to the couple does not appear to be a size in the demand for farm labour, since the size of the farm was unrelated to the number of household members of labour force age (15–65 years).[9]

Summary

Clay and Johnson's findings concerning the priority of farm size or family size as the causal variable have led them to the conclusion that the size of a farm does affect marital fertility. To the extent that a larger farm usually results in larger families, farm size is the causal factor. However, the obverse effect, that increases in family size will result in increases in farm size, is rejected based on a substantial study comprising farming families in 42 different countries. One is led to conclude, then, that just increasing the size of one's family by having more children does not necessarily lead farmers to increase the size of their farms.

There could be any number of reasons why increasing a family's size does not lead to increases in farm holdings, such as the unavailability of additional land, or the prohibitive cost of adding to the present landholdings. In any event, Clay and Johnson's study will be a useful point of reference for the present research. In the case of Irish farms in Ontario, however, there were options for increasing farm size that did not exist in the African countries considered by Clay and Johnson.

It is evident from this brief review that attempts to ascertain the determinants of family size extend over a wide range of approaches or "explanations" – cultural, economic, and demographic, among others. Although many more studies could be reviewed here, a reasonable conclusion that could be reached is that much of the previous literature on the subject of family size suffers from several defects. As an example, a number of these studies attempt to examine a database that is much too varied. Anthropologically speaking, a study such as that conducted by Clay and Johnson (1992), which attempts to understand family processes in more than 40 African countries in a single journal article, covers far too much social and cultural territory to be of much comparative value.

Similarly, an evaluation of family size that extends throughout a 200-year period, such as Gagnon and Heyer's (2001) study, is apt to to be too unfocused to be useful. Although one would think that it is beneficial to encourage a diachronic perspective or a synchronic one, socio-cultural tendencies that are more restricted to specific generations are apt to be missed in such a wide-sweeping approach. In addition, a "cultural" approach, applied in an indiscriminate manner is apt to lead to the notion that cultural processes result solely because of individual decision-making, or simply because people "wish" to have large families, as Salazar (2003) argues in his study of demographic growth in Ireland.

It is furthermore a possibility, or even a probability, that any single determinant of family size does not exist; rather a combination of several elements is at work to produce any given pattern of family characteristics. It is this possible mix of factors, some economic, some cultural, that interest us here.

Major Points of Orientation

The preceding review of literature concerning the various characteristics of the Irish family leads to the following points of orientation that will be used as a guide for the discussion of research in the remainder of this study. There are no clear-cut reasons that can be derived from the scholarly literature for the variety of family forms that exist around the world, and to assume that one explanation, or even several associated ones, could serve to account for family organization is probably not possible. Certainly there has been a lively debate among scholars in the sociological, historical, and anthropological literature concerning the nature, functions, and origins of the Irish family. Limited space precludes a more extended discussion of this literature, but, for the purposes of the analysis in the following chapters, certain key themes are mentioned here as points of orientation.

1 The debate in the literature concerning Irish family composition has apparently suffered from a preoccupation with Irish families in Ireland only; looking at Irish families elsewhere, in Canada in this case, would offer new insights into underlying conditions. In fact, new data involving a comparison between Irish family organization in both Canada and Ireland would serve as a basis for examining the fluidity of such families, beyond that which the Ireland studies alone would suggest.
2 The new data made available by the present study of Irish family farms in Renfrew County open the possibility of helping to clarify the protracted controversy in the anthropological, historical, and sociological literature on the fundamental importance of the stem family organization for the Irish, whether they lived in Canada or Ireland.
3 The present study seeks, in addition to the above, to examine the post-Famine adaptation and settlement of Irish immigrants to eastern Canada, in this case the Ottawa Valley region of southeastern Ontario, to determine the characteristics of the Irish family and farming that developed in their adopted country. This examination, in turn, allows for a comparison of the resulting adaptation with the sorts of family and farm practices prevalent in Ireland, in order to determine if these adaptations could in any way account for variation in the composition of Irish farming households.
4 A longitudinal study is proposed, rather than a static, more synchronic one, situated at only one point in time, for the historical period roughly centred on the decades covering 1851–81, to ascertain possible long-term trends in the composition of Irish household types. The argument here is that this longitudinal, out-of-Ireland approach, has not been undertaken in the previous literature, and therefore stands as an innovative research strategy for illuminating the long-standing stem family controversy.
5 There has been a protracted debate extending across many disciplines concerning the determinants of family size, without any clear conclusions being reached. Many of these studies suffer from defects in the authors' use of comparative methods, such that faulty

conclusions are drawn because either far too many different cultures are used as a basis for comparison, or the comparisons cover periods of time that are far too extensive. The suggestion here is that the subject of family size in farming communities be made based on much more controlled variables. In this case the methodology of "controlled comparison,"[10] which has a lengthy historical development in anthropology, restricts the variables here to one culture, the Irish, and to a reasonably limited time frame of about four decades, rather than many centuries. The variations here are mainly in farm size between Ireland and Renfrew County, and in family size between the two locations.

The debate concerning the nature of rural Irish families has extended over at least a 60-year period. Various approaches – demographic, historical, structural, and so on – have been promoted as viable alternatives by different authors over this period. Several pertinent points regarding the literature can be made. First, there is a certain preoccupation with focusing on rural Ireland to the exclusion of other historical/ethnographic settings. This narrow focus serves to severely limit the realm of possibilities and inhibit the search for alternative explanations.

Because of this preoccupation with Ireland alone, it is suggested here that a fruitful approach would be to examine Irish families in other areas, such as Canada, so that we are not so ethnographically bound, as is the case with those studies situated in Ireland itself. In the Canadian context, for example, we have the opportunity to examine Irish families in the context of population expansion, rather than – as been the case with most previous Irish studies – in the context of depopulation. Therefore, it would appear to be beneficial, in a theoretical sense, to study Irish farming communities undergoing growth and expansion as an empirical counterbalance to those studies focused on Irish communities experiencing decline.

Most previous studies have had a very limited historical depth, thus restricting the opportunity to examine long-term trends in the size and composition of Irish households. A longitudinal approach, I argue, should be adopted, one which extends over at least several decades in the same geographical area, so that we can have a better opportunity to bring to light factors responsible for variations in family size and composition through time.

Chapter Three

The Agricultural Conditions of Renfrew County

This chapter discusses the agricultural conditions of Renfrew County, such as soil composition and the climatic and topographical features of the Ottawa Valley region, thus providing details on the habitat and environmental circumstances in which the Irish immigrants were situated after the Famine. Renfrew County, especially Admaston Township, was one of the last areas of southern Ontario where reasonably priced farmland could still be purchased in the early 1850s. However, the agricultural conditions were not entirely propitious, as the land for the most part needed to be cleared of the forest cover before any crops could be planted. This chapter aims to provide a general description of the farming life at this time period, especially in terms of the crops grown, livestock raised, and the various farm strategies that were employed by the recent Irish immigrants of the mid-nineteenth century.

The Irish Immigrant's Choices

Irish immigrants in the post-Famine period of the early 1850s faced two serious and immediate concerns: where to live and how to feed their families. The first problem, about where to live, hinged on whether to live in an urban or rural environment. In Ontario during this time, the urban centres for the most part had not achieved a level of industrial development sufficient to absorb a large influx of immigrants, and if one chose to live in, say, Toronto or Hamilton, it would probably be in one of the many ethnic urban ghettos that were forming in the mid-nineteenth century. Urban life would no doubt have offered fewer favourable prospects; there would have been little chance of finding employment except in the most menial and poorly paid labour jobs. It is probably for this reason that the Irish experience in Ontario, as noted by several authors (Akenson 1984, most notably), was primarily a rural one; this contrasts with the more urban experience of the Irish in the United States, a country where industrial development was more advanced and hence more capable of absorbing new immigrants.

Choosing to live in a rural environment in Ontario offered several possibilities. One option was to seek employment in and around the lumber camps of the Ottawa Valley, but this had its limitations and was not particularly conducive to a raising a family. Employment in agriculture was therefore the obvious choice for most immigrants because it offered several important advantages. In Ontario it potentially offered an individual a modicum of control over his or her destiny; this was unlike the situation back in Ireland, where one was more likely to be subject to capricious absentee landlords.

Another advantage was that, as a landowner rather than a tenant, one could enhance one's position in life, through effort and diligence, so that one's children could benefit from the appreciation of one's landholdings. As Russell (1982: 136) suggests, "The promise of social mobility was there for every smallholder; if he could just get his lot cleared, he would be amongst the richest people in the province." In other words, the two main advantages of farming in Ontario for the immigrant Irish were employment security and the favourable prospects of long-term investments in a burgeoning agricultural economy.

Farming in Ontario's Wilderness

In his authoritative study of the history of agriculture in Ontario, Robert Jones classifies immigrants into three groups or categories (1946: 60–1). The first of these included immigrants with sufficient capital to purchase a farm ready-made. Second were the immigrants who could afford a backwoods lot and were able to support themselves and their families while clearing the land. In the third group were those who needed to labour on someone else's farm for several years until they were able to obtain enough capital to purchase even uncleared land.

From all the descriptions of the Irish immigrants fleeing the ravages of the Famine back in Ireland, there is little doubt that they would fall into the last two classes, that is, new farmers without capital. For a small farm, that is nine acres or less, Russell (1982: 139) estimates that in the pre-Famine period of 1812–42, the range of new farmers with capital would be from one-quarter to one-third of the total. Clearing rates were variable, and it was unlikely that one could transform a small farm into a larger one in less than a decade. Farmland was also much less expensive in Ontario during the pre-Famine period than later, as indicated in this quote from *The Canadian Emigrant* (13 July 1833, qtd in Russell 1982: 129): "The price of land, too, is still so Low, and may yet be had on terms so easy that the poorest individual can here procure for himself and family a valuable tract; which, with a little labour, he can soon convert into a comfortable home, such as he could probably never attain in any other country – *all his own!*"

The availability of arable land at reasonable prices was much more restricted in the post-1850 period. First of all, most of the good farmland in Ontario had already been taken up by then; the more marginal areas bordering the Canadian Shield, such as exists in Renfrew County, were all that was left for the poorer immigrant without the means to purchase a functioning farm outright. Second, immigrants were faced with the prospect of clearing whatever land they could obtain and taking the chance that their labour would uncover suitable land for agricultural purposes. If not, they would be forced to move on and try their luck with other forested land.

Single men had the opportunity to build up capital by working as farm labourers, or in the lumber industry along the Ottawa River and in the building of the Rideau Canal. Men with families needed to take more immediate steps to feed their dependants. Since it would take settlers about twelve to eighteen months after the acquisition of land to attain self-sufficiency in food (McCallum 1980: 10), that is, if prospective farmers could purchase land soon upon their arrival in Ontario, they would still need immediate help just to survive. In most cases, then, the extended family would act as a support group, helping the new arrivals with food, shelter, and possibly labour until they achieved a minimal level of self-sufficiency.

It must be remembered that when virtually all of a new settler's capital would be expended on a landholding, there would be almost nothing left for purchases of equipment, livestock, clothing, or anything else. This fact of life in early Ontario rural life is illustrated in an address delivered in 1849 by Sheriff Rutan:

> Our food was coarse but wholesome. With the exception of three or 4 pounds of green tea a year for a family, which cost us three bushels of wheat per pound, we raised everything we ate. We manufactured our own clothes and purchased nothing except now and then a black silk handkerchief or some trifling article of foreign manufacture of the kind. We lived simply, yet comfortably—envied no one, for no one was better off than his neighbour. (qtd in James 1914: 569)

Clearing Farmland

The settlers' most immediate concern was to clear enough land to begin growing a crop of food to feed their families. Trees were felled and most of the lighter branches burned, the resulting charcoal selling for a small profit. Often the larger trees were clear cut, using the so-called slash-and-burn technique, so that sunlight could eventually penetrate the forest cover. Ultimately wind would topple the dead trees, which was of course a hazard, but at least the fallen trees could be used for much-needed firewood, as well as for building materials for fences, barns, and houses.

The length of time needed to clear an acre of land has been debated in the historical literature. The time taken to clear forest cover often depended upon the farmer's ability to secure help with this task. Sometimes the farmer would have a few days free to devote entirely to forest clearing; or sometimes only a few hours were available after supper, when other chores were completed. One can see from these various factors that, from one farm to the next, the rate of land clearing depended on the availability of labour, the time needed to devote to crop production, or even the density of the forest itself.

As far as rates of forest clearing are concerned, the historical literature offers a variety of calculations. Forest clearing rates were dependent upon what the individual expected to gain from this work. Russell (1982: 130), for example, divides the landowners into three groups: pioneers, land speculators, and farmers. As far as pioneers were concerned, the return on their work was derived from the appreciated capital value of the farm, and not principally from any cash crop that might have been raised. The land speculators' gain derived from the enhanced value of their lands as neighbouring farms were cleared. In the case of the land speculators, land clearing was usually a mandatory aspect of establishing title. Establishing title in the case of land grants required a three-acre clearing after a period of several years. As for the farmers, our principal interest in this study; their economic position depended upon the amount of cultivated land that could be cleared (Jones 1946: 54; Guillet 1963: 303–6; Strickland 1970: 136).

Farmers themselves can be classified into two groups: those who participated in the commercial economy and those who farmed for subsistence purposes (Russell 1982: 136). For the commercial farmer, the amount of cleared land was of much more importance than the total amount of land owned. During the 1850s in Ontario substantial profits could be made growing wheat, which was mainly exported to the United States and, to a lesser extent, Britain. With yields of 30 to 40 bushels per acre, the commercial farmer could make a considerable profit from his land each year (McCallum 1980: 9–24). Subsistence farmers grew some wheat but this was mainly for their own consumption rather than for the commercial market; thus, they had little agricultural surplus.

"Early settlers in Ontario," McCallum (1980: 9) concludes, "had little agricultural surplus since only 5 to 10 acres of land could be cleared each year." Other historians, such as Edwin Guillet (1963: 312), offer estimates of land clearing that are much higher, such as 10 to 12 acres of trees chopped in a four-month period, or 10 acres of cleared, seeded, and fenced land in a year. Robert Jones (1946: 71–3) suggests that about four to five acres could be cleared in a year if a farmer worked by himself. Russell (1982: 136–8) used assessment rolls and found that the average rate of clearing was much lower – about 1.2 acres per farm in 1822 to about 1.5 acres cleared per farm in 1842. These figures for average land clearing derived from government documents, Russell (1982: 137–8, 144) claims, "seriously challenge the conventional view that the backwoods of Upper Canada could rapidly transform a pauper immigrant into a yeoman farmer ... In fact, at one and a half acres a year, it would take a healthy, hardworking immigrant working by himself just over thirty years to create a fifty-acre farm. [In other words] it took a lifetime for anyone lacking either a large family, or sufficient capital, to clear a farm of 50 acres and so provide a comfortable living."

For the period 1822–42, Russell (1982: 133) determined the number of farms and the average number of cleared acres for 15 Ontario townships using assessment rolls. During this time the number of farms increased from 2,006 in 1822 to 6,540 in 1842, which is a threefold growth; yet, perhaps surprisingly, the average farm size increased only slightly, from 33.6 acres of cleared land in 1822 to 34.7 acres in 1842. This statistical average is not a matter of many bigger farms and many smaller farms. In fact, the range of farm size is quite narrow. Over this 20-year period the largest farm comprised 54.4 acres and the smallest 13.3 acres of cleared land, but the size of most farms fell within a narrow range somewhere in the middle of these two figures. Further statistical analysis could be done here, but the reader gets the point: the farms in this period were virtually all the same size. The question is why?

Unfortunately, Russell does not engage in further analysis of the reasons for this narrow range of farm size because his primary interest was in studying property values through tax assessment rolls and ratepayer statements. For my own purposes here, the reasons for the narrow range of farm size is of interest as a basis for comparison of the Irish farms in Admaston Townships in the period just after the 1840s. As far as the reasons for the average of about 34 acres of cleared land, one can only offer a few suggestions.

One reason for the 34-acre average of cleared land could be that families were relatively small during this early period in Ontario's history, meaning that it took only about 34 acres of cleared land to adequately feed a small family. The farmer was not motivated to clear more land, having sufficient acres cleared to feed his family, which would then free up time for other important tasks, such as building barns and fences and raising livestock. Once these other requirements were taken care of, the farmer would then be in a position to start clearing more land again.

A second reason could pertain to Chayanov's assertion that the consumer/producer ratio determines crop production. Once the subsistence needs of the farmer's family were met, and having a limited opportunity to produce and sell a surplus, the farmer would devote the additional time to leisure activities. This supposition may run counter to the ideology of the Protestant work ethic, which would see the farmer working from dawn to dusk, with limited time spent with his wife and children.

A third factor concerns the reasons land was cleared in the first place. In the Assessment Act of 1819 cultivated land is defined as "every acre of arable, pasture, or meadow land" (qtd in Russell 1982: 132). Cultivated land was assessed at 20 shillings per acre, while uncultivated land was assessed at 4 shillings per acre. Given that, it is not likely that a farmer would be motivated to clear additional land unless he had a potentially profitable use for this land, since his taxes would increase five times for each acre of cultivated land. The farmer also had to consider factors related to need. For example, a growing family may necessitate increased crop production, while investing in more livestock would require additional pasturage. It is unlikely that a farmer would expend his valuable energy clearing additional farmland if there was no reason to do so, if this added land could not be put to productive use, given the additional tax money that would be required.

A fourth factor concerning the reasons for clearing new land has to do with where in the farm cycle the farmer found himself. One would presume that initially the farmer would work feverishly to clear as much land as possible because of the urgent need to feed his family. As time went on these consumptive pressures began to diminish so that the matter of cleared land was less urgent than during the initial habitation period. If one were to construct a graph of time spent on land clearing, activity would peak in the early years but would decline over time to reflect fluctuating need.

All of these factors had an important bearing on the rate at which farmland was cleared. It was not just a matter of clearing as much land as possible to increase the value of one's farm; there were additional costs involved with each acre cleared. It is reasonable to assume, then, that each acre of farmland that was cleared was done so with a purpose and not as some sort of free-time activity for the enjoyment of the exercise or as a matter of pride in cultivating a larger farm.

Agricultural Production

Agriculture production relies on a number of interrelated factors such as soil conditions, climatic features, labour force skills, types of crops grown, and the use of various tools. The most important of these are soil and climatic conditions, since even the most skilled farm labour cannot overcome deficiency in soil fertility or disadvantageous weather. On the other hand, given a climate suitable to the crops grown and suitable soil conditions, labour skills, and agricultural knowledge can be important factors in increasing agricultural production.

These factors were especially important for the time period of the mid to latter nineteenth century, a time in which farm mechanization was minimal compared to today. Fields were ploughed with oxen and horses. Extra labour was hired when needed if the farmer could afford it, or a labour exchange system, called *cooring* in Irish, would serve to reduce the costs of harvesting. This chapter examines the agricultural conditions of Renfrew County, focusing particularly on Admaston Township, to arrive at an assessment of which factors most specifically affected the situation of the Irish farmers during the period after the Famine.

Soil Conditions, Climate, and Topographical Factors

In many places the clearing of forest land is a requisite step in creating an area for growing crops. It is only after the forest is cleared and crops are grown that a farmer can make an assessment of the soil's productivity in general and the specific soil types suitable for different types of plants. In addition, the previous forest cover can have an effect on the nutrients in the soil. In spruce and pine forests, for example, the accumulation of fallen needles mixed with rain water results in fairly acidic soil conditions, conditions that may not be appropriate for growing certain plants. It is for this reason that archaeologists conducting excavations in the boreal forest often find that, since soil acidity quickly dissolves organic material, human remains are not available for further study.

Another factor not often considered is that much of a forest's nutrient content is held in the trees themselves. As a tree grows it draws nutrients from the soil, and when the tree dies the nutrients that it has accumulated are returned to the forest, which in turn supports the future growth of trees. Removing the trees, then, also eliminates an important source of soil nutrients. This is a problem with reforestation projects. After the trees have been cut down and removed there are often insufficient nutrients remaining in the soil to support a secondary growth of trees, resulting in sparse or stunted growth. Burning the felled trees, as in the slash-and-burn technique, returns some nutrients to the soil; however, the wood is often needed for heating and construction purposes. Without a significant source of nutrient replacement, or a scientific approach to crop rotation, soils may become depleted of the necessary requirements for crop production in a short period of time.

Other common soil problems are related to various topographical factors, such as moisture deficiency and retention; salinity resulting from low precipitation, which affects leaching; and shallow soil depth, a common problem in and around the Canadian Shield. The latter is a result of the scouring effects of the receding glaciers during the last ice age, or of swampy areas caused by poor drainage, especially in lowland soils. Without the use of artificial fertilizers nutrient deficiency would result in a consistent drop in crop yields over time. No doubt Ontario's early farmers were aware of these problems and would attempt to cope with their consequences by adding nutrients to the soil through composting with livestock manure or organic nitrogen fertilizers, such as soybean and fish meal. Or they would employ crop rotation or vary the use of different sectors of a farm area, such as switching to pasturage in the wetter areas.

Soil conditions are assessed by agronomists, specialists in the study of the interaction of plants, soils, and the environment; these specialists have worked out a well-defined scheme for evaluating existing soils utilizing a classification system based on the physical properties and chemical nature of particular soils. This system of soil classification is used to develop typographical maps which show existing soil types in a region and can be utilized to determine the suitability of various areas for crop production. The most fertile soils, for example, are found along the margins of streams where there has been an accumulation of alluvial soils. The running water removes nutrients farther up a watershed and deposits them downstream.

Other types of soil are affected by the accumulation of more or less decayed organic material, such as peat, which is composed of highly fibrous, partially decomposed plant material. Rich prairie soils are largely responsible for the success of cereal production in North America. These soils are built up over time from mulch composed of dead grasses. Sandy soils tend to be easily worked but suffer from low nutrient retention because of the leaching caused by the relatively heavier rainfall in the eastern part of Canada. Sandy loam soil, which consists of a mixture of sand, clay, and decayed plant material, is relatively fertile and thus was a favourite of the corn-growing Huron.

The soil conditions and general agricultural economy of Renfrew County were studied by Harry Cummings and Associates (2000), of the School of Rural Planning and Development, University of Guelph, in a special report prepared for the Ontario Ministry of Agriculture, Food, and Rural Affairs.[1] Even though this report was conducted recently, it is still useful for assessing the agricultural conditions in the nineteenth century; certain factors would have remained fairly constant over this time period, such as the distribution of soils of various types, general topographical characteristics, and, within a certain range, climatic conditions. The conditions for growing wheat, say, would have remained pretty much the same today as they were when the immigrants first farmed Renfrew County. Of course, yields of various crops and grains have increased since these times because of the later introduction of farm machinery, artificial fertilizers, and a more scientific approach to agricultural performance.

The most notable topographical feature of Renfrew County is that, with over half of the land area situated within the Canadian Shield, there is a limited availability good soil. The top soil classes in this area cover less than 15 per cent of the total land area. In Renfrew County the municipalities that are located along the Ottawa River, as far north as Pembroke, typically have larger parcels of land where soil conditions permit the cultivation of a wider variety of field crops than other areas of the county, and therefore provide a more diverse agricultural base.

In general, field crop production is limited by the crop heat units in the area; this is especially the case with Renfrew, which is rated as a relatively low 2,500 crop heat unit (CHU) area.[2] Thus, the length of the growing season is a significant factor in crop production. Agriculture Canada (2014) has a website devoted to the "Length of the Growing Season in Ontario" which helps to situate Renfrew County's climatic conditions relative to other locations in Ontario as far as agricultural production is concerned.[3]

According to Agriculture Canada the length of the growing season (LGS) is measured in days starting from the estimated seeding date (10 days after the average daily temperature is above 5°C) until the fall frost (minimum daily temperature 0°C) or until 31 October, whichever comes first, or the length of the frost-free period (LFFP). Here are some comparative figures for southern Ontario:

Table 1 Length of growing season, Southern Ontario

	LGS (days)	LFFP (days)
Niagara peninsula	212	158
Essex Co.	207	155
Guelph	189	126
Muskoka	182	123
Renfrew Co.	188	119

The conclusion that could be reached here is that in terms of climatic conditions, Renfrew County has probably the shortest growing season in southern Ontario, or at least comes very close to it. This places Admaston Township, on a relative scale of southern Ontario farming areas, as quite marginal given the restricted growing season and the types of crops that can be grown under these conditions.

During the time period of Cumming's study (1991–6), one-third of all farmland in Renfrew County was under cultivation, with beef farms accounting for over 50 per cent of all farms. The remaining farms in the study area consisted of dairy and miscellaneous specialty farms, such as those producing hay, maple syrup, and Christmas trees. The profile of farming in Renfrew County was changing during the study period, with field crop and miscellaneous operations steadily increasing in number and beef farms steadily declining.

In terms of farm size, data suggest that the average farm size in Renfrew County (269 acres/farm in 1996) is larger than the provincial average (206 acres/farm). In fact, the average size of Ontario's farms has increased as smaller farms are sold, resulting in fewer, but larger farms. This has evidently been the case throughout most of Ontario for a number of decades; however, the average farm size in Renfrew County has declined slightly over the previous (1986–96) decade. These details are mentioned here simply for comparative purposes; they will be useful for the discussion in later chapters concerning farm size during the 1850s and later decades in the nineteenth century.

Soil Capabilities

Renfrew County, the largest county in the province, comprises an area of 1.9 million acres, with the Canadian Shield extending across a large portion of this total land area. The agricultural capability of soils is based on the Canada land inventory (CLI) classification system which groups soils into seven classes according to their potential and limitations for agricultural use (Environment Canada 1980; Hoffman and Noble 1975). The most highly rated soils are those having no significant limitations on crop production and are therefore designated as class 1. The soils in this class hold moisture well, are relatively deep, and are well drained. They also rate high in productivity for a wide range of field crops under good management. Soils in the class 2 and 3 categories can be cropped with little difficulty; however, they suffer from some limitations in terms of the range of crops that can be grown, the timing of planting and harvesting, and methods of conservation.

Soils in classes 4 to 6 have a declining order of capability for agricultural purposes. For example, class 4 soils are considered marginal for sustained agriculture, as they are considered low to fair in productivity for a range of crops; however, some specially adapted crops may be successfully grown under certain conditions. Class 5 soils are capable of use only for permanent pasture and hay, especially in producing native species of perennial forage plants. Class 6 soils are capable of use only for grazing, as the terrain may be unsuitable for the production of field crops. Class 7 soils are considered unsuitable for agriculture, although certain specialty crops, such as tobacco, can thrive under controlled conditions. Often these areas are too rocky for practical farm use, or contain non-soil areas such as swamps or other small bodies of water.

In terms of the acreage of soil capabilities in Renfrew County as a whole, the approximately 1.9 million acres contain no soils which are rated in class 1, and about 234,000 acres in soil classes 2 and 3, or about 12 per cent of the total land area. The largest area falls into soil class 7 (unsuitable for agriculture), representing 1.2 million acres or 65 per cent of the total. Soils in classes 4, 5, and 6, those suitable for growing hay, pasturage, and grazing, therefore represent the remaining 23 per cent. So, to summarize, only about one-third of Renfrew County soils are suitable for agricultural usage. Of these, soils suitable only for pasturage and hay production are twice as common as soils capable of sustained crop production.

The better classes of soil in Renfrew County are largely located along the Ottawa River, and tend to be concentrated around the towns of Arnprior, Renfrew, and Pembroke. On average the allocation of farmland for crops in Renfrew County is substantially less than for either eastern Ontario or Ontario as a whole. This is likely due to a combination of factors, most importantly the relatively low percentage of the top three soil classes and the relatively low number of crop heat units (CHU) in this county. Consequently, farms in the western parts of Renfrew County typically have a lower proportion of farmland devoted to crop production.

From a comparative perspective, Renfrew County in 1996 had 412,000 total acres in farmland, 141,000 acres of which land was devoted to crops, or 34.2 per cent of farmland in crops. For Ontario in its entirety, 63.1 per cent of farmland was in crops, and 49.1 per cent of farmland in crops for eastern Ontario. In other words, on a percentage basis, Renfrew County had about 50 per cent less of its farmland in crops compared to the province as a whole (Hoffman and Noble 1975: 45; Cummings 2000: 12).

In Admaston Township, which is the more specific focus of our study, the total area of 80,940 acres contains 26,216 acres, or 32.4 per cent, of soils in class 2, and none in soil classes 1 or 3. Soils in classes 4 and 6 represent only 2,251 acres or 2.8 per cent of the total area. By far the largest area falls into soil class 7, comprising 50,958 acres, or 63.0 per cent of the total available land in Admaston. Thus, about one-third of the land area in Admaston Township is suitable for crop production for a fairly wide range of crops; that is, it is well supplied with nutrients and has good moisture retention and moderate to high productivity.

Thus, comparing Admaston Township with Renfrew County as a whole, about the same percentage (about 65 per cent) of the total land area in both cases is unsuitable for agricultural uses. However, Admaston, on average, has nearly three times the land area favourable for crop production (12 versus 32 per cent), but far less acreage (2.5 versus 23 per cent) that would be suitable for hay production and pasturage. The conclusion, then, is that Admaston Township is a far more favourable area for crop production than the average agricultural land in Renfrew County, but far less favourable for growing hay and for pasturage.

Land areas that could be devoted to pasturage, grazing, or hay production are severely restricted in Admaston Township, and therefore present a challenge for raising livestock without the purchase of additional feed. Most of the land area of this township, representing just over 60 per cent, contains either extremely rocky soil, terrain unsuitable for agricultural usages, or swampy conditions. However, this area may be of use for woodlots and other non-agricultural purposes such as hunting and fishing, foraging for nuts, berries, or medicinal plants; these may be valuable resources for the operation of the farm.

As far as comparative statistics are concerned, the first three soil classes in Renfrew County comprise just 12.5 per cent of the total land area. Admaston Township, which comprises 32 per cent of soils in these three favourable categories, thus has almost three times the county average. Aside from Admaston, there are 18 other townships in Renfrew

County, of which Admaston is sixth largest by land area. In percentage of the three top soil classes in the county, Admaston ranks seventh overall, ranging from Raglan, with none of the top soils classes, to Pembroke, with 78.6 per cent of its total land area comprising the top classes of soil.

It would be helpful to have research available indicating if there was a correlation between the percentage of soil types in the top categories and the history of settlement; such research might shed light on whether early settlers were able to determine and compare soil productivity on a comparative basis before they chose to farm in any one township in Renfrew County. If they could, then the likely settlement pattern would be one in which the township with the top percentage of the most productive soil types would be settled first, and the others would follow in a sequence of habitation according to their soil classes, from better to worse. However, even given the luck of some farmers in choosing the most favourable soils in Admaston Township, the climatic conditions in Renfrew County as a whole would be the same for everyone. The county is one of the most marginal in southern Ontario in terms of the length of the growing season, thereby restricting crops to those capable of surviving the relatively cool summer temperatures of the Ottawa Valley.

Of course, the early farmers would not have had access to maps of Renfrew County's soil classes or climatic conditions, nor would they have had much more than anecdotal information on how productive the soils were in the various townships, or on the average summer temperatures of the region. Settlement patterns, though, were made mostly based on what was available on a first come, first served basis. All in all, the early farmers migrating to Renfrew County would no doubt be aware that this was one of the last areas of southern Ontario in which there was available farmland. The obvious reason for this is that the soil characteristics, climatic conditions, and general topographical features were less desirable than in other parts of Upper Canada, much of which was already inhabited.

Statistical averages, in any event, might mean little to the individual farmer. Two brothers, for example, might purchase two adjoining farms of 50 acres each. After several years of cultivation one brother finds that his farm has 80 per cent of the best soil classes, while his nearby brother has only 20 per cent. Statistics have meaning in terms of informing us about aggregate totals, but have little meaning on an individual basis, just as rates of life expectancies areas are probably not going to have a measurable impact on our individual lives – we all expect to live long and prosperous lives, regardless of what the mathematicians tell us are our odds of doing so.

Speaking of statistical averages, one might ask at this point what the carrying capacity of Admaston Township might be for a farming population in the latter half of the nineteenth century. For starters, the total land area of Admaston comprises 80,940 acres. Assuming an average farm size of 100 acres, which could probably support a family of eight persons, the 809 farms would be theoretically capable of supporting 6,475 persons. These are useful figures to keep in mind for the later discussion of farm size and agricultural capabilities.

Land Area Classified by Use

To reiterate, in 1996 Renfrew County comprised 34 per cent of its farmland in crops, compared with 63 per cent for the province of Ontario. Furthermore, about 34 per cent of the land area was devoted to pasture and the remaining land was not put to any agricultural use. As far as Admaston Township is concerned, it ranks somewhat above the Renfrew average with 39 per cent used for crops and 35 per cent used as pasture. In total there were about 1,500 farms, averaging 269 acres per farm in Renfrew County. Admaston had a total of 120 farms, with an average farm size of 315 acres (Cummings 2000: 22–8; orig. Canada, 1996, Census of Canada, Agricultural Profile of Ontario).

Farms classified by type reveal that for Admaston 23 per cent were devoted to the raising of dairy cattle (24 farms) and beef cattle (48 farms), 6 per cent to field crops (19 farms), and the remainder, less than 1 per cent, to miscellaneous use. In fact, 65 per cent of all dairy farms in Renfrew County as a whole were found in four townships; Admaston is one of these. Given the preponderance of dairy and beef farming, it is not unexpected that hay is an important field crop in Renfrew County; it is one of only five counties in Ontario with over 100,000 acres of farmland in hay production. Farms in Renfrew County also generate substantial sales of forest products, with only two other counties in Ontario (Huron and Bruce) generating higher sales. Other significant sources of revenue in Renfrew County were derived from the sheep and lamb industry. In sum, by the late 1990s, the most significant source of farm revenue was derived from the dairy and beef industry; the sale of field crops, while still substantial, was of secondary importance.

In terms of farm size, the range in Renfrew County in 1996 was between 82 acres and 680 acres (which includes owned and rented land). Farm size in this area has not increased as rapidly as other areas of Ontario, partly because of a local emphasis on the preservation of family-operated farms. The study by Cummings (2000: 55–6) noted a trepidation that farmland in eastern Ontario would be taken over by large corporate interests, such as feed and other farm supply companies. Farmers also expressed their opinion that intensive farming, with its large capital costs, would make it difficult for future generations to shoulder the costs of taking over the family farm.

Conclusion

Renfrew County as an agricultural area has historically faced several important challenges. Probably the most important of these is that the potential for agriculture is limited by the lack of quality soils in the region; less than 15 per cent of the soils fall into the top three soil classifications, those which are judged to be capable of sustained agricultural production. By comparison, near the city of Ottawa, over 50 per cent of the soils fall into these top three classifications (Cummings 2000: 91).

The main reason for the paucity of the top soil groups in Renfrew County is that more than half of its land area is within the Canadian Shield, with the result that about 65 per cent of the land area is unsuitable for most agricultural uses. However, there are five or six townships situated along the Ottawa River, including Admaston, which possess larger parcels of land where soil conditions permit more agricultural diversity. Besides soil conditions, another limiting factor in field crop production is that the cold climate in Renfrew County restricts the growth of certain plants; the average crop heat unit figure (at 2,500 CHU) is generally lower than for the rest of southern Ontario.

Renfrew County represented some of the last available farmland in southern Ontario at the time of the Irish Famine. If a potential farmer was able to secure land in the eastern portion of the county, he would find that soil conditions were generally favourable. Admaston Township, for example, contains of 26,000 acres (32.4 per cent of total land area) of class 2 soil, which is rated as moderately high for a wide range of crops and can be managed and cropped with little difficulty. Another 2,500 acres of land fall into soil classes 4 and 6, which have limited agricultural use and are rated as low to fair in productivity of field crops but could be used for sustained grazing for farm animals. However, 63 per cent of the just over 80,000 acres in Admaston Township fall into class 7, designated as having no capability for agriculture or permanent pasture because of rocky conditions, shallow soil, or small bodies of water and swamp. Thus, the early farmer who lacked modern soil maps would find choosing a farm to purchase a risky business, especially if the forest cover had not yet been cleared and the land had not been previously tested with some crop production. Farming in the more western parts of Renfrew County, with its predominantly class 7 soil conditions, could prove to be an economic disaster.

Chapter Four

Land Use and the Allocation of Resources

Many factors affect agricultural production. Some of these are related to the vagaries of weather – extreme temperatures, too much rain, not enough rain – or the presence of predatory insects, birds, and mammals. There are important decisions to be made concerning which crops to plant, the needs of livestock, time devoted to building and maintenance of farm structures, and an almost limitless list of other concerns. Wrong decisions can have disastrous results on a farm family, and can even threaten the family members' very existence.

Choice and Risk on the Family Farm

Farmers make choices that are largely based on personal experience and knowledge passed down from one generation to the next, through processes of cultural transmission. This transmission of behavioural patterns and traditions is known as *enculturation*. New ideas also result from *acculturation* processes, which are transmitted through cultural contact between members of different societies. Farmers use information passed down from previous generations, lessons learned from their own personal experiences, and coping techniques shared by their own peers. These processes combine to form the *adaptive strategies* that are utilized to shape the patterns of human-environmental interactions. The assumption made in anthropology is that groups with the most effective adaptive strategies are more likely to have higher survival rates than those with less effective adaptive strategies (Bates 1998; Moran 2000).

Farmers formulate a set of expectations or probabilities about the outcomes of their farming decisions based on previous personal, social, and cultural experiences. Of course, unexpected or fortuitous events may occur: variable climatic conditions such as humidity, sunshine, rainfall, and temperature, or crop pests such as locusts, rats, fungi and birds, can affect crop yields. In most agricultural communities, crop loss is part of the yield calculation; as a result, farmers usually plant more than they think they would need under optimal conditions.

The yields that a farmer expects are not solely dependent upon the acreage planted. Farmers have little or no control over the exogenous factors that affect crop yield from year to year. Yet, as Wharton (1971: 160) explains, "under the usual conditions of traditional or subsistence agriculture, the farmer's knowledge of the average yields and their probability distribution is greatest. When a new crop or technology is introduced, it affects the first two variables [i.e., yield and cost variations] most significantly." These variabilities of yield and cost condition the farmer's decisions and provide the environment in which attempts are made to control risk and uncertainty in agriculture.

This conceptual analysis, in which an analytical distinction is made between risk and uncertainty, can be traced to Knight's (1965 [1921]) economic treatise in which he discussed the idea that "measurable uncertainty" can be assigned numerical probabilities, and can be referred to as "risk." However true uncertainty cannot have numerical probabilities assigned to it. These concepts have informed subsequent analyses concerning the decision-making processes in subsistence agriculture. For example, in an economic paradigm, life decisions could be understood in the context of the allocation of scarce means to competing ends.

Farmers make decisions every day about allocating their resources, labour, and time, all of which are in limited supply, although they probably do not do so in the context of formal economics but in the everyday context of living their lives, based on what they know and expect to happen. Whether this allocation process is objectively rational, or seen as not entirely rational, the choices made nonetheless take place in the context of a farmer's consideration of such variables as the degree of uncertainty, expectations held about outcomes, and the assumption of risk. A reasonable supposition about subsistence agriculture is that farmers will work to reduce risk and increase security within the parameters of their life experiences.

Farmers' Decisions about Land Use

The literature on agricultural economics and the factors responsible for farm productivity has emphasized crop yields and quantity of cultivated acreage, to the neglect of other important factors that influence farmers' decisions. When one includes other vital factors that contribute to farm productivity it becomes necessary to adopt a more "total-system approach," one that examines the interaction of influencing factors as well as cultivation variables.

Consider, for example, the Irish Canadian farm in eastern Canada in the latter half of the 1800s. This farm was generally composed of acreage devoted to the cultivation of food crops such as potatoes, grain crops such as wheat and barley, pasture fields to feed livestock, and a sizeable woodlot for firewood and building supplies. To understand the decision-making of the farmers during this time period, it is instructive to examine land use patterns that have been recorded during the various decades from 1850 to1880 in order to study the evolution or transitions in land use allocation.

In the early 1850s an immigrant to Renfrew County might have had the choice of purchasing farmland that had already been cleared. Probably, though, given the limited resources of most immigrants, especially among the Irish fleeing the Famine, this sort of property was out of reach. The main alternative was to buy land under a land grant program that required the clearing of trees and brush prior to cultivation. The immediate need, then, was to clear a few acres as quickly as possible, perhaps with the help of others, and plant a crop of potatoes so that one's family could avoid starvation.

It is not possible to ascertain how quickly the first settlers to Admaston Township would have been able to clear the forest to plant their first crops. It was noted earlier that Admaston was not completely surveyed until 1842, although there were several Scottish families already living there before the completion of the survey. The census of 1851 was based on an enumeration of 1850, so one can establish that even the earliest settlers would have had no longer than eight years to begin the settlement process. Also, given the previous discussion (i.e., Russell 1982: 136–8) of land clearing in Upper Canada, such as 1.2 acres per year in 1822 to 1.5 acres in 1842, then it is reasonable to estimate that the largest area that could be cleared of forest in Admaston Township during this eight-year period (i.e., 1842–50) would have been about 12 acres, using the figures that Russell (1982) derived from assessment rolls.. Of course, it is important to note that other authors use estimates that are much higher that this, such as Jones's (1946: 71–3) 4–5 acres, McCallum's (1980: 9) 5–10 acres, or Guillett's (1963: 312) 10–12 acres cleared per year. Using a range of 1.5 acres, on the low side, to 12 acres, on the high side, yields estimates for the eight-year period (1842–50) of 12 to 96 acres cleared in total. These rough calculations, then, give us a baseline for forest clearing, from which to assess the impact of the arrival of the Irish in Admaston Township.

Much useful information on Irish settlement is provided in family histories, such as Carol Bennett's (1992) *Founding Families of Admaston* and her later work, *The Kerry Chain* (McCuaig 2003). From these sources I compiled a list of 219 Irish family heads in Admaston, based on enumerations between 1851 and 1871 (Canada 1851, 1861, 1871). Several families, including the Cardiffs from Northern Ireland, arrived in Canada in 1820, settling in Lanark County before moving to Admaston. Many others, though, arrived in the latter part of the 1840s. These included the Bolgers from Wexford (four heads of households, namely, John, Martin, Patrick, and William, in 1845), John Carty (1848), Andrew Crozier (1847), Christopher Crozier (1848), James Fitzmaurice (1846), Patrick Fitzgerald (1851), Michael Kelly (1851), Jeremiah Lynch (1847), Thomas Lynch (1846), Timothy Lynch (1847), Willian Morrow (1849), Martin Mulvihill (1846), James O'Connar (1848), Daniel O'Dea (1848), Edward O'Hare (1847), Thomas Rowan (1847), Michael Ryan (1847), James Sammon (1846), and James and Patrick Whelan (1847).

Another way to obtain information on immigration is to examine the ages of children born in Canada. The Canadian census did not require respondents to list their children's names upon arrival in this country, as was the case with the censuses used in the United States. For example, a married Irish couple might have one or two children born in Ireland, and then others born in Canada. If one looks at the age of the last child born in Ireland, and the first child born in Canada, one can determine within a year or two when the family arrived in Canada. For instance, John Culhane arrived from Ireland with his wife and four children, the youngest six years old. They then had four more children born in Canada; the first was age four in 1850–1, which suggests that the Culhanes arrived in Admaston in 1846 or 1847.

In another example, Roger Culhane and his wife arrived with three children; their first child born in Canada is listed as three years old in 1850–1, which suggests the family arrived about 1847. Patrick Dillon and his wife arrived from Ireland; their first child born in Canada was listed as age two in 1850–1, which suggests an arrival date of about 1848. John Fumeau and his wife arrived from Ireland with six children; one child born in Canada was listed as three years of age in 1850–1, which suggests an arrival date of 1847.

One could cite many more similar cases. Two points are made here; first, that with the opening of Admaston Township to settlement in 1842 it only actually received a preponderance of Irish settlers during the Famine years of 1847–50, and second, given the above, that the upper limit of land that could be cleared during this period was probably

Figure 1 Land use in Admaston Township, 1851

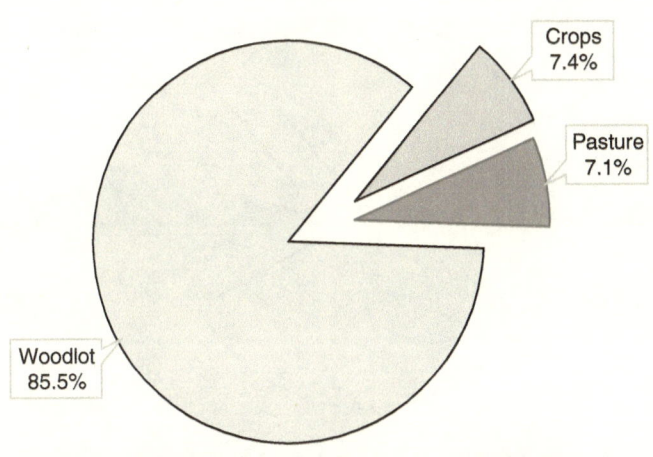

CATEGORIES	ACRES	PERCENTAGE
CROPS	485.5	7.4
PASTURE	468.5	7.1
WOODLOT	5,646.0	85.6
TOTAL ACREAGE	6,600.0	100.1

about 15 to 20 acres per household or less, rather than the aforementioned maximum of 40 acres cleared per household.

The 1851 census report for Admaston Township lists 410 persons of Irish descent. Virtually all adults listed were born in Ireland, with many of their children born in Canada. Of this population, 108 males are listed between the ages 15 to 59 (that is, those physically capable of chopping down trees and otherwise clearing the forest). If we assume, on average, an arrival in Admaston of three years before the census, then 108 men at the rate of 5 acres per year could clear about 540 acres per year, or 1,620 acres over this period.

The agricultural land use pattern for the Irish of Admaston Township is depicted in figure 1. In total, the farms inhabited by the Irish comprised 6,600 acres, of which 85.6 per cent (5,646 acres) remained as woodlot. Land cleared (termed "under cultivation" in the census report) consisted of 7.4 per cent (485.5 acres) in crops and 7.1 per cent (468.5 acres) in pasture. Cleared land, then, amounted to a total of 954

Figure 2 Land use in Admaston Township, 1861

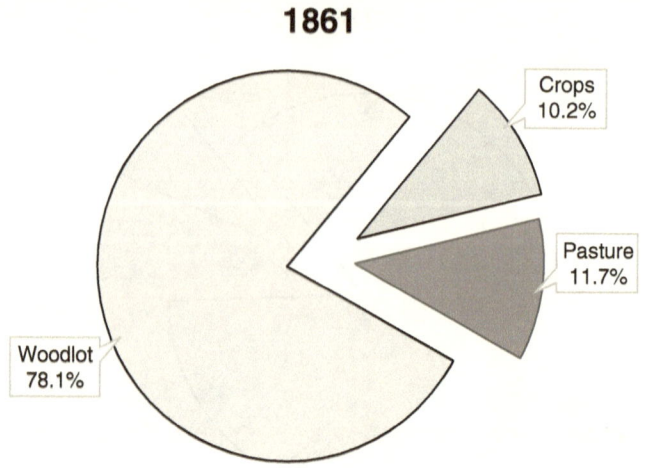

CATEGORIES	ACRES	PERCENTAGE
CROPS	1,768.2	10.2
PASTURE	2,032.8	11.7
WOODLOT	13,589.5	78.1
TOTAL ACREAGE	17,390.5	100.0

acres. One could, therefore, adjust the clearing rate from 5 acres to 3 acres per year over a three-year period (between 1847 and 1850), to arrive at 972 acres, or, alternatively, adjust the time period from three to two years, which leads to 1,080 acres cleared. Note that we are adjusting our assumptions here to fit the facts, rather than the other way around. A reasonable conclusion would be that the Irish who arrived in large numbers during the 1847–8 period had available only about two years to clear land before the census enumeration took place in 1850. According to this census report on land use, it took about 500 acres in crop production to feed about 400 people, or more precisely, 1.2 acres (485.5/410) of crops to feed each person.

Ten years later, according to the 1861 Admaston census, the Irish population more than doubled (from 410 to 898 persons, which is an increase of 54.4 per cent). Land use also changed accordingly, as illustrated in figure 2. In the years after the first census of 1851, land area devoted to crop production increased from 485.5 to 1768.2 acres (3.6 times). Acreage devoted to crop production increased from 1.2 to 2.0 acres per person,

Figure 3 Land use in Admaston Township, 1871

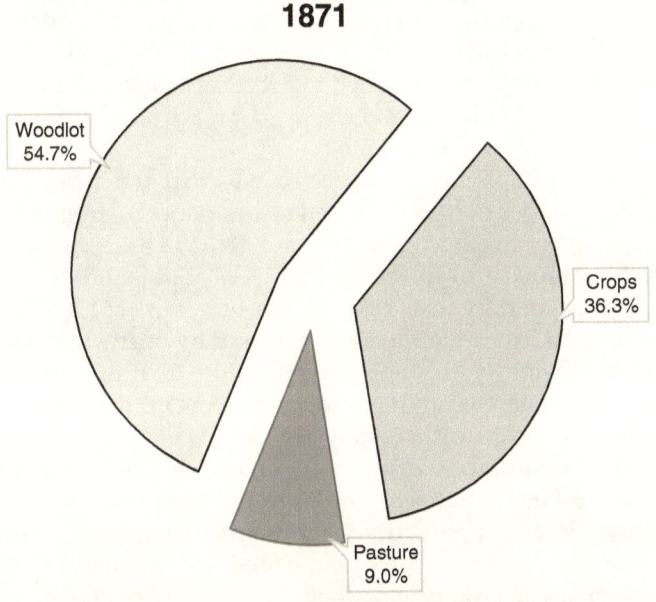

CATEGORIES	ACRES	PERCENTAGE
CROPS	8,337.8	36.3
PASTURE	2,057.5	9.0
WOODLOT	12,551.5	54.7
TOTAL ACREAGE	22,946.8	100.0

a gain more or less proportional to the corresponding doubling of the population. Pasture also increased from 468.5 to 2,032.8 acres, representing an enlargement of 4.3 times. Total farmland increased by over 10,000 acres, with cultivated land increasing from 15 per cent of the total farmland in 1851 to 22 per cent a decade later. As a percentage of the total farmland, the woodlot area, as might be expected, decreased by 7.5 per cent, at the expense of the expansion in cultivated acreage.

By 1871 the Irish population growth levelled off, increasing by only 93 persons (10.4 per cent) over the ensuing decade, to a total to 991 persons. One might expect that with a smaller population increase that land use patterns would also begin to stabilize as well, but this was not the case. As illustrated in figure 3, crop production increased by 6,569.6 acres, an increase of 4.7 times, and now amounted to 36.3 per cent of the total farmland (from 10.2 per cent in 1861).

84   After the Famine

Pasture area remained about the same, at just over 2,000 acres for both time periods, suggesting that livestock acquisitions did not increase. The total acreage of farmland increased as well, from 17,390.5 to 22,946.8 acres, which represents an enlargement of over 5,500 acres, or 32 per cent. Woodlots continued to decrease in size accordingly over the decade, by 1,038 acres, and dropped proportionally from 78.1 to 54.7 per cent of the total farmland.

What was perhaps most unexpected was that the area devoted to crop production per person increased so dramatically, from 1.2 and 2.0 acres respectively for the years 1851 and 1861, to 8.4 acres per person in 1871. In summary, even though the Irish population of Admaston Township increased by just 10.4 per cent between 1861 and 1871, the acreage devoted to crop production increased by nearly five times over this period. Obviously, this unexpected result – that the Irish between 1861 and 1871 began to produce crops well beyond their consumptive requirements – merits further analysis.

The most important question, then, emerging from the changes in Admaston land use patterns from 1861 to 1871 concerns the nearly fivefold increase in crop production over the previous decade. Surely the people were not eating five times more food, so what motivated such a startling increase in crop production?

It could be that the extra crops were sold to other farmers, but given that probably most people were eating the same basic vegetables this seems unlikely. The consumption needs for basic crops was fulfilled at about 1,700 acres, since the overall population increased only marginally during 1861 to 1871 period, which suggests that the additional land put under cultivation was not used to feed the people but was used for crops with some retail value, such as wheat and barley. This idea is worth pursuing, but requires an examination of specific variations in crop production. Another possibility is that a portion of the crop was fed to animals, such as pigs (peas) or horses (oats). There are a variety of possibilities that could be explored to explain the increase in crop production. Thus, a detailed examination of the individual crops grown during the various time periods between 1851 and 1871 is required.

Variations in Crop Production

Comparative crop production, or what might be termed the "relative productive efficiency" of a region, can be assessed according to various measures. One of these could be the volume of production in bushels, another could be the area or acreage over which a crop is planted, and another could involve a combination of the two, which is to say the number of bushels per acre produced by farms or the regions as a whole. Here the various crops that were grown in Admaston Township during the period of 1851 to 1871 are examined according to the enumeration of the agricultural censuses. In particular we are interested in the relative rise or decline of production of various crops over this time period and the possible reasons for the changes taking place.

Wheat

The earliest domesticated wheat was grown about 10,000 years ago in the Fertile Crescent of present-day Iraq, Turkey, and Iran. Soon after the crop appeared farther west, reaching Greece and Germany, about 7,000 years ago (Diamond 1999: 97, 123–4). Today more land is used for the cultivation of wheat than for any other commercial food and is the leading source of vegetable protein in the human diet. According to statistics provided by the United States Department of Agriculture for 2017–18, the world trade in wheat (761.9 million metric tons) is greater than for all other crops grown for human consumption combined and is second only to rice (494.9 million metric tons) as the main human food crop. Corn (or maize) (1,077.98 million metric tons) is the world's largest food crop but is primarily used for animal feed. Canada in 2017–18 ranked third among the world's wheat exporters and sixth among wheat producers (https://www.fas.usda.gov/data/world-agricultural-production).

Wheat is the main food crop of the Western Hemisphere; it grows best in cool, temperate climates with moderate soil fertility. Before the industrial production of fertilizer, crop rotation was commonly practised and manure was added to the soil to maintain nitrogen levels. Soil and climatic conditions vary widely over the different areas of North America; consequently, wheat production also varies widely from one region to another. For example, in a study of wheat yields across 10 states during the 1938–48 period, Texas had the lowest production at 12.4 bushels per acre and Washington the highest at 26.3 bushels per acre, with an average across the United States of 17.0 bushels per acre (Wilson and Meyers 1954: 116). (This time period was chosen here because the crop yields then, before climate warming, the introduction of GMOs, the widespread use of commercial fertilizer, and the industrial mechanization of farming, are probably closer to those of the period of the present study than to those of today.)

The claim has been made "that farm prosperity was commonly related to wheat production in mid-nineteenth century Ontario ... Wheat production has popularly been associated with the frontier of

Table 2 Wheat production, Admaston Township, 1851–71

	1851	1861	1871
Total acres	177	1,290	702
Bushels	2,782	16,015	4,448
Bushels/acre	15.7*	12.4**	6.4
Per cent of farm production	20.9	17.3	18.1
No. of farms	51/53	139/148	128/154

* Jones (1946: 86) estimates that wheat production in 1851 for Upper Canada as a whole was 16.1 bu/acre.
**Includes both fall and spring wheat. Fall wheat: 256 acres, 4,567 bushels, 17.8 bu/acre. Spring wheat: 1,034 acres, 11,448 bushels, 11.1 bu/acre; 31 farms (31/148) planted both.

settlement. It was said to be the crop of new farmers" (McInnis 1992: 62). McCallum suggests that "Ontario wheat was perhaps the most successful staple crop in Canadian history ... the land and climate of southern Ontario were admirably suited to the growing of wheat. New land yielded thirty to forty bushels of wheat per acre, and the average yield of the 1820s was as high as twenty-five to thirty-five bushels" (1980: 8–9). He also notes that "close to three-quarters of the cash income of Ontario farmers was derived from wheat [but] by the 1870s Ontario's wheat trade had run its course" (p. 22).

The following table describes wheat production in Admaston Township between 1851 and 1871.

Wheat yields in 1851 at 15.7 bushels/acre were commensurate with the United States average of 17.0 bushels/acres of a later period in the 1930s, as well as Jones's (1946: 86) estimate of 16.1 bushels/acre for Canada West as a whole. McCallum (1980: 20) comments that "by the time of the census of 1851 the average for the province had fallen to sixteen bushels per acre, and only three of the forty-two counties had averages of twenty bushels or better." He furthermore includes a quote by the president of the (Ontario) Agricultural Association, who claimed that "most of the farms in the old settled areas bordering on Lake Ontario were 'worn out,' [and that] vast areas of the most fertile land have been rendered absolutely unproductive by continual wheat cropping" (ibid.: 20). By 1866 barley had largely replaced fall wheat in much of the province. The behaviour of Ontario's wheat farmers was furthermore described "as practicing a destructive style of agriculture" because they did not grow wheat in a soil-conserving manner (Kelly 1971: 97).

Land Use and the Allocation of Resources 87

The practices of the Irish farmers of Admaston Township were apparently no different from those of the rest of the province. Production in 1851 of 15.7 bushels/acre could be considered quite acceptable given the agricultural deficiencies of climate and topography of Renfrew County. In 1861 wheat production had declined to 12.4 bushels acres, but the areas devoted to wheat production grew dramatically (by 7.3 times) from 177 acres in 1851 to 1,290 acres in 1861. The number of bushels produced also grew substantially (by 5.8 times), from 2,782 bushels in 1851 to 16,015 in 1861. Such yields were apparently not sustainable and wheat production fell by half, to 6.4 bushels/acre in 1871. Those farmers who wished to continue growing wheat would immediately have to begin to practise soil conservation measures or give up planting wheat altogether.

Oats

Oats are primarily grown to feed working animals, especially horses, although they are also grown for human consumption. Oats do well under a variety of conditions and are especially suited to cooler climates. They can also be grown in relatively poor soil and thus have an advantage over wheat, which requires richer soil.

In an assessment of the value of oats in agriculture, it has been noted that "probably no other grain crop is so universally seeded under adverse conditions or on relatively poor soils ... and where the farmer would not consider seeding a more exacting crop such as wheat" (Wilson and Myers 1954: 147). Thus, oats are often considered a secondary crop, although yields are frequently lower than farmers might hope for given the less than favourable conditions under which it is grown. All in all, however, oats appear to be a crop particularly suited to the soil and climatic conditions of Renfrew County.

For comparative purposes, it can be pointed out that oat yields in the United States for the years 1939–48 were highest in Wisconsin (41.3 bushels/acre) and lowest in Texas (21.8 bushels/acre), yields which probably reflect the advantages of growing oats in a cooler climate and in an area with more fertile soil. The average yield in oat production across the United States during the period from 1939 to 1948 was 32.8 bushels/acre (Wilson and Myers 1954: 144). A proviso that is frequently made in agricultural texts concerning oat production is that although oat yields may be higher than those of wheat, the latter crop is more densely packed and thus weighs more by volume, as when measured by bushels per acre.

Oat production from 1851 to 1861 in Admaston (see table 3) increased over five times, while maintaining levels of production in terms of 23 to 25 bushels/acres. These figures are significantly lower than the

Table 3 Oat production, Admaston Township, 1851–71

	1851	1861	1871
Total acres	176.5	1,057	*
Bushels	4,360	24,260	7,260
Bushels/acre	24.7**	23.0	*
Per cent of farm production	32.8	25.2	28.5
No. of farms	15/53	126/148	92/154

*Acreage for oats grown not enumerated for 1871.
** Jones (1946: 86) estimates that oat production in 1851 for Upper Canada as a whole was 27.6 bu/acre.

average of 32.8 bushels per acre for the United States as a whole, but closer to Jones's estimate of 27.6 bushels per acre in 1851. Unfortunately, in the 1871 census only the total number of bushels produced was recorded and therefore a figure for bushels per acre cannot be calculated for Admaston Township using this data. However, by 1871 production of oats declined by about three times from the previous decade. It would be interesting to know if the decline in the rate of production in terms of bushels per acre was similar to that which occurred for wheat. Notice also that there was a substantial decline in the number of farmers growing oats, from 126 to 92; one wonders if declining productivity of oats over the previous decade was the reason for this decrease. Livestock production (discussed later in this chapter) may also be a factor.

The decline in the production of oats could be associated with the timber trade of the Ottawa Valley. Jones (1946: 116–17) notes that "as early as 1830, the demand of the expanding timber trade of the Ottawa Valley outran the local agricultural production ... hay and oats were too bulky to be brought such distances [from southwestern Ontario]. This factor ... gave the farmers of the lower Ottawa Valley a virtual monopoly in these two products." Jones also estimates that for 1854–5 one timber company, John Egan and Co., employed 3,800 lumberjacks, 1,700 horses, and 200 oxen. The horses and oxen consumed 60,000 bushels of oats and 1,200 tons of hay. Feeding the men required 10,000 barrels of flour per year and 6,000 barrels of pork (ibid.: 11). The first phase of the timber trade focused on the production of squared timber, which lasted into the 1850s, with a second phase, focused on sawed lumber, ending about 1900. The timber trade of Renfrew County in the Ottawa Valley and its possible effect on the county's agricultural production are worthy of further consideration although outside the purview of the present study.

Potatoes

Potatoes were first cultivated in the Andes of Peru. The potato requires a cool growing season with moderate moisture and well-drained sandy loam soil with a moderately high level of fertility. It has been noted that "potatoes are generally the most heavily fertilized of all field crops" (Etheridge 1928: 492). Potatoes were first introduced in England and Ireland in the late sixteenth century, they were not immediately popular because the farmers did not know how to grow them. In Ireland, the loss of the wheat crop due to war forced the people to learn to grow potatoes, which could be used as a substitute for bread. Dried potato meal has a composition similar to flour. It has been further noted that "Next to wheat the potato is the most important food crop in the world. In weight the potato crop of the world exceeds even corn by millions of tons ... about 90 per cent of which is grown in Europe" (ibid.: 490). Potatoes are also used in the manufacture of starch, alcohol, and flour, and are sometimes fed to livestock when prices are low. When potato plants are fertilized with sufficient quantities of nitrogen, phosphorous, and potassium, yields of between 114 and 286 bushels per acre can be obtained under optimal conditions (ibid.: 493).

For the Irish fleeing a devastated homeland, it must have come as an immense relief, even a matter of joy, that their beloved potato yielded bountiful harvests in their new country. No more the putrid, fungus-ridden crops they had left behind. The potato thrived in Admaston Township, becoming the main food source, producing over 5,500 bushels of food in 1851, a larger yield than any other crop (table 4).

The total Irish population of Admaston Township more than doubled between 1851 (410 persons) and 1861 (898 persons) and then remained much the same over the next decade (991 persons in 1871). Considering that the potato was the main source of sustenance for the Admaston population, production was 12.9 bushels/person for 1851, 28.1 bushels/person in 1861 and 11.5 bushels/person in 1871. Thus, the amount of potatoes available per person in 1851 and 1871 remained about the same. Between 1851 and 1861 potato production increased five times while the overall population doubled in this period. However, between

Table 4 Potato production, Admaston Township, 1851–71

	1851	1861	1871
Total acres	78.5	210.5	180.8
Bushels	5,540	25,389	11,196
Bushels/acre	70.6	120.6	61.9
Per cent of farm production	41.7	51.5	44.0
No. of farms	48/53	129/148	134/154

1861 and 1871 potato production decreased by over half, even though the overall population remained about the same.

Production levels of the potato were not sustained beyond 1861 levels, a trend that has been previously noted for other crops as well (wheat: 16,015 bushels produced in 1861, down to 4,448 bushels in 1871; oats: 24,260 bushels produced in 1861, down to 7,260 bushels in 1871; potatoes: 25,389 bushels produced in 1861, down to 11,196 bushels in 1871). This drastic decline in production over a 20-year period is puzzling.

The Irish certainly knew about maintaining fertile fields through crop rotation and manure fertilization. In terms of the role of the potato in crop rotation, O'Neill (1984: 86) notes that for agricultural production in Ireland of the 1840s, "The potato filled an almost magical combination of needs for the Cavan farmer. It brought rough land into tillage, provided a major part of the farm's vegetable food, served as the major form of animal fodder, and acted as a restorative root crop which replenished land exhausted by successive cereal crops. It cannot be stated too strongly that the potato, when grown by farmers, was not solely or even largely a subsistence crop in Cavan."

O'Neill also stresses the importance of the practice of regular oats-potato rotation in Cavan during the pre-Famine times of the 1840s. (ibid.: 86). This system of cultivation would begin with an unmanured crop of potatoes, followed by a manured crop of potatoes. The following year a crop of oats would be planted. This pattern would extend over the next three years. In the seventh year, grass would be grown (or the land would be manured), followed by a return to potatoes to begin the process again.

The point to be made here, based on research in Ireland prior to the Famine, is that a pattern of potato and oat rotation was well developed in the Irish immigrants' home country. Since both oats and potatoes

Table 5 Other crops grown, Admaston Township, 1851–71

	1851	1861	1871
Barley			
Acres	11	114	N/A
Bushels	277	1,794	83
Bushels/acre	25.2	15.7	N/A
No. of farms	9/53	46/148	5/154
Peas			
Acres	23	446	N/A
Bushels	377	5,385	2,323
Bushels/acre	14.7	12.1	N/A
No. of farms	15/53	91/148	86/154
Hay			
Production (in tons)	120.5	560.0	1,431.0
No. of farms	23/53	104/148	142/154

were both grown in abundance in Admaston Township, and the necessity of crop rotation and manuring was apparently well known to the Irish of Admaston Township, it is difficult to understand the reasons for the precipitous decline in the production of both potatoes (25,389 bushels produced in 1861 and 7,260 bushels in 1871, a decline of 71.4 per cent) and oats (24,260 bushels produced in 1861 and 11,196 bushels in 1871, a decline of 53.8 per cent). It surely would be ironic if a decline in potato production in Admaston Township had the same adverse effects there as it did in Ireland. This was probably not the case, however, in that the Irish had many other options in their new homeland, such as changing their subsistence strategy from one based on food crop production to one based on livestock production.

Other Crops

While wheat, potatoes, and oats generally accounted for about 95 per cent of the crop production in Admaston Township between 1851 and 1871, it should be noted that several other crops were also grown. It is not known if growing these other crops was an attempt to forestall the decline in production of the major crops, or whether this was an attempt to fulfil a niche in farm food needs. Table 5 includes summary figures for barley, peas, and hay production.

Miscellaneous Crops

Rye: In 1851, 30 bushels were grown on 2 acres. In 1861, 10 bushels were grown on 1 acre. Used for making bread, rye grows well on poor land, needs less fertilizer than wheat, and can be grown where the severity of climate makes production of wheat uncertain. Growing conditions seem ideal for Renfrew County. Nevertheless, bread was probably made from wheat.

Turnips: In 1861 570 bushels were grown. Turnips grow best in cool, moist climates and in loose, sandy soil. They make excellent feed for livestock, especially sheep.

Corn: In 1861, 135 bushels were grown. Corn is North America's most abundant crop, and is far more valuable in aggregate value than any other commodity. Corn requires an abundance of nitrogen and yields are best in soils high in organic matter. Renfrew County's relative short growing season makes corn largely unsuitable for cultivation.

Barley

Barley has the advantage of maturing earlier than wheat, which may make it suitable for the relatively short growing season of Renfrew County. Barley has some use in making bread and in malting, but is now primarily used as feed for livestock, especially hogs, whose digestive system cannot utilize other rougher, more fibrous feeds as well as ruminants, such as cows and sheep. In Admaston Township, 277 bushels of barley were produced in 1851, yielding about 25 bushels per acre, which is considered about average production. By 1861 barley production increased to 1,794 bushels, an increase of over six times, but by 1871, for unknown reasons, production dropped to a mere 83 bushels.

Peas

A distinction can be made between field peas and garden peas, with the former used for livestock feed and the latter for human consumption, although the biological difference between the two is slight. Peas grow best in cool climates and in well drained soils. In order to increase the yield, peas are often sown with oats so that the vines do not settle on the ground; however, this makes for difficulty in harvesting. In 1851 only 377 bushels of peas were harvested, but production increased sharply to 5,385 bushels in 1861, then decreased by about half, to 2,323 bushels, in 1871. This trend suggests a continuing need for livestock feed over these decades.

Hay

Hay is the one crop that did not suffer the dramatic decrease in production between 1861 and 1871 typical of all the other field crops. Production in hay amounted to 120 tons in 1851, increasing by nearly five times to 560 tons in 1861, and then increasing again by nearly three times to 1,431 tons. It is interesting to note that in 1851 only about half of Admaston's farms (23/53) reported growing hay, but in the two subsequent decades over 90 per cent (142/154) of the township's farmers reported growing this crop, suggesting an increasing importance of livestock production in the local farming economy. Hay plays a central role in maintaining a stable livestock production program. It is necessary for winter feeding, and for periods of low production of other feed crops due to drought or other hazards. Thus, hay production is more important for farms in the more northerly latitudes than for those in more southern climates, which would have earlier access to pasture.

Hay production is particularly important for raising dairy cattle, which require more and better forage than do beef cattle and sheep. For example, it has been noted that "All classes of livestock derive about 16 per cent of their total nutrients from hay, while dairy cows derive from 35 to 38 per cent of their nutrients from this source" (Wilson and Myers 1954: 508).

Summary Comments on Crop Production

It is of course not possible to travel back in time and interview the Irish farmers of Admaston Township about their farming decisions. However, even if you could conduct such interviews it might still not do you much good – they would likely say that were simply feeding, housing, and clothing their families as best they could. That said, the statistics that were collected in the 1851 census, and in later decades, are no doubt fairly accurate and reflect the results of the farmers' decisions. In other words, the numbers are what they are, regardless of how they got that way.

Looking at the numbers, then, there were about 400 Irish people living in Admaston Township in 1851. This population more than doubled (to about 900 people) over the next decade to 1861, and then stayed about the same for 1871. If one examines the agricultural production over these decades, a good place to start would be to examine the potato crop; since this crop was only for domestic consumption, potatoes had no real commercial value, unlike other crops. Since the human population more than doubled between 1851 and 1861, it is reasonable

94   After the Famine

to assume that the potato crop would follow this pattern: people can consume only so many potatoes a day, and the surplus, if any, has no sale value beyond the individual household.

As the census statistics illustrate, while the overall population increased by slightly more than twice between 1851 and 1861, the potato crop increased by over four times. Then, while the overall population remained virtually the same over the next decade to 1871, the potato crop decreased by over half. No doubt the Irish in Ontario, unlike the poor farmers in Ireland, ate more than potatoes, but it is difficult to determine what the consumption patterns would have been. The production of potatoes in 1851 amounted to 13.5 bushels/person, in 1861, 27.9 bushels per person, and in 1871, 12.3 bushels per person.

Comparative figures are difficult to find. Gallagher (1982: 23) estimated that in Ireland each person consumed on average 8 pounds of potatoes per day, or 2,920 pounds per year. A bushel of potatoes weights about 60 pounds, so converting the Irish figures means that each person in Ireland would consume 48.7 bushels of potatoes per year. In Admaston, the production of potatoes ranged from 12.3 bushels per person in 1871 to 27.9 bushels per person in 1861. So, even at the highest level of production in Admaston, the potatoes produced would be between a third to one-half of what was required in Ireland. Clearly the Irish of Admaston ate a more varied diet.

As far as the other major field crops were concerned, oats were consumed primarily by livestock, especially horses. According to various estimates, oats generally weigh 32 pounds per bushel. Mares weigh about 1,000 pounds and stallions about 1,200 pounds. A horse weighing about 1,100 pounds would, when working, consume about 2.5 pounds of oats daily; it would consume about 22 pounds of hay when nutrient requirements are less. Assuming that a working horse would be fed oats for about eight months of the year when engaged in ploughing, harvesting, and other heavy chores, a horse weighing 1,100 pounds would consume about 600 pounds of oats over that period of time, amounting to about 18.8 bushels, or about 28.5 bushels if fed oats the entire year.

At the rate of 18.8 bushels of oats for eight months, oat production in Admaston could support 232 horses in 1851 (or 153 horses for the year), 1,290 horses in 1861 (or 851 horses for the year) and, finally, 386 horses in 1871 (or 255 horses for the year). The purpose of these calculations is to set a baseline for the consumption of oats by livestock. It is possible that oats were grown in excess of local needs in order to sell to markets supporting the Ottawa Valley timber trade. In any event, these calculations appear to be the only way to determine the existence of excess production.

Livestock Production

Animals, aside from dogs, were domesticated about the same time in human history as plants. Wheat and peas, for example, were domesticated around the same time as sheep and goats, about 10,500 years ago. Rice and millet were domesticated along with pigs and cattle about 9,000 years ago (Diamond 1999: 98–103, 158–61). Horses, first used as a source of winter food, then for transportation, were domesticated about 6,000 years ago, at about the same time as potatoes, corn, beans, and oats (Anthony 2007).

Horses became the chief means of long-distance transportation across Eurasia and, when later hitched to the newly invented wagon or chariot, became a formidable military force, allowing the early Indo-Europeans to move across Europe and dominate the autochthonous peoples of the region. As Diamond (1999: 91) explains: "Before animal domestication, the sole means of transporting goods and people by land was on the backs of humans. Large mammals changed that: for the first time in human history, it became possible to move heavy goods in large quantities, as well as people, rapidly overland for long distances ... [horses] may have been the essential military ingredient behind the westward expansion of Indo-European languages." It could be argued, then, that the domestication of animals played a role every bit as important in human history as plant cultivation.

Livestock production contributes three significant aspects to the family farm. First, there are the various goods and services that animals contribute, such as ploughing, transportation, wool, dairy products, leather, meat, and manure. However, animal husbandry can have adverse effects on farm fields through overcropping, leading to soil erosion and deforestation of natural habitats. There is also the potential of ground water contamination from agricultural run-off and of other environmental impacts such as water shortages; especially in arid regions, water diversion projects used to support livestock production can limit the availability of water for other needed uses, such as growing and sustaining orchards.

Second, farm animals are a form of investment. They can increase a farmer's wealth through their propagation. Selective breeding can contribute to the accumulation of wealth through the production of more highly prized animals to be sold at livestock auctions, stock shows and fairs, or commodity markets. Selective breeding can be a source of such intangibles as social value and prestige for the farm owner. Animal husbandry in many areas of the world is also a means of maintaining cultural traditions and ways of life. In addition, when farms also grow

Table 6 Livestock production, Admaston Township, 1851–71

	1851	1861	1871	+/– 1851–71
Sheep	408	1,208	1,249	+306.1%
Pigs	228	612	313	+137.3%
Milch cows	196	538	450	+229.6%
Horses	57	287	239	+419.3%
Cattle	188	561	415	+220.7%
Oxen	145	208	45	–322.2%
Totals	1,222	3,144	2,711	Avg. +165.1%
Livestock	43/53 (81%)	136/148 (92%)	134/154 (88%)	

their own feed stock, these field crops are then also a source of cash income, albeit an indirect one (Bennett 1982: 111–27).

Third, while livestock production can serve as a source of income for the family farm, it also provides additional economic value by contributing to food security; livestock is a source of protection against the risks involved in growing crops. Crop yields can be diminished by drought, extreme temperatures, excessive rainfall, wild animals, disease, or insects. Fluctuations in market conditions can reduce the value of cash crops. Livestock production therefore serves as a form of diversification and an economic buffer; it enhances the income security of a farm (Johannesen and Skonhoft 2011).

Livestock production in Admaston Township from 1851 to 1871 is depicted in table 6. The advantage of this longitudinal approach, covering several decades, is that one can study the changing transformation of farm production, something a more synchronic approach would not be able to illustrate. In Admaston Township, for example, the most pronounced changes over these two decades is the dramatic increase in the number of horses owned, by over four times, and the coincident decrease in oxen, by three times. There can be little doubt that the two trends are related.

In a study of developments in ploughing technology in nineteenth-century Canada, Skeoch (1982: 160) aptly describes the replacement of oxen by horses in Ontario's early agricultural history: "In Canada, horses did not displace oxen until the 1850s when farming was passing from the pioneer phase. The root-strewn fields of pioneer southern Ontario could be handled better by oxen than by horses. But once these fields were converted to neatly cleared plots of land the horse was the more efficient of the two."

Of course, there were trade-offs that a farmer would need to consider. Oxen ploughed fields at a slower pace than horses, so in that sense horses were more efficient. This was an important consideration if a farmer wished to expand his landholdings from, say, an initial 50 acres, to 100, or even 200 acres. In other words, there is an economy of scale at work that a farmer must consider that favours using horses. On the negative side, horses were more expensive to maintain, as they needed to be fed oats, which had to be grown or bought, whereas oxen could be set free to forage on rough ground or pasture. Horses were also initially more expensive to buy than oxen, so money needed to be saved up. Of course, horses also had other non-agricultural uses. They could be used to transport goods, as in pulling wagons to carry produce to more distant markets; they could also be used to transport people, on horseback or in carriages to church, nearby towns, or social gatherings.Horses had social and entertainment value in that they helped to ease the isolation of life on the farm.

Interestingly, this transition from oxen to horses was not abrupt, as one might expect. In fact, the number of oxen owned between 1851 and 1861 actually increased, by 30 per cent, at the same time that horse ownership was also increasing, by 80 per cent. Thereafter, between 1861 and 1871, the ownership of oxen decreased by 80 per cent, while horse ownership levelled off. The steady increase in the number of oxen owned during the first decade probably occurred because of the establishment of new farms and the expansion of old farms onto new, undeveloped acreage. After 1861, the dramatic drop in oxen ownership would then indicate that the farmlands of Admaston Township were reaching a more mature state, one in which horses could manage the ploughing on a more efficient basis than oxen. These trends in oxen and horse ownership are also consistent with the increase in acreage devoted to crops over the decade, from 486 acres in 1851 to 1,768 acres in 1861, an increase of nearly four times.

Ownership of sheep increased steadily by three times from 1851 to 1871. Sheep are raised principally for their meat (lamb and mutton) and wool. They can be raised in temperate climates, especially in arid zones, and usually are grazed on land devoted to pasture. The sale of wool can be a major source of income for a farm. In fact, the agricultural census of 1861 showed that 1,827 pounds of wool were produced by Admaston farmers, most of which was probably sold in local markets.

The number of milch cows doubled over the two decades, yielding over seven tons of butter during 1861. The number of pigs owned increased by about three times from 1851 to 1861, but then declined by 50 per cent from 1861 to 1871. In reference to Cavan, Ireland, O'Neill (1984: 87, 92–3) noted that a relationship existed between the size of a farm and the number of pigs owned. For example, farms of 1 to 5 acres had the highest number of pigs, whereas farms of over 30 acres had the highest cattle stocking, yet he found that "there is no simple linear relationship here" (p. 92). Nonetheless, farms of under 5 acres had too small a capacity to exploit the cereal market. In addition, the smallest Irish farms were heavily invested in potatoes for use as pig fodder, whereas the larger farms were more pasture-oriented.

Thus, if such trends were also prevalent in Admaston Township, a 50 per cent decrease in pig ownership between 1861 and 1871 is probably reflective of a general increase in farm size. This trend could be associated with a more general focus on raising milch cows and beef cattle, along with an increase in hay production to feed them, in lieu of raising animals, such as pigs, that do not eat hay and must be fed relatively expensive grain, such as barley and oats. In sum, the general trend in livestock production is a substantial increase in horse ownership over oxen, and an increasing emphasis on raising animals, such as sheep, cattle, and milch cows, whose dietary preferences are more suited to pasturage.

Agricultural Production: Admaston and All-Ontario, 1851–1871

The *Historical Atlas of Canada* offered an insightful observation in comparing agricultural conditions in eastern Ontario with those in the rest of the province during the middle to late nineteenth century:

> Eastward a distinct agricultural boundary separated eastern Ontario from the rest of the province. Here farms had adopted a hay-oats complex similar to that of Quebec. Although the complex existed throughout the two provinces, its dominance from eastern Ontario eastward suggests a major divide in the agriculture of central Canada. (G.J. Matthews and R.L. Gentilcore 1993: 131)

What are the implications for the present study, if any, of the differences referred to above? Given the statistical data presented in the *Historical Atlas,* and the agricultural census reports for Admaston Township, we are able to make comparisons first for crop production and second for livestock ownership for the period 1851 and 1871.

Crop Production (excluding Hay)

We are now in a position to provide observations comparing agricultural performance in Admaston Township to that of the province of Ontario as a whole for the 1851 to 1871 period:

Land Use and the Allocation of Resources 99

Table 7 Crop production, Admaston and All-Ontario, 1851–71

	1851		1871	
	Admaston %*	Ontario %**	Admaston %*	Ontario %**
Wheat	21	45	18	25
Oats	33	27	29	28
Potatoes	42	15***	44	23***
Barley	5	–	10	12
Other	–	13	–	12
Totals (%)	101	100	101	100

* Percentages for Admaston are based on total bushels produced.
** Percentages for Ontario are close approximations derived from bar graphs. Units of production were not indicated.
*** Includes corn.

1 *Wheat*: The precipitous decline in wheat production of almost 50 per cent for Ontario between 1851 and 1871 no doubt reflects a corresponding decline in market conditions for this staple crop in the late 1850s. By 1871 the production of wheat stabilized in all areas, including Admaston, at about 20 to 25 per cent of all agricultural production, a situation which probably reflected its use as a subsistence crop. However, in Admaston wheat production declined sharply from 15.7 bushels/acre in 1851 to only 6.4 bushels/acre in 1871. In 1851 wheat production in Ontario as a whole averaged about 16 bushels/acre (Jones 1946: 86; McCallum 1980: 20), suggesting that Admaston farmers were averse to practising soil conservation. Apparently, to maintain production levels of wheat, more acreage was devoted to growing this crop, increasing from 177 acres in 1851 to 702 in 1871.
2 *Barley*: "By 1866 barley replaced fall wheat in much of the province" (Kelly 1871: 97); however, for 1851, barley is not even listed as a crop grown. By 1871 production of barley increased to 12 per cent of the provincial total. For Admaston, barley was a very minor crop; only 83 bushels were produced in 1871. Since barley is mainly used as a feed for hogs, with minor amounts used for malting, the increase in barley production indicates its growing importance as feed for livestock.
3 *Oats*: Since oats are used to feed working livestock, especially horses, one could expect that fluctuation in oat production would reflect the number of horses owned. Oats are especially suited to

cooler climates, such as that found in Renfrew County, and, unlike wheat, oats thrive in relatively poor soil conditions. In 1851 oat production for Admaston amounted to about 25 bushels/acre, which compares favourably to production in all of Ontario at this time of about 28 bushels/acre (Jones 1946: 86). In Admaston, oat production increased by five times between 1851 to 1861, after which there was a decline in production up to 1871, by three times. The reasons for this decline are difficult to ascertain, however a decrease in oat production might be related to the diminishing supply requirements of lumber camps of the upper Ottawa Valley; production may have been curtailed owing to transportation difficulties, as suggested by Jones (1946: 116–17). Nonetheless, oat production in Admaston and across all of Ontario was maintained at a fairly consistent level between 1851 and 1871, at between 27 to 33 per cent of total crop production.

4 *Potatoes*. Over 40 per cent of agricultural production in Admaston Township was devoted to growing potatoes, amounting to 5,500 bushels in 1851; this is not surprising given the Irish origins of its inhabitants and the nutrient value of this crop. As Gallagher (1982: 21–2) indicates, "As a vegetable the potato is a potent source of calories ... It is also a remarkable source of protein, amino acids, and all the important mineral elements." This was also a crop that was familiar to them in terms of its growing requirements, and the cool climatic conditions of eastern Ontario were well suited to this crop. In addition, as O'Neill (1984: 8) indicates for Cavan, Ireland, potatoes "served as a major form of animal fodder"; they were presumably also used, along with barley, as feed for hogs. By contrast, in the rest of Ontario potatoes were not a significant aspect of agricultural production; the *Historical Atlas* combines potatoes with corn in the "other" category, amounting to between 15 per cent in 1851 and 23 per cent in 1871. While further research would be necessary to arrive at broader conclusions, it is possible that other Ontarians had much more animal protein in their diet than did Admaston farmers and their families during the mid-nineteenth century.

In sum, for the Irish of Admaston between 1851 to 1871, wheat, potatoes, and oats accounted for 95 per cent of all agricultural production. In all of Ontario, wheat and oats accounted for over 70 per cent of agricultural production in 1851. By 1871 wheat production declined by 20 per cent province-wide because of restrictions on exports and soil depletion. Production of oats remained virtually the same, at just under 30 per cent of all agricultural production, for both time periods; however,

Table 8 Livestock production, Admaston and All-Ontario, 1851–71

	1851		1871	
	Admaston %	Ontario %	Admaston %	Ontario %
Cattle	43	55	34	50
Horses	5	20	9	30
Swine	19	13	12	12
Sheep	33	12	46	8
Totals (%)	100	100	100	100

barley production, increasing to 12 per cent of crops produced in 1871, took up the slack left by the drop in wheat. The conclusion, then, is that aside from the emphasis on potato production among the Irish, crop production in Admaston and all of Ontario was largely similar in both 1851 and 1871; the principal crops were wheat, oats, and later barley, all of which comprised over 50 per cent of all agricultural crops grown for both time periods.

Livestock Production

For all of Ontario, according to the *Historical Atlas*, livestock production for the 1851 and 1871 census periods was relatively consistent in that numbers of cattle, horses, swine, and sheep, in that order, were maintained over this 20-year period. There was a slight decline of 5 per cent in cattle owned over this period, with a 10 per cent increase in horses. Swine and sheep were next in importance, averaging about 20–5 per cent.

For Admaston, cattle were the most important livestock in 1851 but their numbers declined by 10 per cent over the next two decades. It is in the production of sheep that the largest contrast lies between Admaston and all of Ontario. Sheep amounted to 33 per cent of total livestock in 1851, rising to 46 per cent in 1871. These percentages stand in sharp divergence to those for all of Ontario, for which the figure is no more than 12 per cent. For all of Ontario, horses comprised 20 to 30 per cent of all farm animals owned, but in Admaston horses never amounted to more than 10 per cent. However, these percentages are deceiving, giving the impression that horses were less important in Admaston than in the rest of the province. If one looks just at the bare numbers, in Admaston only 57 horses were owned in 1851, but this number increased to 239 horses by 1871, an increase of nearly five times. The contention posited here is that the increase in horses owned in Admaston is a direct result of changing agricultural requirements. As the quality of land improved between the ground-breaking period (around 1851) to the much easier ploughing conditions of the 1870 period, horses were much preferred over oxen because the former could plough fields at a faster rate. This is also indicated by the sharp decline in oxen owned in 1851 (145) to only 45 in 1871, a decrease of three times.

Unfortunately, a breakdown of the cattle category is lacking in the *Historical Atlas*; we are thus at a disadvantage in determining the changing dynamics of different types of livestock ownership across the province. In Admaston, horses as a percentage of livestock owned never amounted to over 10 per cent; overall the figures were masked by the dramatic increase in sheep production, whereas horses owned increased by five times. Similarly, for Admaston, the cattle category shows a 7 per cent decline in animals owned, yet milch cows increased by 2.5 times (196 to 450), and beef cattle increased by over two times (188 to 415) between 1851 and 1871. In all, it was the drastic decline in oxen owned in Admaston (145 in 1851 to 45 in 1971) that disguises a 10 per cent drop in cattle owned. The point here is that if the all-Ontario figures for cattle had used the more animal-specific figures available for Admaston, we would be in a much better position to determine the internal dynamics of livestock production as a whole.

We now turn to the major conclusion of the *Historical Atlas*, quoted above, which indicates "a distinct agricultural boundary ... a major agricultural divide in central Canada" between the oats-hay complex of eastern Ontario and the rest of the province. The question, then, is how do the Admaston agricultural data inform us about this assertion? With reference to oats, we note that there is no major difference in their overall rate of production in Admaston (33 per cent in 1851 and 29 per cent in 1871) and the rest of Ontario (27 per cent in 1851 and 28 per cent in 1871). However, basing assessments only on fluctuations in percentages can result in misleading conclusions; for example, the acreage devoted to cultivating oats in Admaston increased by six times between 1851 (177 acres) and 1871 (1,057 acres), even as the percentage of oats in Admaston's overall crop production declined by 4 per cent over this period.

Unfortunately, the *Historical Atlas* does not provide production figures for hay. For Admaston, there was a major surge between 1851 (120 tons) and 1871 (1,431 tons), an increase of twelve times. Dairy cows derive almost 40 per cent of their nutrient requirements from hay. Hay is also used as a source of winter feed for horses. These figures suggest that a dramatic increase in hay production is associated with a corresponding increase in the number of dairy cattle and horses; in fact, in

Admaston milch cows increased by two and a half times between 1851 and 1871 and horses by over four times. These increases are also associated with Admaston's land use patterns; acreage devoted to crops (including hay) increased by nearly five times between 1851 (7.4 per cent) and 1871 (36.3 per cent). In conclusion, these figures indicate that the assertion in the *Historical Atlas* about a "distinct agricultural boundary" between eastern Ontario (as far as Admaston Township is concerned) does not correspond with the facts and should be revisited by further research.

The Importance of a Farm's Woodlot

As one explores the history of agricultural development in southern Ontario, the general theme seems to be that the pioneer farmer's approach upon acquiring his plot of land is to clear as much of the forest as possible, and in the quickest amount of time, in order to convert the apparent wilderness into farmland. Various statistical figures on the rate of forest clearance can be used as a measure of farm development.

For the modern scholar of agricultural economics, the study of forest clearance seems like a reasonable approach to understanding colonial history. This approach, however, is a faulty one because it is predicated on the requirements of today's farmers, who do not need a woodlot. In the pioneer days, I wish to suggest, the woodlot was just as important as the land devoted to crops or pasture. It is a mistake to regard the area set aside as woodlot as wasted space or as an unproductive farm area, and as such to give it negligible consideration. The woodlot area was every bit as important as the food grown on cultivated areas, and thus the size of the woodlot enters directly into the farmer's decision-making and subsequent farm productivity.

It is no doubt correct to view much of the woodlot area as unsuitable for agricultural purposes, yet it is significant that over the 20-year period from 1851 to 1871 the woodlot area of Admaston never fell below half of all the township's farm acreage (1851, 85 per cent; 1861, 78 per cent; 1871, 55 per cent). Certainly, over this 20-year period most of this wooded area could have been cleared if the farmers desired to do so, yet for some reason they never did. Part of the reason is that there was an expansion of cultivated areas (crops and pasture) by 80 per cent over the 20 years (1851, 2,142 acres; 1861; 3,800 acres; 1871, 10,394 acres). Even by 1871 the total amount of cultivated area, at just over 10,000 acres, was not even half of Admaston's total of 26,000 acres of the top-rated soils of the class 2 variety (there were also another 2,500 acres of land suitable in Admaston for pasture).

In other words, by 1871 the sustainability of farming in Admaston Township had reached just over a third of its maximum capability, with the assumption that the remaining available fertile land could have supported an additional population much larger than the existing one. Under these conditions, decreasing the woodlot further was not necessary because the cultivated land area, expanding at its current rate, was sufficient to support the existing population. The conclusion one could reach is that Admaston's population would have to increase by three times before further clearing of the existing woodlot was necessary.

The problem with this line of reasoning, which is to say that a farm's woodlot was just another area into which increasing cultivation could take place, overlooks the fact that even without expansion of a farm's cultivated area, the woodlot would nonetheless diminish over time. The reason is that, for the Irish farming household of eastern Canada, a woodlot was indispensable for survival; it provided wood not only for cooking but also for heating fuel, without which existence in the harsh Canadian winter would not have been possible. Often overlooked in studies on agricultural production is the fact that the wooded area was also a source of additional food for the farming household, such as deer, moose, rabbits, partridge, berries, medicinal plants, waterfowl, and fish.

In addition, the woodlot provided building materials such as lumber for houses, barns, and sheds, and for poles for fences and railings. A critical decision that farmers needed to make therefore concerns achieving and maintaining a balance between cultivated areas and the woodlot, since both are necessary.

The farmer may expand the cultivated area of his farm at the expense of the woodlot, thus depleting the supply of firewood or building materials. The farmer may then be able to grow additional crops to be sold at local markets, but this would mean having to buy firewood; in reality this could be a zero-sum game. On the other hand, additional acreage could be purchased, thus preserving the woodlot, but that would require increased productivity to create income to purchase the land. Either way, the size of the existing woodlot is an important factor to consider, regardless of which expansion strategy is followed.

This dilemma for the farmer represents a classic example of an *opportunity cost*. The farmer, as a rational decision-maker, is faced with two production possibilities, that is, to decrease his woodlot in order to produce more crops, or, alternatively, preserve the woodlot and lose out on the possibility to increase food production. In either case, whichever decision the farmer makes, he invariably loses the opportunity to expand production in another area.

The question, then, is as follows: How can the woodlot as a production factor in the assumption of farmer's risk be assessed? A reasonable approach would be to calculate the size of a woodlot needed by the family farm, depending upon the size of the family that the woodlot needs to support for heating and other needs, and then attempt to calculate the rate at which the woodlot would decrease as these various needs are met.

Such an analysis was conducted during my own ethnographic fieldwork in an Anishinaabe (or Ojibwa) community located in northern Ontario (situated about 250 kilometres north of Thunder Bay in the subartic forest); in this village every household at the time of the research (in the 1970s) heated its log cabin with firewood (see Hedican 1986, 2001). Most of the inhabitants lived in one- or (rarely) two-room cabins. The cabins were kept small in order to conserve firewood. The Irish houses of Admastown, according to information in the Canadian census, were referred to as "shanties": these were small log buildings of two to four rooms, comparable in size and structure to the Aboriginal cabins of my fieldwork. After a series of calculations involving the quantity of firewood in an average acre of woodlot, based on a set volume of a standard "bush cord" (4'×4'×8'), and assuming certain rates of reforestation (such as that found in Hilts and Mitchell's 1999 study of woodlot management), a reasonably accurate estimate is that the average farming household required about two acres of woodlot per annum to meet its need for fuel and construction uses. At this rate, an average wood lot of, say, 50 acres could be expected to last an estimated 25 years, or about one generation.[1]

It is also important to understand that a diminishing woodlot does not necessarily lead to an expansion of arable land or a subsequent increase in crop production because of forest clearing; the woodlot likely consists of the least desirable farmland, such as rocky ground or areas of swamp and streams. The total area of a farm is relevant for considering the productive strategies that a farmer makes, not just the cultivated areas that grow crops or pasture animals. The argument here is that an acre of woodlot can be just as important as an acre of wheat, since both yield crops that are indispensable for a household's survival.

If too much of a farmer's woodlot is consumed, and/or turned into cultivated acreage, then replacement wood would have to be bought to meet the farm's needs for heating, cooking, and lumber. In such a case the farm's productivity is therefore the sum of crops harvested *minus* the replacement cost of additional wood. All this leads to the conclusion that an expansion of a farm's cultivated area, at the expense of the woodlot's acreage, is a counter-productive strategy. The woodlot is an important economic asset in its own right.

Conclusion

The Irish family farm of eastern Ontario was a malleable entity moving inexorably through the course of time. Its history involved many cycles – a time to sow and a time to reap, a time to be born and a time to die, to paraphrase *Ecclesiastes*. The repetition of annual cycles tends to obscure the longer-term transitions taking place. It is important to stress that a family farm is an integrated whole of various component parts: land for various uses, and people young and old. These components interact with each other as a total system such that decisions which affect one part are apt to cause changes in the other.

This interactive approach to a farm's component parts has been aptly described for the Irish farmers of north-central Ireland: "It was difficult for Cavan tenants to increase the acreage under grass at the expense of one tillage crop without affecting the other. Pasture had to compete with these crops as a system and not independently" (O'Neill 1984: 90). In sum, a system approach not only makes intelligible the interactive processes of farm life in Ireland, it also applies to the actions and agrarian strategies of Irish farmers of eastern Canada.

Chapter Five

Measuring Agricultural Performance

This chapter revolves around an experiment to develop a measure of agricultural performance. It begins with a discussion of Chayanov's theory that agricultural productivity is primarily determined by the composition of agrarian households, and then attempts to work out or operationalize how this theory might be tested in practice. This exercise can be seen not only as a contribution to the measure of agricultural performance as a form of agricultural economics, but also as a testament to the usefulness of Canadian census materials of the nineteenth century to generate a basis for testing modern theories in the social sciences.

The Malthusian Spectre

At the time of the Irish Famine there were no doubt those who viewed the death of so many millions of Irish countrymen by starvation and disease as an act of God, as a catastrophe divinely inspired to teach the Irish a lesson. Thomas Malthus, an Anglican cleric, perhaps did not hold any animosity towards the Irish themselves, but probably harboured no sympathy to their plight nonetheless.[1]

This catastrophe demonstrated, according to Malthus, a law of nature in which a growing human population would eventually outgrow its ability to feed itself, thus requiring divine intervention as a corrective to rampant human fecundity. In this sense, the mass starvation in Ireland was no different than a foolish human being who ignores the law of gravity by jumping out of a building while flapping their arms. In other words, as Malthus's logic would dictate, the Irish brought this calamity upon themselves. In turn, when half the Irish population was dead or had emigrated, the landowners would feel no shame in returning their lands to the more profitable pasturage that was more compatible with divine design.

Malthus's basic theory was that human population growth would inevitably exceed the ability of agricultural production to meet the demands of subsistence; when the limit is reached, the human population would thereby be reduced by starvation and disease to a level that could once again be sustained by existing agricultural methods. One of the more famous of his critics, Ester Boserup (1965), in her influential work *The Conditions of Agricultural Growth*, reversed the variables in Malthus's dictum by stating that it was population that determined agricultural growth rather than the other way around. She based her theory on the idea that humans will always find new ways to grow more food (necessity is the mother of invention), so that there are no natural laws restricting population growth except the limitations of people's creativity.

Circumventing Malthus's Predicament

In both Mathus's and Boserup's theories, it is the relationship between population growth and agricultural production that is the significant interaction. In the case of the Russian economist Alexander Chayanov (1966), as laid out in *The Theory of Peasant Economy*, his theory does not go beyond the human population itself as an explanatory principle. He suggested, on the basis of his own empirical observations of Russian agricultural production, that it was the consumer/worker ratio that was the most important variable in determining economic activity. Malthus asserted that continued population growth would inevitably confront fixed barriers, which in turn would result in painful adjustments; Chayanov, in contrast, encouraged theorists to look no farther than the internal dynamics of the family farm itself. In Chayanov's perspective an increasing population did not need to end in dire straits, as proposed by Malthus, if the farm family was able to adjust the size of its farm or engage in more labour-intensive agricultural activity.

Economic activity in Russia, Chayanov observed, tended to increase with the number of consumers in an agricultural household. Thus, there was a direct correlation between the size of a family and the size of the farm that fulfilled its subsistence needs. In cases in which there were no opportunities for expansion of the family farm, agricultural productivity could nonetheless be increased by more intensive labour inputs. Chayanov's thesis therefore suggests that the consumptive needs of a growing population are met by an intensification of farm effort, leading in turn to increases in agricultural performance and productivity.

Chayanov's theory is logically convincing because it does not lead into the sophistic trap of necessarily associating population growth with the natural constraints of theories associated with that of an ecological carry capacity. There is no carrying capacity per se, according to Chayanov, only the limits of the human will to work harder to support a farmer's dependants. Thus, Chayanov and Boserup shifted the emphasis away from the limits of agricultural production and the resulting painful rearrangements that human populations choose to make, or have thrust upon them, towards the population itself as the most important factor which controlled agricultural productivity.

The Chayanov model would appear to fit an analysis of agricultural development in Admaston Township among the Irish residents for several reasons. First, there does not appear to be any significant wealth differences in the population, according to the listings of the monetary value of crops, livestock, buildings, and equipment listed in the various census reports. One could suggest, then, that Admaston's Irish population is basically a homogeneous one, lacking significant social differentiation. This is a point, however, that needs to be investigated with empirical evidence. Second, the population is composed primarily of farming families who supply their own subsistence needs, or can trade to obtain what they lack. Third, rather than selling their agricultural products for cash to buy what is needed, the economic system can most accurately be described as a barter economy, as opposed to a capitalist one in which the family farm is oriented towards producing a surplus for sale to outside markets. This does not preclude, however, the earning of small amounts of cash, or the occasional purchase and sale of products, but the transactions are primarily one-time events, such as buying a horse; cash was not used consistently as the primary medium of exchange.

Operationalizing Chayanov's Theory

Given these preliminary assumptions, the question then becomes, how is one to operationalize the Chayanov model under the empirical conditions of agricultural production? Chayanov's theory, which relates consumer/worker ratios with the intensity of agricultural production, is not readily amenable to analysis of specific data sets unless some decisions are made about precisely what is meant by the terms utilized in an analysis. Here is a short list of the most problematic terms and how they might be used.

The term *family farm* is the most common one used in the literature concerning pre-capitalist modes of production; however, it is problematic in a number of regards. For example, in anthropological usage a "family" is usually regarded as a group of people who share ties of kinship, either through blood (consanguineal) or marriage (affinal). Individuals may live in the same household or many miles apart. A family may be nuclear, or extended; in the latter case descent is traced either bilaterally or through the male (patrilineal) or female (matrilineal) line.

As far as the census data of Admaston Township is concerned, it is virtually impossible to determine if those listed are members of the same family. For example, in the house of John and Mary Kelly, there is listed a woman, age thirty-nine, named Julia Kelly. Julia may be related to John and Mary, as one might suppose from the common surname, but then again Kelly is so common a surname that this could be a faulty assumption. In another example, Mary and Thomas Enright live with Helen Shanoutin, age twenty. The different surname may lead one to think that Helen is not related to Mary and Thomas, but actually Mary and Helen are sisters, as Shanoutin is Mary's maiden name.

In some instances, the census taker had the option of indicating the relationship of each person to the head of the household, but this information is not always listed. Under these circumstances it is probably best to dispense with the term "family," except under very restricted circumstances, and replace it with the term "household." A *household* may be defined as people who may or may not share ties of kinship, but who share a living space. These individuals may share preparation of meals, eat together, help cover budgetary items such as food and rent, and contribute labour for the benefit of the household as a whole. The term *domestic group* is commonly used in anthropology and is equivalent to a household in meaning.

As far as the term *farm* is concerned, the designation used in the present study refers to members of the same household who provided for most of their own subsistence needs, such as procuring their own food, supplying labour from their own household in which crops and livestock are raised for domestic use. The common labour needs of the household farm tended to follow a prevailing division of labour based on gender; men were generally the farm operators, engaged in such activities as ploughing, sowing, weeding, and harvesting, and tending livestocks while women were more often responsible for the maintenance and organization of the household and its members, while engaging in such activities as tending a vegetable garden, churning butter, producing clothes, collecting eggs, and milking. These activities did not preclude selling or exchanging produce in order to acquire other products that a farm requires, as long as this exchange or sale was on a use value basis, rather than for the purpose of accumulating capital or profit to be used for further investment.

The social organization of the farming household often consisted of young men staying on the farm to help their aging parents, and daughters marrying farming men outside of their household. Typically, the young women who married moved into their husband's household, a post-marital residence pattern known as *patrilocal residence*. In the case of many Irish farming households, the land base was not large enough to support all of the sons, so the family farm frequently was inherited by the eldest son, with his brothers either emigrating, moving to urban centres, where wage labour might be available, or attempting to earn enough money to purchase their own farm. Another option was for the aging father to purchase additional land for his sons as they became of age, in which case it may have been the youngest son, rather the eldest, who remained on the family farm and eventually inherits the property.

In sum, in assessing the applicability of the Chayanov model to the Irish farmers in this study, the key points are: first, the Irish of Admaston Township operated family farms; second, these farms utilized little or no outside labour; third, agricultural production was primarily devoted to providing for the subsistence needs of the farm family (i.e., was devoted to use value), as opposed to generating profit in a capitalist economy; and, fourth, excess production was channelled back into the farm itself to increase its proficiency. For example, profits were used to buy horses to replace oxen, to upgrade buildings, or perhaps to purchase additional land.

Methods and Procedures of Analysis

To operationalize Chayanov's theory several terms need a more precise definition. One of these is *consumer*. Within the farming household food is typically consumed at different rates by different members, depending on their size and caloric intake. It is impractical, though, to assign a different numerical weight for each person. As a matter of practical expediency for the purposes of this study, adult males were assigned 1.0 consumer unit each, adult females 0.8 units, and preadolescent children, those 12 years of age and under, 0.5 units. As far as *workers* or farm labourers were concerned these were calculated as males 16 years of age and over.

In terms of *acreage cultivated*, the census reports distinguish between "under crops" and "under pasture." Initially, I thought that I would only include the "under crops" category because this would appear to be the most labour-intensive area of a farm's agricultural production;

112 After the Famine

Table 9 O'Hare household, Admaston Township, 1851

Name	Age	Consumer units	Worker units	Acreage cultivated	Ratio consumers/ workers	Acres cultivated/ worker
Hugh	54	1.0	1.0	35		
Mary	50	0.8	–			
Patrick	28	1.0	1.0			
Edward	26	1.0	1.0			
Dennis	19	1.0	1.0			
Ann	17	0.8	–			
Mary	9	0.5	–			
Patrick	2	0.5	–			
Totals	8	6.6	4.0	35	6.6/4.0=1.65	35/4.0=8.75

Note: The O'Hare household is perhaps unusual in having so many mature members, resulting in a somewhat higher proportion of consumers to workers. In the 1851 sample of households used here, the range of consumer/worker ratio was 1.00 to 6.30. In the acres cultivated per worker ratio, the range was between 3.00 and 40.00, thus demonstrating a considerable variation overall.

however, when I examined individual farm cases I soon discovered that some farmers preferred to specialize in crop production, with a minimal concentration on livestock ownership. Other farms had a reverse pattern, with a more substantial concentration on animal husbandry. On this basis it seemed reasonable to include both the acreage under crops *and* pasture as a measure of a farm's agricultural production. Table 9 is an example, then, of the calculations involved.

In an initial attempt to operationalize Chayanov's theory and apply it to the Irish households of Admaston Township, a table was constructed concerning household variation of worker's productive intensity for each of the three census reports between 1851 and 1871 (table 10).

Discussion of Results

This discussion of workers' productive intensity will proceed column by column, assessing the numerical significance of the changes that occurred in the farming households of Admaston Township over the 20-year period between 1851 and 1871. Beginning with the column farthest to the left, the number of household members on average declined steadily from 6.47 members per household to 5.70 members, representing a decrease of 11.9 per cent. A reasonable explanation for a decline

Table 10 Average household variation in workers' productive intensity, 1851–71

	Household members N=	Consumers N=	Workers N=	Ratio of consumers/ workers	Acres cultivated	Acres cultivated/ worker
1851	6.47	4.58	1.53	2.99	15.9	10.39
1861	6.10	4.60	1.60	2.88	26.0	16.25
1871	5.70	4.30	1.60	2.69	51.4	32.13

in household size is that it is due to the internal population dynamics of the farming household themselves. For example, in 1851 there were 121 males age 24 or under who, in 1871, would be between the ages of 20 and 44.

These males, or many of them in any event, would be looking to eventually establish their own farming households. The actual increase in the number of households was from 53 to 154 or an increase of 101 households, which means that there were still possibly another 20 households that could have been established. The manner in which these young men would have obtained land for their new households, either through inheritance or direct purchase, is a matter to be dealt with more fully in a later discussion of the stem family.

The second column shows that the average number of consumers per household also declined, by 6.1 per cent, over the 20-year period. This was probably a result of the newer farmers having smaller families, and the older, more mature families shrinking in size as the children left their natal households upon marriage. In the third column there is hardly any change over the 20 years in the average number of workers per household, increasing slightly from 1.53 to 1.60 workers, which probably reflects the fact that men 16 years old and over are going to be counted as workers regardless of whether they are working in their father's household or their own. The number of workers per household also did not change to any large degree, because the ratio of workers per household remained in direct proportion to the increases in population between 1851 and 1871.

The fourth column depicts the ratio of consumers per worker, which declined by 10 per cent, from 2.99 consumers per worker in 1851, to 2.69 consumers per worker in 1871. Here again, this decrease is a result of a general decline in household size and the number of consumers per household over the 20 years. The implications, however, are significant because a steady decrease in the consumer to worker ratios means that workers have fewer consumers to support on a per capita basis, and with fewer dependants to provide for, workers then have the option of either working fewer hours per day and increasing their leisure time, or working the same number of hours but cultivating more land or otherwise expending more effort in other farm-related tasks.

The last two columns tell us what the farmers decided to do with their spare time; there was a dramatic increase (of 69.1 per cent) in the acres of farmland cultivated over the 20 years, from 15.9 acres per household on average in 1851 to 51.4 acres in 1871. Similarly, in the final column there was an increase of 67.6 per cent in the ratio of acres cultivated per worker (from 10.39 acres in 1851 to 32.13 acres in 1871). The increase was most pronounced in the 1861–71 period, during which there was an increase of 97.5 per cent (from 16.25 acres to 32.13 acres cultivated per worker); however, over the 20-year period farmers were cultivating about three times as much land.

What do these trends say about Chayanov's theory? On the whole the activities of the Irish farmers of Admaston Township confirm the main tenet of Chayanov's assertion, that it is the internal dynamics of the population itself, rather than external pressures, which determine agricultural productivity. While in situations of an increasing consumer to worker ratio, workers will work harder to meet the subsistence demands of their household. In the present case of a declining consumer to worker ratio, farmers have the option of utilizing the extra time to increase agricultural productivity. In accordance with the "use value" approach of simple commodity production, the results of the increased productivity can then be used for the purchase of another use-value commodity that the farmer needs.

This situation leads us, in turn, to reconsider how the farmers were able to increase the number of acres that they were able to cultivate by three times, a seemingly unrealistic feat even if they worked harder or longer. The answer is that they increased their productive capacity by ploughing their fields faster using horses than oxen, especially in the decade of 1861–71. Also, as was noted earlier in figure 3, crop production increased from 1,768 acres in 1861 to 8,337 acres in 1871, an increase of almost five times the area. Livestock production, listed in table 8, shows that the largest increases were in sheep, about three times, and horses, four times, while oxen decreased by three times, over the 1861 to 1871 decade.

The conclusion that can be drawn here is that a declining consumer to worker ratio led farmers to increase their agricultural productivity by switching from the slower oxen to the faster horses, which in turn allowed for even more land to be cultivated. The extra revenue from this increased agricultural productivity was then reinvested in further livestock purchases, such as sheep, which produced a saleable commodity in the form of wool. In this sense, Chayanov was correct in asserting that workers could be compelled to work harder, or increase their agricultural output, given the proper incentives that are internally generated by the population itself, either in terms of meeting the subsistence needs of an increasing household population (1851–61), or making investments in the family farm when a decreasing consumer worker ratio allowed for increased time for productive effort (1861–71).

Towards a More In-Depth Analysis of Labour Intensity

The previous discussion gives a broad overview of the Admaston Township farm economy in terms of domestic production. A further step in this analysis is to examine each of the various census years individually, using a more in-depth research strategy. It is necessary to begin with the generally accepted assumption in the methodology of the social sciences that conclusions concerning a data set must be drawn on the basis of a *systematic sample*, rather than on the basis of information that could be discursive, subjective, or otherwise biased.

A sample strategy is therefore necessary in order to make certain inferences about some larger population from a smaller one (the sample). The most generally accepted approach is to formulate a simple *random* sample, one in which each element in the population must have an equal and independent chance of inclusion. One begins, first, with a full listing of every element, in our case farm personnel, in the total population to be investigated. Once this list has been constructed, a procedure is decided upon; it is then used to randomly select elements from the total list. In *systematic* sampling, every nth name is selected from the list. The interval between the names is usually determined by dividing the number of persons desired in the sample from the total population under investigation. Choosing the interval between names selected from the full population does not compromise or bias the selection process because the name of every person has an equal chance of being selected over any other name on the list (see Dressler and Othes 2008; Russell 2002; McNeill 2005 for sampling procedures in the social sciences).

The present study begins by documenting all of the individuals recorded in the Canadian censuses as living in Admaston Township in the years 1851, 1861, and 1871. This constitutes the total population from which the subsequent samples are drawn. The enumerators recorded the names, ages, and other pertinent information for each member of a household, and then apparently moved on to the next nearby farm. If one looks at the location of each of the Admaston households on a map the only observable systematic pattern in the collection of household data by enumerators is their proximity to one another.

The information on Admaston households was then encoded on spreadsheets so that the data could be analysed in various ways. The main components of this information related to household size and composition, the age of family members, farm size, acreage cultivated, acreage devoted to pasture and woodlots, and the various crops grown and livestock cared for. The households were then arranged in alphabetical order for ease of retrieval, a system which also had the statistical effect of randomizing the sample. The sample was then organized into two groups; Irish and non-Irish, with Irish meaning all individuals born in Ireland and their first-generation offspring.

For the 1851 census a sample size of 30 households was chosen, starting with the first household on the list; then every second household was selected. For the 1861 census every fifth household was selected; for the slightly larger 1871 population, every sixth household was selected, yielding a sample size of 30 households for each of the decades. If for any reason the sample selected contained ambiguous or otherwise faulty data, the next one was then selected. Data on each of the 30 Irish households selected for each of the three census years were then subsequently organized according to acreage cultivated; the resulting consumer/worker and cultivated acreage/worker ratios were then calculated (tables 11, 12, and 13).

Based on this information, graphs were constructed on domestic variations in labour intensity, where the y-axis indicates cultivated acres/worker, and the x-axis the corresponding consumer/worker ratio for each household (figures 4, 5, and 6). As Sahlins (1971: 34) explained, "In principle, intensity per worker must increase by the labor equivalent of the per-capita consumption quota for every increase of 1.00 in the domestic ratio of consumers to producers. The law [the theoretical law of domestic economy], then, is $I = k (c/w)$, where 'I' is intensity, 'k' the average social labor required to maintain one person at normal consumption, and 'c/w' the dependency ratio."

If Chayanov's theory suggests that the intensity of labour varies inversely to the relative working capacity of the producing unit, then the Chayanov slope on each graph is C = acres/worker x consumers/worker = acres/consumer. For example, the graph of household variation in labour intensity for 1851 (figure 4) shows the acres cultivated/workers on the vertical y-axis and the ratio of consumers/workers on the horizontal x-axis.

Table 11 Household variation in labour intensity, Admaston Township, 1851

House-hold	Number of members	Number of consumers*	Number of workers#	Total acreage cultivated	Ratio of consumers/ workers	Acres cultivated/ worker
1	8	7.1	3	20	2.37	6.66
2	7	4.6	1	40	4.60	40.00
3	8	5.1	1	20	5.10	20.00
4	9	7.9	4	30	1.98	7.50
5	7	5.6	3	12	1.87	4.00
6	4	3.1	1	2	3.10	2.00
7	9	5.9	1	20	5.90	20.00
8	9	5.9	1	8	5.90	8.00
9	10	6.3	1	30	6.30	30.00
10	7	4.3	1	5	4.30	5.00
11	7	4.3	1	15	4.30	15.00
12	7	4.3	1	5	4.30	5.00
13	4	2.8	1	4	2.80	4.00
14	8	5.4	1	4	5.40	4.00
15	5	3.3	1	12	3.30	12.00
16	7	5.4	3	16	1.80	5.33
17	9	6.4	2	20	3.20	10.00
18	4	2.8	1	10	2.80	10.00
19	7	4.3	1	8	4.30	8.00
20	5	3.3	1	8	3.30	8.00
21	4	2.8	1	8	2.80	8.00
22	6	5.4	3	20	1.80	6.67
23	6	5.3	4	80	1.33	20.00
24	2	1.8	1	5	1.80	5.00
25	8	5.3	1	8	5.30	8.00
26	7	4.6	1	20	4.60	20.00
27	4	3.3	2	6	1.65	3.00
28	1	1.0	1	10	1.00	10.00
29	7	4.6	1	16	4.60	16.00
30	8	5.1	1	16	5.10	16.00
Avg.	6.5	4.6	1.5	15.9	2.99	10.39

* Adult males counted as 1.0 units, adult females 0.8 units, and preadolescent children (12 years of age and younger) 0.5 units.
# Workers calculated as males 16 years of age and older.

Table 12 Household variation in labour intensity, Admaston Township, 1861

Household	Number of members	Number of consumers*	Number of workers#	Total acreage cultivated	Ratio of consumers/ workers	Acres cultivated/ worker
1	4	3.1	1	10	3.10	10.00
2	8	7.1	4	111	1.78	27.75
3	3	2.3	1	8	2.30	8.00
4	6	4.3	2	5	2.15	2.50
5	5	3.3	1	40	3.30	40.00
6	8	4.8	1	42	4.80	42.00
7	6	4.9	1	12	4.90	12.00
8	4	3.4	1	9	3.40	9.00
9	11	8.1	3	15	2.70	5.00
10	5	3.3	1	7	3.30	7.00
11	3	2.8	2	50	1.40	25.00
12	4	2.8	1	15	2.80	15.00
13	10	6.9	3	12	2.30	4.00
14	3	2.8	2	40	1.40	20.00
15	8	6.4	3	32	2.13	10.66
16	7	4.3	4	21	1.08	5.25
17	2	1.8	1	4	1.80	4.00
18	6	5.0	1	8	5.00	8.00
19	5	4.6	1	40	4.60	40.00
20	5	4.3	2	14	2.15	7.00
21	4	9.6	2	76	4.80	38.00
22	8	5.4	2	16	2.70	8.00
23	8	5.7	1	10	5.70	10.00
24	6	3.8	1	45	3.80	45.00
25	8	5.1	1	8	5.10	8.00
26	9	5.8	4	30	1.35	7.50
27	7	4.3	1	10	4.30	10.00
28	10	5.6	3	45	1.86	15.00
29	7	4.3	1	29	4.30	29.00
30	5	3.3	1	18	3.30	18.00
Avg.	6.1	4.6	1.6	26	2.88	16.25

* Adult males counted as 1.0 units, adult females 0.8 units, and preadolescent children (12 years of age and younger) 0.5 units.
\# Workers calculated as males 16 years of age and older.

Table 13 Household variation in labour intensity, Admaston Township, 1871

Household	Number of members	Number of consumers*	Number of workers#	Total acreage cultivated	Ratio of consumers/ workers	Acres cultivated/ worker
1	4	3.3	1	40	3.30	40.00
2	3	2.8	2	80	1.40	40.00
3	4	3.3	1	40	3.30	40.00
4	5	3.3	1	8	3.30	8.00
5	10	6.6	1	20	6.60	20.00
6	11	8.5	2	90	4.25	45.00
7	5	4.6	2	50	2.30	25.00
8	7	6.2	3	50	2.10	16.66
9	3	2.3	1	40	2.30	40.00
10	12	7.6	2	120	3.80	60.00
11	8	5.3	2	100	2.65	50.00
12	3	2.3	1	30	2.30	30.00
13	5	3.3	1	45	3.30	45.00
14	3	2.6	1	70	2.60	70.00
15	7	5.1	1	50	5.10	50.00
16	9	8.2	3	80	2.73	27.00
17	2	1.8	1	40	1.80	40.00
18	4	2.8	1	100	2.80	100.00
19	4	2.8	1	15	2.80	15.00
20	8	6.7	1	40	6.70	40.00
21	8	5.3	1	50	5.30	50.00
22	8	5.8	3	40	1.93	13.00
23	1	1.0	1	10	1.00	10.00
24	2	1.8	1	60	1.80	60.00
25	1	1.0	1	8	1.00	8.00
26	10	8.2	1	80	8.20	80.00
27	5	2.3	2	30	1.15	15.00
28	8	6.7	1	80	6.70	80.00
29	6	3.8	1	30	3.80	30.00
30	5	3.3	1	45	3.30	45.00
Avg.	5.7	4.3	1.6	51.4	2.69	32.13

* Adult males counted as 1.0 units, adult females 0.8 units, and preadolescent children (12 years of age and younger) 0.5 units.
\# Workers calculated as males 16 years of age and older.

Figure 4 Household variation in labour intensity, Admaston Township, 1851

The numerical values of these two ratios were previously calculated in table 11 in the two right-hand columns. For household 1 in this table the ratio of consumers/workers is 2.37, and the acres cultivated/worker is 6.66. These two values, i.e., 2.37 on the x-axis, and 6.66 on the y-axis, are then plotted as coordinates on the graph as a conjunction of the two points. Similarly, every other of the 29 households is also plotted on the graph. For 1851 the Chayanov slope is calculated as follows: C = total acres cultivated/consumer = 478/137.3 = 3.48/1.00. In this instance the Chayanov slope is figured as a line beginning at X = 1.00, Y = 3.48, and rising to the right by the value of 3.48 acres for every increase of 1.00 in the c/w ratio. Once these various values for the 30 Irish households are subsequently plotted on the graph, one can visualize patterns in the labour intensity of farmers for 1851.

The pattern depicted in the graph of figure 4 shows that 3 of the 30 households fall on the line of expected worker intensity, 6 are above this line, and 21 are below it. One way to interpret these results is that 70 per cent (21/30) of the farmers in 1851 had difficulty in maintaining a consistent pattern of worker intensity as the number of consumers that they needed to support increased. Looking at the results a little more carefully shows that over half of the sample, 16/30, hovers around the

Figure 5 Household variation in labour intensity, Admaston Township, 1861

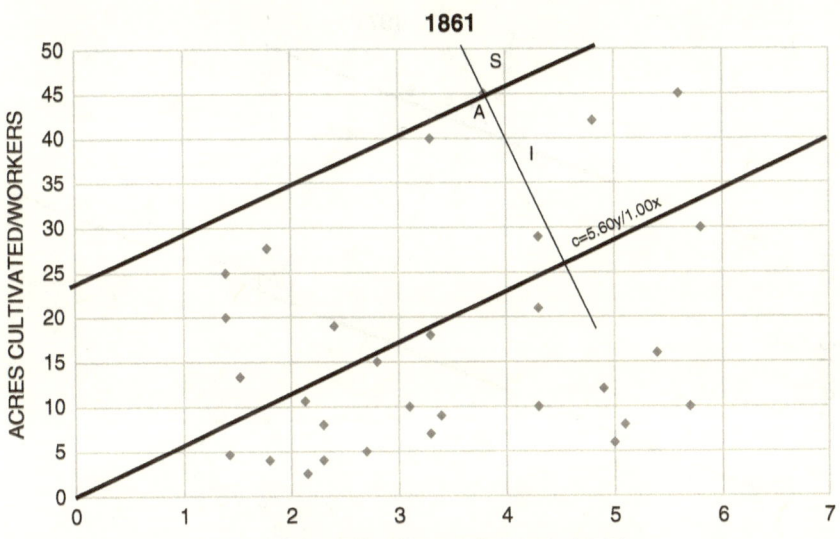

expected line of worker intensity, and when the 6 above the line are added in, this shows that 73 per cent (22/30) of the farmers are either working at or above the line of productive intensity.

For 1861, the pattern (C = 5.60y/1.00x) shown in figure 5 illustrates a marked increase in farmers' productive intensity over the previous decade. For this year farmers are now working at a rate of 5.60 acres cultivated per consumer, an increase of 2 more acres cultivated per consumer over the previous decade. Also, there are a greater number of farmers (10/30 or 33 per cent) who are working above the expected level of worker intensity, with an additional five households performing very near the line of expected intensity. However, in 1861, half of the households (15/30) struggled below the level of acres per consumer that was the norm for that year.

The pattern for 1871, as illustrated in figure 6, shows interesting comparisons with the previous two decades. In this year the line of worker intensity (C = 11.98y/1.00x) shows that each farmer in the sample was able to increase production to nearly 12 acres for each consumer, doubling the output for the previous decade. In addition, in 1871, there was a greater percentage of farmers working either at or above the line of productive intensity (23/30 or 77 per cent), with a

Figure 6 Household variation in labour intensity, Admaston Township, 1871

correspondingly small number of households performing below the line (7/30 or 23 per cent).

Thus, when one compares the relative changes in the ratio of acres cultivated per consumer over the three decades, one cannot help but be impressed by the steady increases in worker intensity, from 3.48 in 1851, to 5.60 in 1861, to 11.98 in 1871. In over two decades, representing about one generation of farm households, farmers' productive intensity increased by about three and a half times as indicated by the ratio of consumers to workers.

Measuring Social Differentiation

The term *social differentiation* refers to the variations or distinctions in wealth, power, and status in a society. It differs from the term *social stratification*, a term which is equivalent to institutionalized inequality; a stratified society is one divided into two or more categories of people who are ranked higher or lower relative to one another. Societies that are stratified can be contrasted with *egalitarian societies*, societies in which private property tends to be either absent or nearly so, and in which there is a virtual lack of distinction in regard to status, power, and privilege. Based on these definitions it is apparent that the Irish farmers of Admaston Township lived in a differentiated society but not a stratified one; each person could move up or down a scale of wealth based on their own productive efforts.

The graphs depicting household variation in labour intensity, which has been a topic of discussion thus far, offer insights into the differences in the distribution and intensity of domestic agricultural production. This production varies according to the ratio of consumers to workers and, in turn, to the ratio of cultivated acres per worker. Ultimately by plotting these different points on a graph, one arrives at a median line through the graph, representative of the "Chayanov slope," a line which shows incremental increases in acres cultivated per consumer. The household positions plotted on each graph give an idea of the relative intensity of domestic production, which is situated either above or below the Chayanov norm (line "C" on each graph).

Those households operating above this norm produce a surplus within the local domestic economy; they exceed the normal intensity of labour requirements. While the points on each graph offer the reader a visual impression of the socio-economic differentiation in the local Irish population, one can press this analysis further by attempting a more precise measure of this differentiation. For example, with reference to figure 4, representing the distribution of household labour intensity in 1851, it can be observed that the surplus production is at its highest point at 4.60x, 40.00y, which can be referred to as point "A" on the graph. Then a perpendicular line "I" can be drawn through point A to line "C" below, intersecting this line at a 90° angle.

The length of "I", which can be regarded as a measure of intensity, can then be calculated; it represents the limits of the upper and lower bounds of worker surplus production in 1851. A formula can then be developed to calculate this relative surplus production. One needs only to draw a parallel line, call it "S" (i.e, for surplus labour capacity), through point A equidistant from line C below. In fact, any point along line S would have the same measure of labour intensity as point A, regardless if this point is to the left or right of point A because the distance between lines S and C remains constant. This fact also holds true for any other points between lines S and C which can be connected by a line (I) parallel to line C.

A formula can then be used to calculate a relative degree of intensity:

$$I = S - C$$

Thus, for point A, I = (40.00y/4.60x) = 8.70 − 3.48 = 5.22, which is a measure of the range of surplus labour capacity between lines S and C; that is, the acres cultivated per worker above consumer needs. Similarly, the other points above line C and below line S can also be

124 After the Famine

Table 14 Household surplus labour capacity above Chayanov norms, 1851–71

	Households N =	Household Surplus Production	
		Per cent of households	Above consumer needs
1851	6	20	5.22
1861	10	33	6.24
1871	13	43	23.73

calculated about these households' surplus domestic intensity. These are the households which are producing above their own labour requirements, or the amount of a household's surplus domestic labour. There were six of these households in 1851, which represents (6/30) 20 per cent of the households in the sample utilized for the calculations.

For comparative purposes, one can then study the surplus labour requirements in the other decades. For 1861, the highest point above line C is situated at a point A, with coordinates 45.00y, 3.80x. Using the formula above, $I = (45.00y/3.80x) = 11.84 - 5.60 = 6.24$, which is the distance between S and C and as such is a measure of the range of surplus labour production. For this year there were 10 of these households (10/30) or 33 per cent of the households working above the Chayanov norm.

For 1871, the highest point above line C is situated at point A with the coordinates 100.00y, 2.80x. In this case $I = (100.00/2.80) = 35.71 - 11.98 = 23.73$, or the range of surplus labour capacity. There were 13 (13/30) or 43 per cent of the Admaston households in this sample working above capacity for their labour requirements. These various statistics on household labour are summarized in table 14.

One interpretation of this analysis is that from 1851 to 1871 there had been a progressive differentiation of the Irish farming population of Admaston Township over the two decades after the initial settlement of most of its population after the Great Famine. An increasing number of farmers were working at surplus capacity, which is to say, working above the strict consumer needs of their families. This trend is particularly evident in the decade between 1861 and 1871, during which the surplus production of farm workers increased by nearly four times.

Of course, farmers who wished to increase their production had the capacity to do so in Admaston Township, either by purchasing more land or working the land they had more intensely both unlikely options back in Ireland. The statistics presented in this chapter demonstrate clearly that, given the opportunity and sufficient resources, Irish farmers in Admaston were capable of progressing well beyond the immediate subsistence needs of their families. The foregoing analysis refutes the idea, expressed by many at the time of the Famine, that Irish farmers were inherently lazy and therefore deserved their fate.

Discussion

The focus of this chapter has been as much on methodology as on illustrating any specific aspects of Irish agricultural production in Admaston Township. This chapter looks at the various tools that have been developed in anthropology to understand populations in the historical past and demonstrates how they, and the discipline as a whole, can make contributions that are unique to the study of historical processes.

As far as Chayanov's theory concerning farmers' productivity in relation to the ratio of workers to consumers is concerned, the question is not so much whether or not this theory is appropriate but whether or not it is useful. Does the theory provide insights into historical populations that would not be obtainable using other existing methodologies? The answer is, Yes, his theory is useful, and beyond what one might expect. As O'Neill (1984: 6) explains, "Chayanov's model is particularly important, both because of its highly empirical origin and its wide influence ... Chayanov's thesis can be extended and used to argue that an increase in population should lead to labor intensification across a population, and hence to a rising level of agricultural productivity." And furthermore, as Durrenberger (1984: 12) suggests, "The potential of Chayanov's analysis has hardly begun to be developed."

The present analysis of Irish farmers in Admaston Township illustrates a somewhat hidden aspect of Chayanov's theory. I had set out to conduct an empirical study of the Admaston population along various dimensions, such as acres cultivated per consumer or to study the rising level of economic activity as the number of consumers per family unit increased. What I had not expected to find was such a marked differentiation in the Irish farming population over the decades between 1851 and 1871. My initial assumption was that a certain level of productivity would be reached as the Irish adjusted to their new land and were sufficiently comfortable feeding their families without fear of food shortages similar to those which they were escaping in their home country.

However, contrary to my expectations, I discovered a continual rise in agricultural productivity, one that was most pronounced between 1861 and 1871, when population growth levelled off. Certainly, one can find reasons for this increased productivity, for example in farmers' switch from oxen to horses, but such an exploration still does not explain why the Irish felt compelled to go beyond their immediate needs. Lacking the ability to go back in time and conduct interviews with the people concerned, we will never know their reasons for sure, but the facts are there in the census reports of the mid-nineteenth century. Whatever the reasons, the Irish worked much harder than they needed to fulfil their basic subsistence requirements. Perhaps they felt invigorated at the seemingly unlimited prospects that their new life afforded, freed from the centuries of repression that they and their ancestors had experienced. One wonders what the Irish farmers in Ireland could have accomplished had they not suffered the Cromwellian land confiscations of the mid-seventeenth century and the subsequent political repression.

Conclusion

In the case of the Irish farmers, Chayanov would predict that if agricultural production was based on a one-to-one correspondence between the consumer/worker ratio and some set unit of production, such as acres cultivated/farmer, then the expectation would be that any increases in production would follow increments approximating a rise of about 45 degrees if depicted graphically. There are many farmers whose production approximates this expected result, but there are also those falling below this expected output and others who rise above it. In fact, when the results of agricultural production are plotted on graphs for 1861 and 1871, there is a sharp rise in farmers producing far above the expected norm.

A key question here is: How can this dramatic increase in agricultural production, with its associated increase in social differentiation, be explained? While there are no doubt many possibilities, the two main contenders would be either (a) an attempt to improve the farmer's life by providing better housing, equipment, and domesticated animals, which is to say, an attempt to increase the use value or simple commodity production of a farm. The alternative explanation (b) is that the change during the 1861–71 decade was a matter of capitalist production to generate profit. My contention throughout this study is that (a) is the most reasonable explanation. Therefore, based on the data presented in this chapter, the increasing social and economic differentiation among the Irish farmers of Admaston Township is a very prominent finding of this study. However, an associated conclusion concerning this increase in social and economic differentiation is that when there were profits from farming these were then directed back into improving the infrastructure of the farm enterprise, rather than retained as a source of capital accumulation (see McInnis 1982: 9–49).

In *Unequal Beginnings*, John McCallum's (1980) insightful comparison of agricultural development in Quebec and Ontario during our study period (circa 1870), it is noted that "Ontario farmers purchased livestock and improved their buildings during the boom years of the mid-1850s" (1980: 52); this strategy was also adopted by the Irish farmers of Admaston Township. In southern Ontario and Quebec, the lucrative wheat trade virtually collapsed by the mid-1860s because of the "triumvirate of land shortages, soil exhaustion, and western competition" (ibid.). Admaston farmers, many of whom had just fled the Famine in the early 1850s, were just beginning to clear their fields at the time of the wheat boom in the 1850–65 period. Thus, the Irish of Admaston were not able to take advantage of this lucrative source of capital. The economic situation for Quebec farmers was like that of the Admaston Irish farmers; both groups tended to lack investment opportunities. As McCallum states, "Quebec farmers ... could have found no major investment outlets under the hopeless market conditions that confronted Quebec agriculture in the first half of the nineteenth century" (1980: 52–3).

An associated point concerns the possible market demand from timber camps farther north in the Ottawa Valley; Admaston farmers could profit from the sale of hay, oats, horses, and meat to the lumber camps in this area. This could explain the increasing economic differentiation of Admaston farmers. However, the historical facts do not support this suggestion for the Irish of Admaston Township.

Robert Jones, probably the foremost authority on the history of agriculture in Ontario, points out that the requirements of the lumber industry were met by "The timber squatters who followed the industry up the river ... and since these crops [hay and oats] could not be transported long distances local farmers faced no serious competition ... [meeting the needs of the timber industry] remained no more than an off-season activity of the farmers [of the region]" (McCallum 1980: 11, see also Jones 1946: 77, 125–34). The conclusion that could reasonably be drawn here is that provisioning of the Ottawa River lumber industry was largely the preserve of farmers located near to this economic activity, and that the Irish of Admaston Township, who lived in the southern portion of Renfrew County, were too far removed to take advantage of this economic opportunity. Thus, the Admaston Irish farmers operated in a somewhat closed economic system. They arrived too late to take advantage of southern Ontario's wheat boom of the 1850s, and were too far removed geographically to benefit from the more northerly lumber industry.

Chapter Six

Population and Family in Transition

As a starting point for the discussion in this chapter, the term "Irish family" is used here to refer both to the families of people living in Ireland during the time of the Famine in the mid to late nineteenth century and to the families of Irish people who emigrated to Canada, along with the first generation of descendants, during this time period. As far as the reasons why certain families are structured the way they are, as I noted previously, there is considerable debate in the literature, a debate which ranges across a number of disciplines, such as history, anthropology, sociology, and demography.

The point, then, is that it is hardly possible to determine with any degree of certainty why one group of families is structured one way and not another; it is also difficult to exactly determine the various historical processes that are involved in in the development of family structures. Suffice to say that economic expediency is an important factor in shaping families. It is commonly recognized that nuclear families are more highly mobile units, and thus more adaptable to an industrial economy, with its need for a transient labour force, than the larger extended families of previous centuries, which were more useful in an agricultural context.

One must also consider the cultural background of a society's families. There is a certain "force of tradition" that compels people to hang on to social forms that were comfortably used in the past. The sheer variety of families that anthropologists have encountered in various cultures shows that humans have explored just about every possible variation conceivable: families whose members live with the husband's – or wife's – relatives, families whose members trace their descent through the male – or female – line, or through both lines, and numerous other permutations.

One could also add to this list of explanations certain sociological factors, such as what could be termed the "gendered division of labour." In this case a division of labour involves one spouse (often the male) working in a wage economy and another spouse (frequently the female) working in the domestic domain. These roles may vary from society to society, but the point is that, from a sociological perspective, a family involves certain roles that contribute to the overall good of its members and lend importance to people's existence.

In the context of Irish families, the literature on the "stem" families has been discussed at some length in the introductory chapter. We now examine the structure of Irish families in Admaston Township in more detail, with the goal of addressing some unresolved issues that have arisen in the literature.

Population Structure

The population structure of Admaston Township in 1851 is largely a reflection of the family composition of Irish emigrants who arrived from Ireland in the two or three years during and immediately after the Famine. As figure 7 and table 15 illustrate, the total Irish population living in Admaston during the census year of 1851 was 410 persons. Those under 19 years of age comprised 55.4 per cent of the population. In the middle-age categories, those between ages 20 to 49, there were 82 males and 71 females, comprising 36.3 per cent of the total population. The elder category, those over 50 years of age, comprised 8.3 per cent of the population.

Thus, the population structure of Admaston in 1851 is largely composed of young families, with a very large child and adolescent population. This bears out earlier suggestions that the typical family of Irish immigrants who came to Canada during the Famine years comprised a married couple with one or two children born in Ireland. Later, through the next decade, more children would be born into this family, so that the initial parents, who were probably in the 20 to 29 age group in 1851, would now be 10 years older. The relative scarcity of those in the older age group, those more than 50 years of age, at 8.3 per cent of the population, probably reflects a lack of desire on the part of older people to leave Ireland and endure the hardships of beginning life anew in the Canadian wilderness, or is a reflection of the higher-than-normal death rate of elderly people making the voyage on the "coffin ships."

A decade later, by 1861, the Irish population of Admaston increased from 410 to 898 persons, representing more than a doubling of the Irish population (figure 8, table 16). Over this decade the percentage of the population under 20 years of age remained just about the same as in 1851 at 58 per cent, indicating in both census years a very bottom-heavy

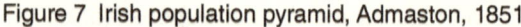

Figure 7 Irish population pyramid, Admaston, 1851

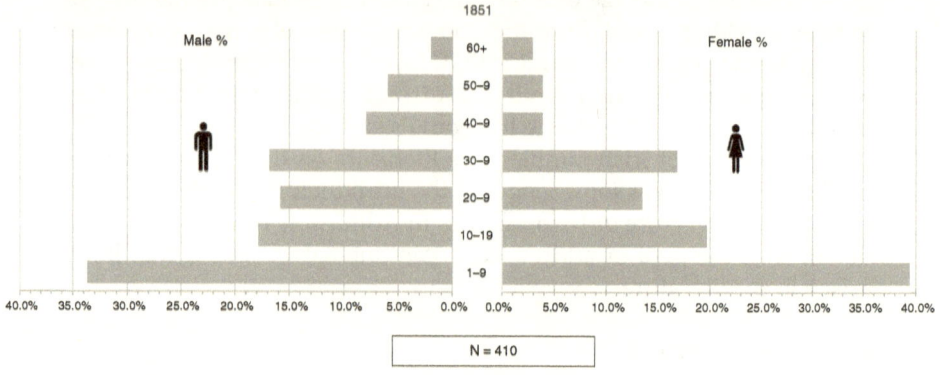

Table 15 Irish population by age and sex, Admaston, 1851

Age	Male	Female	%
0–9	68	82	36.6
10–19	36	41	18.8
20–9	32	28	14.6
30–9	34	35	16.8
40–9	16	8	5.9
50–9	12	8	4.9
60+	4	6	2.4
Totals	202	208	100.0
N= 410			

population pyramid, with great potential for future growth. A relatively small proportion of this population (9.4 per cent) was 50 years of age or older, a slight increase from the 8.3 per cent of a decade earlier.

The population structure of 1871 (figure 9, table 17) suggests that the Irish population had levelled off, increasing by just 93 persons, to a total population of 991, a dramatic cessation in population growth compared with the increases during the 1851 to 1861 period. The younger age group, comprising those individuals under 20 years of age, continued to form the bulk of the population, at 55.2 per cent of the total, while the elder age group, those age 50 and older, showed the largest gain, increasing by 52 persons between 1861 and 1871, and now forming 13.6 per cent of the population. The overall population gain, of just

Figure 8 Irish population pyramid, Admaston, 1861

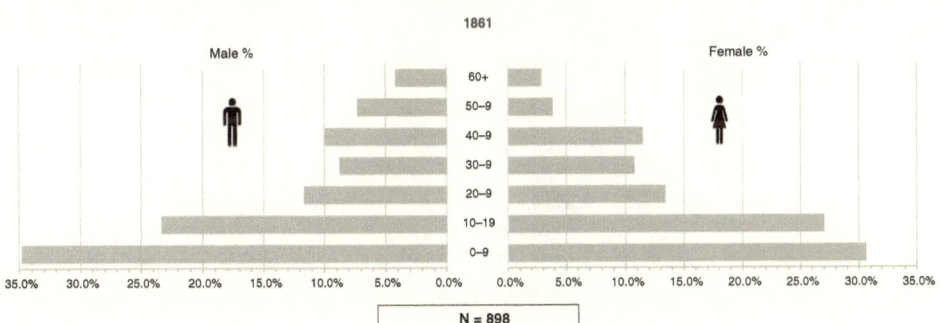

Table 16 Irish population by age and sex, Admaston, 1861

Age	Male	Female	%
0–9	167	128	32.9
10–19	112	113	25.1
20–9	56	56	12.5
30–9	42	45	9.7
40–9	48	48	10.7
50–9	35	16	5.7
60+	20	12	3.7
Totals	480	418	100.3
N= 898			

over 9.4 per cent for the decade between 1861 and 1871, suggests that this growth was due to local births, rather than to migration into the area. Certainly, the overall immigration of Irish people to Canada decreased significantly for the 1861–71 period as a whole, compared with the late 1840s, with its massive influx of post-Famine immigrants from Ireland.

In summary, the younger generation (under 20 years of age) remained remarkably high as a proportion of the total Irish population, hardly varying at all between 1851 (55.4 per cent) and 1871 (55.2 per cent). Even though the Irish population of Admaston levelled off during this last decade between 1861 and 1871, there remained much potential for growth in the future. One would expect to find in the decades ahead, as this large

Figure 9 Irish population pyramid, Admaston, 1871

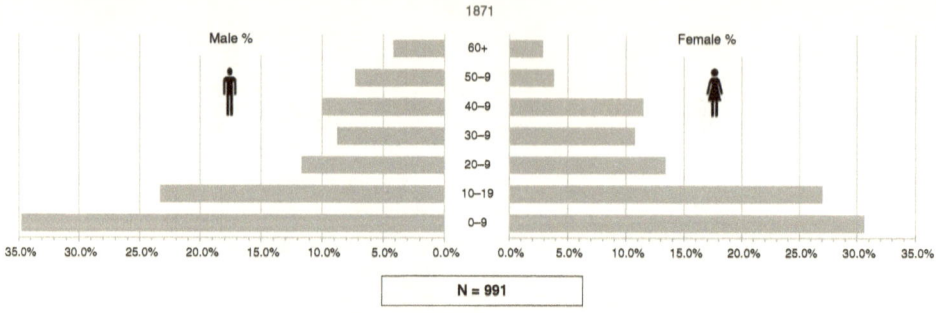

Table 17 Irish population by age and sex, Admaston, 1871

Age	Male	Female	%
0–9	148	123	27.3
10–19	152	124	27.9
20–9	69	83	15.3
30–9	38	40	7.9
40–9	35	44	8.0
50–9	51	37	8.9
60+	32	15	4.7
Totals	525	466	100.0
N= 991			

population of children and youth grew to adulthood and began to have their own families, that there would be a further "echo boom" in the population. Such an expansion would subsequently cause a strain on the availability of existing resources, especially in regard to arable land in Admaston Township, suggesting that the second generation of Irish in Renfrew County may well be forced to sell off their parents' farms and migrate elsewhere. In fact, many Irish did move to the American West, especially the Dakotas in the mid-1880s, to begin farming anew.

The other two generations saw a shifting of population percentages. The older generation (over 50 years of age) increased from 8.3 per cent in 1851 to 13.6 per cent in 1871, while the middle generation (20 to 49 years) decreased from 36.3 per cent in 1851 to 31.2 per cent in 1871, which suggests an aging of the local population over age 20 over the two decades.

Implications of Irish Population Structure

It would be interesting to find out if the Irish population structure of Admaston was different from or like that of similar residents of other areas. Finding equivalent data on populations is difficult. The age categories are often different, or the categories too broad or undifferentiated (e.g., grouped generically as "children," "young adults," "elderly adults"). Fortunately for the present study useful population data have been found for the Killashandra Parish, County Cavan, in 1841 (O'Neill: 1984: 197).

Before looking at these figures, I tried to hypothesize about what the population structure in an Irish community in 1841 would be like. This was a period, before the Famine, in which population growth in Ireland was still relatively high, reaching about 8.5 million for the country as a whole. The population was also more "mature" than that which one would expect to find among the Irish of Admaston; one could reasonably assume that there would be more persons in the elderly, post-50s population, than one would find in Admaston. On this basis my preliminary estimate would be that those in the post-50s age group would comprise about 15–18 per cent of the Cavan population. An estimate as to the size of the younger generation, those under 20 years, would be somewhat less than that of Admaston, say about 50 per cent of the population, leaving about 35 per cent for the middle (20–49) sector of the population.

The total farming (labourers excluded) population of Killashandra Parish in 1841 was 3,870 persons, which is a substantial sample size. In terms of the percentages in the different age categories, 58.8 per cent were 20 and under (notice the one-year difference from Admaston, at "under 20"), 29.6 per cent were 21–50, and 11.5 per cent were over 50. Evidently my initial assumptions about an Irish population in the 1840s were wrong. The figure for the youngest sector of the population (0–20 years) in Killashandra, at 58.8 per cent, was virtually the same as that of the Irish of Admaston (1851, 55.4 per cent; 1861, 58.0 per cent; 1871, 55.2 per cent). The oldest sector of the population (over 50 years), at 11.6 per cent for Killashandra Parish, was comparable to the Admaston population (1851, 8.3 per cent; 1861, 9.4 per cent; 1871, 13.6 per cent). The figure for the middle sector (21–50 years) was 29.6 per cent for Killashandra, comparable to Admaston's at 36.3 per cent in 1851, 32.6 per cent in 1861, and 31.2 per cent for 1871. (These details are summarized in table 18)

The Admaston population between 1851 and 1871 was experiencing an increase in its elderly population and a corresponding decline in the middle-age population, while the percentage of the youngest persons

Table 18 Age categories, percentage of population, Cavan (1841) and Admaston (1851–71)

Age Group	Cavan* 1841	Admaston 1851	Admaston 1861	Admaston 1871	Avg.
0–19	58.8	55.4	58.0	55.2	56.9
20–49	29.6	36.3	32.6	32.2	32.7
50+	11.6	8.3	9.4	13.6	10.7
Totals	100.0	100.0	100.0	101.0	100.3

* Age categories for Cavan (Killashandra Parish) are 0–20, 21–50, 51+.

remained about the same for each period. After two decades of settlement, then, the Admaston Irish achieved a population distribution comparable to that of an Irish population a decade earlier. By 1871 the immigrant Irish population of Admaston eventually reached a population structure, in terms of the distribution of the various age groups, that was virtually the same as the pre-Famine population in Ireland. (Of course, further research would be needed to verify this point.)

The conclusion that the population distribution of age groups in Admaston was virtually the same as that of pre-Famine Ireland has further implications for our theoretical investigation. For example, as far as the continuation of a stem family structure comprising three generations of people brought over from Ireland is concerned, there were just not enough people in the post-50 age category to perpetuate this family pattern even if there was an inclination to do so.

If, as indicated in my initial working hypothesis, the Irish population of Admaston in the post-Famine period could not be considered a "natural" one, that is, one which evolved over many generations on the same land, the stem family would have needed many more years to replicate itself, even if there was already a "cultural" tendency to do so. Since it has now been shown that persons in the post-50s population formed virtually the same percentage for both Admaston and Killashandra, then a reasonable hypothesis going forward would be that the percentage of stem families in Admaston would be about the same as that existing in Ireland itself.

Thus, the major difference between the Irish farming family in Ireland and that of Admaston is that in Ireland the older generation was more likely able to hold on to their farm, forcing their younger male children to relinquish a possible claim to the inheritance of the farm upon the parents' retirement or death. In Canada, it was the younger family members who initially bought the family farm, perhaps with some financial help from their parents, but the key point is that the older people came to Canada as "extra" family members, as opposed to farm owners. In this case, the younger people could start their own farms, probably with the financial help of the government's pre-emption program, rather than having to wait for their parents to retire or die.

Another major difference between the Irish farmers of Ireland and of Canada has to do with the relative deficiency of economic opportunities in Ireland, and the effect that this situation had on marriage age. Setting aside the argument that marriage age in Ireland was primarily tied to inheritance, it was nonetheless difficult for a younger male to start a farm of his own because of the lack of opportunities to purchase one, even if he had the funds to do so. If he decided to rent rather than purchase farm property, he was subject to rent increases and the stigma of poverty; his marriage prospects were thus more limited, at least until middle age, at which time he might have been able to accumulate the necessary assets to allow him to marry.

Marriage Age

According to O'Neill's (1984: 178) study of Killashandra in Cavan, the mean marriage age in Ireland in 1841 for all farmers was 26.0 years for males, and 21.7 years for females. While age at marriage statistics are not available for the Admaston population, we can roughly estimate these figures for 1851 by deducting two years from the age of the parents when their first child was born. The procedure is first to draw up a list of all married couples in the Admaston census of 1851. This list includes married couples with children who live on a farm. Deleted from this list are all couples not living on a farm, married couples without children (because the age of the first child was used as a guide to determine the age of the parents' marriage age), or widowed individuals.

It is unfortunate that the actual year of marriage for the farming couples was not recorded in the census forms, yet most couples would probably have had their first child within the first two years of marriage, if they were going to have any at all. It is also possible of course that a couple's first child might have died and therefore was not recorded. Yet, with this proviso, and lacking any other means of determining the age of couples at marriage, the procedure followed here is no doubt the best option for comparative purposes.

When first considering a comparison of Irish married couples in the Killashandra Parish of Cavin for 1841 with the Irish of Admaston in 1851, I could think of two competing hypotheses or assumptions about what to expect in terms of the data that would emerge. In the first instance, it seemed reasonable that the Irish of Admaston would have married at an earlier age than their Cavan counterparts. The reasoning behind this was that the Irish fleeing the Famine would have arrived in their late teens or early 20s and were probably able to make a quick start to farming because of the relative ease of purchasing a farm as a result of the existing pre-emption program. Following this line of thought, the marriage age for the Admaston Irish would have been two to five years younger than for their Cavan counterparts, who would have been delaying marriage until a farm was secured.

On the other hand, the Admaston Irish could have had a higher age at marriage than their counterparts in Cavan because of the arduous struggle to escape the Famine, the time taken to secure the funds to travel to Canada, and the subsequent delay in finding a spouse in the absence of a ready social community. So, there are two competing hypotheses that one could draw on, each with its own rationale. Table 19 presents the comparable marriage figures for Cavan and Admaston.

The most striking aspect of table 19 is the similarity in marriage ages for Ireland in 1841 and Admaston in 1851, especially for the age at marriage for males. For all farmers in both groups, males marry at 26 years in Cavan and 26.8 in Admaston. For small farmers in both groups, males marry at 27.1 for Cavan and 27.6 for Admaston. In every instance, the marriage age for males in Cavan and Admaston does not differ more than .80 of a year for the two groups, or 9.6 months. Also significant is the similarity between the marriage ages in relation to farm size. In both instances the marriage age is high for small farmers, drops by one or two years for medium farmers, then rises again to its highest level for large farmers.

The somewhat higher marriage age for small rather than medium farmers was also remarked upon by Arensberg and Kimball (1940: 106). They noted, for example, that in terms of occupation and marital status in County Clare, "the longest delay in marriage is found among the small farmers ... No other occupational class, not even the professional class, delays marriage so long or has so many celibate members."

While males show a remarkable degree of consistency between Cavan and Admaston in terms of age at marriage, there is a much greater degree of discordance among females. While there is only a one-year difference overall between females (21.7 years for Cavan and 20.7 for Admaston), there are greater differences in the age of females in the individual groups. The largest variance is in the age of females who marry farmers with small holdings (23.8 years for Cavan versus 20.0 years for Admaston females). This difference of almost four years

Table 19 Mean marriage age, Cavan (1841) and Admaston (1851), by farm size

Group	Cavan (1841)		Admaston (1851)	
	Males	Females	Males	Females
Farmers (all)	26.0	21.7	26.8	20.7
Small farmers*	27.1	23.8	27.6	20.0
Medium farmers	25.6	21.6	26.0	22.3
Large farmers	28.4	22.7	27.8	24.7

* Farm size in Admaston was calculated as "small" (100 acres), "medium" (150 acres), and "large" (200 acres). For Killashandra, Cavan, O'Neill (1984: 156) divided the farming community into the three groups of "small" (1–12 acres), "medium" (13–25 acres) and "large" (more than 25 acres). Also, useful for comparative contextual purposes are O'Tuathaigh's (1972: 206) statistics on the size of landholdings in Ireland: 1–5 acres, 44.9 per cent (1841); 15.5 per cent (1851); 5–15 acres, 36.6 per cent (1841); 33.6 (1851); 15–30 acres 11.5 per cent (1841); 24.8 (1851); above 30 acres, 7.0 per cent (1841); 26.1 per cent (1851). Thus, "small" (1–15 acres) holdings declined from 81.5 per cent in 1841 to 49.1 per cent in 1851, and "large" holdings increased from 7.0 per cent in 1841 to 26.1 per cent in 1851.

is difficult to explain, except perhaps to resort to the explanation given by Arensberg and Kimball, that small farmers in Ireland, both male and female, are more likely to delay marriage than farm couples in the other two categories of farm size; a situation which apparently does not apply to Admaston women in the small farm category.

Curiously, a corresponding discrepancy occurs among large farmer couples: the marriage age in Cavan is two years lower than in Admaston. In fact, the marriage age of Admstaon women, at 24.7 years, is the highest among all of the categories of females in both Ireland and Admaston; however, this later age also corresponds to the later age at marriage of all males (28.4 in Cavan, and 27.8 in Admaston) in the large farm category.

The importance of these statistics on the age of marriage among the different farm groups is that the later a person marries in life, the fewer children they can be expected to have; this is owing to the fact that those who marry late have a shorter period of fertility than those who marry at a younger age. Thus, family size can be positively correlated with the age of the marrying individual. Ireland, however, poses a conundrum in this regard. As Arensberg and Kimball (1940: 106) explain, "strangely enough in a declining population, fecundity is very high. Although there are fewer married women of childbearing age per 1,000 inhabitants [of Ireland] than in other countries ... the fertility of these women is remarkably high." Despite this great fecundity in Ireland, "the balance between high fertility and few and late marriages keeps their numbers down" (ibid.: 106–7).

Neither of my initial assumptions about possible differences between Cavan and Admaston appear to be valid in explaining the facts at hand. Overall, in both areas, the tripartite grouping of farmers offers the most plausible explanation for the situation in both Cavan and Admaston, regardless of the geographical differences involved or the 10-year gap between the censuses. Simply put, the age of marriage of men in both areas is virtually the same, which is also about four to six years greater than the age at which females were married.

One can conclude from these age differences that men were under greater pressure to accumulate resources before marrying than women. In general, men, after accumulating. sufficient resources, were ready to marry at about 26 years of age, while women were ready to marry at an earlier age, at about 21 years of age. These statistics relating to the marriage age of Irish men and women reflect the types of household and family composition that emerged.

The Childhood Dependency Ratio

The previous discussion of the population structure of Irish people living in Admaston Township between 1851 and 1871 presents the necessary empirical evidence for any assessment of family dynamics involving changes in size and structure. The tables on the Irish population illustrate the internal dynamics of population movement by age, sex, and year of birth, factors that are necessary components of our understanding of family groupings, but the figures in these tables primarily offer background information of the dynamic forces underlying family change. For this reason, it would be prudent to use the population figures in another manner, such as examining the ratio of children (younger than 15 years) to adults in the prime child-rearing age category (20–45 years). The result of such an analysis would yield what could be called a *dependency ratio*, a number which would allow for a view of Irish parental responsibilities. Such an analysis would also allow for a better understanding of the fluctuations in family size and the general fertility or fecundity rate of the Admaston population.

The fecundity of a population can be measured in different ways. Aside from the age of women at marriage, another index of fertility is the ratio of women to children, or more generally, adults to children. Data on the ratio of children (0–14 years) to adults (20–45 years) are set out in table 20 for the Irish population of Cavan, Killashandra Parish, for 1841, and Admaston Township for the years 1851–71. This table also

Table 20 Ratio of children (0–14 years) to adults (20–45 years), Cavan (1841) and Admaston Township (1851–71)

	Cavan*		Admaston						Avg.
	1841	N=	1851	N=	1861	N=	1871	N=	
All adults	1.51	1156	1.38	145	1.63	256	1.54	268	1.52
Females	3.01	581	2.94	68	3.12	134	2.88	143	2.99
Males	3.04	575	2.60	77	3.43	122	3.30	125	3.09

* The data for Cavan (1841) are derived from O'Neill (1984: 197) "farming female age structure," Table A.1, combined with "farming male age structure," Table A.2. O'Neill uses 10-year increments, so for the purposes of the present table his age grouping of 11–20 for both males and females was divided by two. Similarly, the 41–50 age grouping was also divided by two in order to correspond with my own age structure data for Admaston, which use 5-year increments. As such, the Cavan population figures are deemed to be reasonably accurate estimates.

indicates the so-called dependency ratio for all the adults in each category, as well as for females and males separately.

Based on these data sets, several observations can be made. First, for all adults the childhood dependency ratio is lowest for Admaston in 1851 at 1.38 children per adult. This ratio then increased substantially (by almost 20 per cent, to 1.63 children per adult) by 1861, during which the adult population of Admaston increased by 77 per cent. After this period there was a marginal decline in the dependency ratio (1.54) in 1871, corresponding to a more minimal increase in the adult population over this decade. For the Cavan population of Ireland in 1841, the dependency ratio of 1.51 for all adults, is virtually the same as the average including the Admaston population. The Cavan childhood dependency ratio is higher only for Admaston in 1851, but less than for Admaston in either 1861 or 1871. This trend would indicate that the size of farming families was low in 1851 because most families during this time were just beginning their growth cycle. However, for the next several decades between 1861 and 1871, families matured and became larger, even larger than the pre-Famine Irish families, which were experiencing a high growth rate as well.

Second, there are significant differences between adult males and females in the dependency ratio across the two decades. Probably this is accounted for by the fact that the Irish families in 1851 were smaller than in later years, meaning fewer children for each adult to support. Here again the dependency ratio for both females and males is lowest in 1851, except for the one instance of females in 1871, which is due to the high number of adult females in this year. For Cavan the dependency ratio is higher than for Admaston in 1851, but, except for the instance just noted, is significantly lower for both males and females.

The dependency ratio is highest for females over males in 1851, but then for the 1861 to 1871 decade this ratio is significantly lower for females. This may have to do with the relatively small population; a small population accentuates certain proportions than would be the case with a larger population. For example, adult males (53.1 per cent) constitute a proportionately higher population in 1851 than females (46.9), but then there is a reversal of this proportion in 1861 (males 47.7 per cent, females 52.3 per cent) and in 1871 (males 46.6 per cent, females 53.3 per cent). Nonetheless, regardless of the vagaries of small populations, a high dependency ratio still means that a person in this category has more work to do in raising children, proportionate to others with a lower ratio.

A third observation concerns the range of the childhood dependency ratio across the various decades between 1841 and 1871, and across both females and males during this time period. The highest ratio in all these cases and time periods is for males in 1871 (at 3.30 children per male) and the lowest occurs with males in 1851 (at 2.60 children per male). The range at these extremes is not particularly large, at less than one child per adult, indicating that in both Ireland, in the Cavan case, and Canada, in the Admaston case, during this 30-year time period (which extends before and after the Famine), each adult on average has about three children to support, not a particularly onerous burden for farming families of this time period and circumstance.

A fourth observation is that across these cases, in and out of Ireland, and across this 30-year time period, females outnumber males. This discrepancy is most evident in Admaston, where females outnumber males (in the 20–45 age category) by 10 per cent in 1861 (134 to 122), and by about 15 per cent (143 to 125) in 1871. These differences between males and females would obviously have an impact on the childhood dependency ratios for the sexes, leading to a higher ratio for males because of their smaller numbers. This means that on a per capita basis each man had a greater number of children to support than women. Thus, there were more men to shoulder the burden of raising children than there were for women. The possible reasons for the rather large, disproportionate numbers in the adult child-rearing category, however, remain obscure and require further research. It is possible that the mortality rate is higher for men because of the rigours of farm life in the nineteenth century, although this has not been proven. One would think on the other hand the number of male deaths on the farm would be offset by the relatively high number of deaths of women in childbirth, at least compared with today.

In terms of the male/female sex ratio for children (under ten years of age), for Admaston in 1851 females outnumbered males by 82 to 68, representing a 10 per cent difference in females over males. However, in 1861, males outnumbered females by 167 to 128 (a difference of 13 per cent in favour of males) and, finally, in 1871, males again outnumber females (148 to 123, or a 9 per cent difference). These differences in the male/female sex ratio of children do eventually even out through the different age groups; for example, in 1851 males represented 49.3 per cent of the overall population, and females 50.7 per cent. By 1861, the overall sex ratio again favour males (53.5 per cent) over females (46.5 per cent), and in 1871 males outnumbered females (53 per cent for males, and 46 per cent for females). By comparison, for the Cavan farming population of 4,081 persons in 1841, males outnumbered females by 4.6 per cent overall; in the 0–10 age group males comprised 15.4 per cent of the population, and females 14.6.

Given the small populations involved, a few more individuals born of one sex or another can distort the overall percentages, yet it is nonetheless worth considering if there are any implications regarding Irish families in terms of the variable numbers of men and women. One suggestion, proposed by O'Neill (184: 174–6), is that infant mortality is the root cause of these variations in sex ratios of the Irish population during the nineteenth century. As he explains, a problem with any studies of demographic change and fertility among the Irish "is its vulnerability to distortion created by high rates of infant mortality ... unfortunately, nothing can be assumed about infant mortality in pre-famine Cavan" (1984: 172).

O'Neill's research for Cavan found that his figures "for farming children indicate a normal ratio, with boys outnumbering girls in the early stages" (1984: 174). This was also the case with the Irish of Admaston, as in the 0–9 age group, boys outnumbered girls by 167 to 128 in the 1861 census, and by 148 to 123 in 1871. However, in 1851, the reverse is true, in that year girls outnumbered boys, by 82 to 68. For Cavan, O'Neill also reported similar imbalances among the numbers of male and female children. His conclusion was that "Such a distorted sex ratio in the early years of childhood could have resulted either from poor reporting or from high infant mortality" (ibid.). He discounts under-reporting as a cause of the distorted sex ratio, arguing instead that the cause is the result of malnourishment among mothers and their children.

Furthermore, in the cases in which female children outnumber their male counterparts, as is the situation with Cavan in 1841 and

Admaston in 1851, O'Neill suggests (1984: 174–5) that "As male fetuses are known to suffer a disproportionately high incidence of miscarriage and stillbirth, a population which is malnourished or unhealthy would produce an inordinate percentage of female births." He supports this conclusion with several research studies linking breastfeeding patterns and infant mortality. While conceding that "virtually nothing is known about child-feeding in Ireland [during this time]" (ibid.), he does offer the opinion, based on the research that he consulted, that in a dairy culture farming women would tend to bottle-feed their infants earlier than women of the labouring class, who had more limited access to cow's milk. This leads O'Neill, referring to sources in *Science* (i.e., Knodel 1977) and *Demography* (Knobel and Kintner, 1977) on the relationship between breastfeeding and population growth, to "an assumption of bottle-feeding in pre-famine Ireland [such that] the transition from breast to bottle characteristically resulted in dramatic increases in infant mortality, an increase which would more than offset any increase in natural fertility."

Are there any conclusions, then, that could be drawn about the disproportionate sex ratios of children in Admaston? If we can rely on the research results presented by O'Neill for Cavan in 1841, and the further research reported in such reputable journals as *Science*, then it could be suggested that the Irish of Admaston in 1851, having for the most part just arrived in Canada from their Famine-stricken home country, suffered from malnutrition of both mothers and children, resulting in a relatively high (yet unproven) number of cases of infant mortality, as suggested by the greater number of young female to male children in that year. In the later decades of 1861 and 1871, the ratio is largely reversed, with male children outnumbering their female counterparts. If O'Neill's assumptions, and the research literature upon which his opinions are based, are correct, then improvements in the nutritional health of the Admaston Irish provide a reasonable explanation for this reversal.

Any factor, or combination of factors, which tends to distort the sex or age distribution of a population, especially a factor as high infant mortality, will doubtless influence the main theoretical initiatives which are discussed in this book. An assessment of Chayanov's theory of agricultural productivity will be affected by changes in the dependency ratio of children to adults, or in factors which alter the distribution of males to females. To the extent that children could generally be regarded as consumers-dependants and, adults as the farmworkers, then the dependency ratios depicted in table 20 illustrate enough internal variation in the Admaston population to prompt us to ask several pertinent questions.

The most important of these questions centres on Chayanov's position that an increase in the consumer/worker ratio would result in a corresponding increase in worker productivity: Is agricultural productivity higher among the Irish people with a higher childhood dependency ratio? Also, did productivity increase among all adults between 1851 and 1861 because of a corresponding increase in the child/adult ratio, and did it decline between 1861 and 1871 because of a decline in this dependency ratio? Here again, we are led by such questions to seek answers internally, that is within the social system itself, rather than to consider large-scale external factors that could be seen to control, in a causal or deterministic manner, local-level social and economic phenomena.

These sorts of data allow us a better understanding of what makes a family one size or another, a size which is ultimately a reflection of the internal dynamics of population structure and child-to-adult dependency figures. There is obviously a need to further our understanding of such dynamics by a deeper or more thorough search for the underlying factors responsible; these include, for example, the discordant population figures in certain age categories that may ultimately lead to differences in family size.

Household Structure and Composition

As a research strategy, we might reasonably look at the internal dynamics of household and family structure itself. For the Irish of Admaston Township, household composition can generally be classified according to various groupings as shown in table 21. At this point in the survey a decision was made to broaden the scope of the investigation to include the census material for 1881, in addition to data for the 1851-71 period, which have comprised the usual data set up to this point, as well as the 1841 population data from Cavan, Ireland. Unlike previous discussions in this book, the discussion here attempts to focus more explicitly on the distribution of household types among the Admaston Irish over these three decades. It was felt that focusing on three decades rather than two would more effectively cover the household transitions for a complete generation of Irish after the Famine.

Rather than seek the causal factors of family size or other characteristics of the Irish family in such exogenous factors as the size of the family farm, we might reasonably look at the internal dynamics of the family structure itself in terms of the integral aspects of family composition. For the Irish of Admaston Township, household composition can generally be classified according to three groupings. The first of these could be understood in terms of "remnant" families, that is,

144   After the Famine

Table 21 Composition of Irish households, Admaston Township, 1851–81

Household Type	1851	1861	1871	1881	Totals	Per cent
Individuals	2	10	7	15	34	5.33
Single parents	4	5	12	12	33	5.17
Solitary couples	4	15	12	11	42	6.58
Nuclear families	45	103	122	134	404	63.32
Stem	5	6	4	7	21	3.29
Extended						
Other*	14	24	11	53	104	16.31
Total households	74	163	168	232	638	100.00

* Includes the following:
Nuclear family with husband's relatives – non-stem family (2.66 per cent of total)
Nuclear family with wife's relatives – non-stem family (0.63 per cent)
Son as head of household (3.45 per cent)
Nuclear family with help living on the farm (4.23 per cent)
Not classified (5.33 per cent)

households occupied by lone individuals, single parents, and solitary couples, which between 1851 and 1881 formed 17 per cent of Admaston's Irish households. This category of household consists primarily of those individuals who are at either end of the reproductive cycle, such as newly married couples or elderly couples whose grown children have moved out on their own. As might be expected, there are far fewer of these types of household in 1851 (10 altogether) than in 1881 (38 such households), or about four times as many in 1881, as the members of the young families of the earlier decades mature in age, leading to more solitary individuals and elderly couples.

The largest change in household composition over the three decades occurred in the number of nuclear families, which increased by three times (45 in 1851 to 134 in 1881). Extended families of various sorts also increased by three times (19 in 1851 to 60 in 1881). Note that there were also a relatively large number of extended families (comprising 16.3 per cent altogether) that were either difficult to classify or had somewhat uncommon relation characteristics, mainly nuclear families with various other relatives appended to them. An interesting demographic feature overall is that extended families, while decreasing in number between 1851 and 1881, nonetheless maintained the same percentage (3.8 per cent) of total households over the three decades. However, within the extended family category, the number of stem families remained virtually the same (5 in 1851 and 7 in 1881). On a percentage basis, stem families declined from 6.8 per cent of total household in 1851 (5/74) to 3.0 per cent (7/232) in 1881.

In sum, over the three decades after the Famine the clear majority of Irish settlers living in this part of eastern Canada, as illustrated in table 21, lived in household types involving nuclear families: a husband and wife with their offspring alone. After this, there are variations from decade to decade in the predominance of household types. For example, in 1851 the category of nuclear families with help living on the farm was prominent, as was the nuclear family with the husband's or wife's relatives. By 1861, solitary couples became more prominent, as was the case with the 1871 census. The 1881 census data on household distribution comprise a large group that was difficult to discern because of illegibility or other transcribing factors, but sons as head of households were prominent. This latter situation probably is a result of aging parents giving way to their male children as the main farmworkers.

The evidence, then, indicates that nuclear families were becoming the preferred form of household type among the Canadian Irish, whereas extended families such as the so-called stem family, reputed in the literature as the "traditional" Irish household arrangement, were in sharp decline. Of course, this trend towards smaller, less complex family units would not come as a surprise to analysts, except that it runs counter to family tendencies in Ireland during the same time discussed here. Salazar (2003: 272), in a critique of what he refers to as the "cultural factor" in Ireland, indicates that "in pre-famine times, the nuclear family was the characteristic model in the peasant class, but with the structural changes of the second half of the nineteenth century the nuclear family was gradually replaced by the stem family." The argument that he is making is that the stem family is an aberrant form of Irish family life. It is the nuclear family that could be considered "traditional," except for a relatively brief period before the Famine when population expansion and frequent subdivision of the family farm threatened an agricultural collapse. This is a puzzling phenomenon – extended families were decreasing among the Canadian Irish at the same time as they were supposedly increasing in Ireland. Examining several issues concerning the stem family is therefore necessary at this juncture because it bears directly on the larger discussion of family size.

As has previously been stated, the stem family is found primarily in agricultural societies, especially those in which large families are forced to subsist on relatively small plots of land. This situation apparently delays the devolution of property from one generation to the next, with the aging parents holding on to control of the family farm for as long as they are able, and their own children waiting in abeyance, thus delaying or hindering their own marriage. Although there exists some variation in the specific details from one geographical area to another, the term *stem family* has been used to depict a constellation of situations, such as the three-generational household, the delayed age of marriage of the farmer's sons, and the eventual devolution of the property intact (impartible inheritance) to one son after his own marriage and children.

The literature on Irish families has been the scene of a lively debate for many decades. For instance, as previously noted, Fitzpatrick (1983: 384) asserted that Irish rural society before the First World War was characterized by a family structure that was "uniform and distinctive," and that household size in Ireland during this period "remained strikingly stable over the era of post-famine adjustment." Contrary points of view, however, were held by many scholars; for example, Gibbon and Curtain (1983: 380) held the opinion that Fitzpatrick's assessment of Irish families is "extremely tenuous and unconvincing."

One of the more obvious reasons for this sometimes acrimonious debate on Irish families is that the disputants tend to lack common ground regarding the conceptual terminology, a situation that is not easily reconciled. The literature on the Irish stem family, for example, has largely used the term *family* to incorporate both household structure and kinship relations, that is, to conflate them into a single category, despite an obvious need for more precise usage. The term *stem family* has been used far too loosely, encompassing various uses at different levels of abstraction. In any event, the term *stem family household* is more precise in a theoretical sense because it describes, at a moment in time, a household composed of three generations and two married pairs.

This lack of clarity is partly the result of a conceptual terminology that emphasizes family "structures" and "types," rather than its functions. A stem family, for example, can result from a large family undergoing subdivision with the homestead and elderly parents going to one son (a *stem household*), with nearby lands going to other sons. This case, then, would involve nuclear households operating within an extended family framework but not an extended household structure (see Breen 1984: 95–108).

What these various possible situations illustrate is the difficulty in reconciling "structure" with "process." It is household structures that are most observable in the census records; the social processes that foster or generate one family type or another are less visible because they are part of the undercurrent of people's decision-making regarding matters such as whom they choose to live with or whom to leave their inheritance to.

Regarding the suggestion that the availability of land was a crucial factor in determining family structure, land availability explains the lesser prevalence of the stem family only if it could be established that some elderly parents were living in other forms of household arrangements. Nearly 20 per cent of Admaston's households fall into the category of individual or solitary couples (table 21); therefore to understand more fully what has led to a decline in extended families one would also need to have more background on why elderly parents chose to live by themselves as opposed to living with a son and his family. Such knowledge, though, appears to be beyond the reach of our present research capabilities.

A further difficulty is that relying solely on the aggregate totals found in census reports can be misleading. This problem is particularly evident when an attempt is made to link the size of a farm with the size or type of family, leading erroneously to the conclusion that an increase in the former is apt to lead to an increase in the latter.

As far as the data on stem families are concerned, a further conceptual issue is that it is possible to view such families in a "loose" or a "strict" sense, following Birdwell-Pheasant's (1992: 208–10) use of the terms "loose" and "rigid" model of Irish families. The "strict" sense, probably the more conventional view, regards stem families as comprising three generations of the husband's relatives. The "loose" view, a more inclusive one, regards three generational households as also comprising a nuclear family with the wife's parents. For analytic purposes we could term the former as "patri-stem" families and the latter as "matri-stem" families. For whatever reason, I have never seen this distinction in the rather extensive literature on stem families – all previous authors either have regarded stem families as *only* comprising a nuclear family and the husband's relatives, or, for whatever reasons, have not regarded this distinction as important enough to consider. Undoubtedly a case can be made for a certain male bias in previous interpretations of stem families, or in kinship studies in general. I cannot see any valid reason why a husband *and* his wife's elder parents cannot also be included in a discussion of stem families.[1]

One of the most important observations from table 21 that one can make concerning Irish household composition concerns the rather dramatic increase in the number of households overall in Admaston Township over the three decades from 1851 to 1881. First, the household total more than doubled from 1851 to 1861, after which there was only a relatively small increase (a gain of five households) in the next decade to 1871, after which there was another large jump (168 to 232 households, or 38 per cent) over the ensuing decade to 1881. Second, regarding the stem families of the patri-stem variety (2.66 per cent), they far surpass the matri-stem kind (0.63 per cent), but, overall, stem families comprise a surprisingly small proportion (3.3 per cent) of the total Irish households of Admaston Township. Given the relatively large number (10–15 per cent of the total households) of stem families reported for Ireland itself, one of course is led to wonder about the causes or reasons behind this significant discrepancy.

Irish Families in Canada and Ireland

When one studies the underlying differences in Irish family types between those in Ireland and Canada in the post-Famine period there are several important factors to consider. Probably the most important of these relates to the very reason many of the Irish around the time of the Famine left their homeland in the first place. In Ireland the Irish generally lacked sufficient land to support their large families, a situation which forced many to move to less fertile farmland.

Aside from land shortages, the second important factor pertains to the ownership of the land itself. There was a great transfer of land from Catholics to Protestants from the time of the Cromwellian land confiscations (1652–3) onwards; over the course of the seventeenth and early eighteenth centuries many Irish became tenant farmers rather than land owners. The *conacre* arrangement, whereby a tenant could rent land in return for labour, sometimes referred to as the "potato-truck system," frequently kept the Irish poor in a perpetual state of indebtedness, and was therefore an additional factor which worked against Irish farmers gaining any degree of self-sufficiency.

The availability of land and an increasing growth in population influenced not only the structure of Irish families but their size as well. However, the prospect of owning their own land, to become landlords themselves, would have no doubt been incentives for emigration to Canada, even without the "push" effect of the Famine. There was much more farmland available to Irish immigrants in Canada than any of them could ever have imagined owning back in Ireland. And it was not just the availability of land; there was also the chance to break the strict dependency on the potato crop, a dependency which had ultimately led to tragic consequences. In their new country, the greater availability of land allowed for a more diversified farm economy, with a larger variety of crops, as well as more pasturage for sheep and cattle. Of course, the prospect of clearing farmland from virgin forest, coping with the harsh winters, and fending off wild animals would have been daunting indeed. Despite these less than propitious circumstances, the Irish immigrants to Canada not only survived, but flourished, often beyond their expectations.

In terms of the subject of discussion at hand, which is to say the size of farms and the corresponding relationship to family size, in Ireland "small" farms comprised about 10 to 20 acres, while "large" ones consisted of 40 to 60 acres (see Arensberg and Kimball 1940: 30; Birdwell-Pheasant 1992: 212; Gibbon and Curtin 1978: 453). Somewhat lower figures are reported for Cavan, based on acreage reported in the Tithe Applotment Book for Killashandra, with small to middling farms ranging up to 25 acres, and larger ones more than 25 acres, up to an unspecified size (O'Neill 1984: 156). By contrast, farm size in Renfrew County ranged from small, 50–150 acres; moderate, 150–300 acres; and large, 300–500 acres or more. Of course, farm sizes in the Ottawa Valley were somewhat smaller than these average figures in the initial habitation period of the 1850s, but the sizes tended to increase rapidly over the ensuing decades as more forest was cleared and increasingly greater amounts of land were made available for cultivation. Thus, as one traces individual families through the census data, many Irish farms tended to double or even triple in size over the three decades.

The number of Irish households in Admaston also increased accordingly, more than doubling between 1851 and 1861 (from 74 to 163). Certainly one of the main reasons for the expansion of farm lands in Admaston Township was to provide for the growing number of mouths to feed. Over time, expanded farm areas would become easier to manage when a father has growing sons who could act as labourers, reducing or eliminating the need to hire help from outside the household. Yet, as these sons aged, another dynamic would come into play, one that concerns how, or if, the adult sons were to be provided for.

Land expansion, first, plays an important role in meeting the consumptive challenges of a growing family, and second, serves possible future needs in providing for the land requirements of the father's sons. Of course, following the rationale of the stem family, the devolution of land implies an expectation that the aging parents would be cared for by a son receiving such land. The fact that farm size in Admaston doubled or tripled over the course of the period of the present study further suggests that fathers were accumulating land to facilitate partible inheritance. Hence it is important to clarify the issue of land acquisition, since average farm size included other farms and wild lands, and not just acreage for immediate cultivation, that were acquired to set up future generations.

The main conclusion following this analysis is that the most salient difference between Canada and Ireland was most certainly the larger availability of farmland in Canada, compared with the very restricted opportunities in Ireland. What follows is a further conclusion that flows naturally from the first: this is the idea that the very low incidence of stem families in the Ottawa Valley region of Canada was a direct result of a farmer's sons having opportunities to purchase farm properties of their own, without having to linger on their father's estates, often for many years, in hope of an eventual inheritance. In addition, sons in Canada had opportunities to earn cash by themselves, working as labourers on nearby farms or in lumber camps, and consequently could marry at a younger age than their cohorts back in Ireland. This is not to suggest, of course, that fathers did not provide for the land needs of their sons; the point is that for sons who could not be helped by their fathers – whether through a direct transfer of land during the lifetime of the father, or through inheritance – there were other avenues by which sons could earn cash and thereby acquire land, avenues which may not have been available in Ireland.

The role of land, or more specifically, access to land, as an influencing factor in the structure of families was the subject of a lively debate among geographers in the late 1970s. Cole Harris (1977), in an article entitled "The Simplification of Europe Overseas," argued that "Europeans tended to establish overseas drastically simplified versions of European society ... where land was cheap and agricultural markets were poor, the results were foregone: ... a remarkably homogeneous society would emerge around the independent nuclear family" (1977: 481–2). In other words, "the structure of northeastern European societies overseas has more to do with the nature of access to land in colonial settings than with the particular backgrounds of emigrating Europeans" (1977: 469).

In terms of explaining emerging Irish families in Renfrew County, Harris's proposals would appear to have some merit. It has been widely agreed among scholars that the stem family in Ireland was the result of a rapidly growing population with little opportunity for the sons of farmers to purchase new farmland. One would then presume, based on Harris's proposals, that if there were opportunities in Ireland the stem family would not have emerged in the first place, or that such families would revert to nuclear units. However, it is not entirely clear based on the literature, which family form – nuclear or stem – results from the restriction on Irish agricultural land. In other words, it is entirely possible that stem families in Ireland were preferred as an ongoing cultural pattern and did not really have much to do with the availability of land in the first place. Of course, in anthropology, a long history of environmentally deterministic arguments for cultural patterns have made us leery of simplified explanations based simply on a single unified economic or geographic factor.

In the case of the Irish of Admaston Township, the facts clearly show a preponderance of nuclear families, with fewer stem families than existed in Ireland. However, it is easy to jump to conclusions to explain this phenomenon. For example, the 20-year period from 1851 to 1871 was probably too short a time frame to allow for the full emergence of stem families, even if there were cultural tendencies in its favour. The emigrants who arrived in Canada were mainly the young and vigorous, with few dependants. The older members of their families might well have succumbed to the rigours of the transatlantic voyage, or to disease, malnutrition, or other hazards, thus removing the older generation from the family structure.

As far as the "access to land" explanation so preferred by geographers is concerned (note that the commentaries on Harris's [1977] article by Pollack [1979] or Mitchell [1979] seem to accept this explanation), there are always problems with overly simplistic or univariate explanations for complex phenomena. As an example, "land" in itself is not a unidimensional entity. As has been shown in the Admaston context, a survey of farmland has demonstrated at least eight different soil types, from excellent to very poor, as far as agricultural potential is concerned. While it is correct to state that these soil types are not evenly distributed across the township, it would be also right to conclude that "land" in terms of the various soil types can in itself be regarded as having limited explanatory power as a determinant of family types. In other words, "access to land" is far less important as a factor in conditioning various family types, that is, access to *quality* land, than is access to land strictly in terms of its *quantity*.

To reiterate the earlier statistical data in this book on soil capabilities, the potential productivity of Canadian soils is classified into a number of different categories which range from class 1 (soils which have no restrictions on agricultural use) to class 7 (very limited or no agricultural value). Renfrew County has in total 1.9 million acres of land designated for potential agricultural use. In terms of the distribution of the various soil classes, there are no soils in the class 1. Soils in classes 2 and 3 (those capable of sustained crop production) amount to 12 per cent (234,000 acres) of the total area. Soils in classes 4, 5, and 6 are useful only for growing hay and for use as pasture, and comprise 23 per cent of the total. Soils in class 7 (unsuitable for agricultural use) represent 1.2 million acres or 65 per cent of the overall total. Thus, only about one-third of the soils in Renfrew County have any agricultural use at all, and of this area just over 10 per cent is suitable for growing the crops to feed humans and/or animals. The conclusion, then, is that Harris's argument that "access to land" is the single most important factor in contributing to the emergence of the independent nuclear family is somewhat meaningless unless one has access to specific agricultural data on land use, such as that provided for Renfrew County in the present study.

One could also point out that there are other strategies that a family could adopt to circumvent the deleterious effects of a more restricted access to land. As the data for Admaston illustrate, the growing population began to stall around 1871, yet the number of households continued to increase. There is no way of telling if the soil capacity of Admaston had reached a limit in its ability to support the existing population, or if emigration out of the area was responsible for the levelling of the population. Whatever the cause, it is obvious that the Irish in Admaston were formulating new strategies for providing for the agricultural needs of the emerging nuclear family households, and were not reverting to stem families. This is evident by the growing number of households with small farm plots of around 50 acres, in an area where few small farms previously existed. One could conclude, tentatively at least, that a small nuclear family could subsist adequately on a 50-acre farm, especially with possible parental support.

Soil capabilities and knowledge about the distribution of the various soil categories undoubtedly account for important differences in family types in the two geographic areas. In Admaston, the pioneering family, who would first need to clear the forest, would have little knowledge about the underlying soil that they had purchased. It would only be after several growing seasons that the Admaston farmer would be able to ascertain which soils were suitable for crop production, which areas were suitable for pasture, and which areas had no agricultural use because of a limited soil depth, swamps, rocks, or other adverse conditions. In Ireland, on the other hand, soil capabilities would presumably have been well known, as generation after generation of Irish farmers had the opportunity to determine the possibilities for agricultural use on their farms from knowledge passed down over decades, or even centuries.

Rethinking Stem Family Theories

Many theories have been proposed to account for incidences of the stem family in Ireland and elsewhere. These theories take into account factors relating to cultural, economic, and demographic variables, among others, to explain the occurrence of this form of family structure. The suggestion that emerges from the discussion here is that it is primarily the economic factors that account for the low incidence of stem families among the Irish of the Ottawa Valley.

If the Irish were inclined to form stem families as part of a cultural tradition, one would expect a much higher incidence in Canada. This would be the case especially in the early (1851–61) years of immigration after the Famine; this 10-year period would not allow sufficient time for stem families to change to another form, as through assimilation of family features not inherent to the Irish population. The transplanted Irish population in Canada evidently preferred to live in nuclear families regardless of the "traditional" family forms they had so recently left behind in Ireland. One hastens to add, nonetheless, that the idea that the transplanted Irish "preferred" nuclear families over other family forms must take into consideration that the older generation tended not to emigrate, or had already died at home during the Famine years; the general absence in Admaston of the older generation limited the formation of stem families. In the Irish case, the "flight from Famine" had a tendency to skew the population results in favour of younger people, those who had survived the disease and food shortages.

The demographic argument for the stem family has some merit because of differences in population structures between the Irish in Ireland and their counterparts in Admaston, but this difference is likely associated with economic factors. The greater availability of land and money in Canada allowed for an increased overall population growth in conjunction with a lower density of population, as people were allowed to spread out over a country virtually devoid of inhabitants, at least in the early years of the 1850s. However, it is important to consider that conclusions regarding household types must be tempered by the fact that the 1851–61 Admaston population was particularly young during this decade; only about 10 per cent of the population was over 50 years of age. This is a common demographic pattern among immigrant populations, and so regardless of cultural traditions, there was simply a lack of elderly parents in Admaston to form stem families early on, even if there existed a cultural propensity to do so.

While it is suggested here that the availability of land was a crucial factor in determining the prevalence of the stem family structure in the Ottawa Valley, land availability only becomes explanatory of the lesser prevalence of the stem family if it can be established that some elderly parents in 1881 were living in other forms of household arrangements. Notice, for example, that in table 21 over 17 per cent of household types fall into the category of "individual," "single parent," or "solitary couple." A more in-depth investigation beyond the aggregate totals presented in this study would be useful in revealing the extent to which elderly parents chose to live by themselves, rather than within the stem pattern, in which the aging parents live with their son and his family out of economic necessity.

It is not entirely clear without an analysis of the census data on a more detailed basis what the options were for elderly parents aside from living with a married son and his family. It would also be useful to study a map of Admaston Township with a view to determining the extent to which elderly couples had adult children living nearby. Such an exercise would be helpful to clarify the statistical data derived from the census reports. For example, the census reports would appear to indicate that some elderly couples were living entirely independent of their adult children. It is completely possible, however, that adult children provided various forms of support for elderly parents who lived in different households. Viewing such a map could help one to discern if there is a geographical propinquity of households, between aging parents and their adult children, which would offer some of the benefits of a stem family structure, without all of the family members living in the same household. There is obviously room for analysis of the census data beyond that presented here to shed further light on the stem family question.[2]

Inheritance and Family Structure

The present study of aggregate census data illustrates the limitations of the usefulness of such data without the inclusion of specific data on people, events, and situations, as would commonly be done by historians. In other words, a combination of the two avenues of study, one anthropological and the other historical, would therefore probably yield more propitious results. Elliot's (2004) insightful study of Tipperary Protestant Irish migration to the Ottawa Valley provides an alternative perspective. In this case the life paths of hundreds of individual migrants are traced. In a most illuminating section – called "Strategies of Heirship" – Elliot discusses the issue of land availability in terms of purchase versus inheritance:

> Of the 451 sons in 141 families who lived on the Ontario side of the Ottawa Valley in the period covered by this study and who were set up independent of their parents by 1881, just over half obtained their initial stake of land from their fathers, 136 while their fathers were living and eighty-eight by inheritance. Another 15 per cent purchased lands in the area, though whether with parental assistance or not is usually impossible to say. Still another 15 per cent took up a trade or profession, fifty-two becoming tradesmen and seventeen professionals ... Only 10 per cent of sons left the region as young men without acquiring land there. (Elliot 2004: 213–14)

Elliot (2004: 214) then goes on to qualify the information provided in the above quote by indicating that while half of the sons who came of age during his period of study in the mid-1800s were provided land by their family, fewer than a fifth of the families were able to provide for all of their sons in this way. In addition, he notes the importance of early arrival in the region if the parents were to pass on quality properties to their sons. Those situated on lands of marginal productivity were left with a difficult situation; the sons of such families would probably strike out on their own without attempting to secure parental lands of lesser or limited agricultural value.

Elliot's data illustrate that the various options with regard to issues concerning land inheritance versus further land acquisition are immensely relevant to the present discussion concerning stem families in the Ottawa Valley. The aggregate census figures are apt to yield useful information on the internal composition of farming households, but the researcher is then left to make his or her own broad assumptions concerning the reasons why individual families had chosen to live in the sorts of family arrangements that eventually make it into the census reports. The obvious lack of opportunity to question the very people who would be capable of providing the answers to the questions can only result in conjecture on the part of the historian or anthropologist.

However, with the data such as that provided in Elliot's study, one can gain insights into the decision-making and "strategies of heirship," as he phrased it, that provide the underlying conditions of the stem family structure. If, as we believe, the availability of land is crucial to our understanding of the stem family structure, then mere statistics provided by the census reports give us only part of the answer. We also need to know more about family resources in a broader sense than just quantities of land: land use, crops grown, some measure of the relative productivity of the land, and ratios of farm workers to dependants are all important contextual matters.

Provided with such information, one would then be in a more advantageous position to know more about how useful such land would be in terms of supporting one or several sons as they reach their adult years. It is useful to remember also that stem families, in part, are themselves household structures. The type of social structures that emerge are primarily the result, I contend, of decisions made by the members of these families regarding their resources and how they are to be distributed among family members. An emphasis on a family's decision-making processes is in stark contrast to an emphasis on family structures as somehow determined by forces external to the family, or as a result of a society reaching a certain "stage of development."

Summary Comments

An attempt has been made in this book to reconsider explanations for the existence of the Irish stem family from a historical or longitudinal perspective to suggest which of the differing circumstances between Ireland and Canada might have explanatory value. It is now obvious that there are many factors that are relevant to this discussion. I agree in a broad sense with Verdon (1979) and Connell (1962) that the Irish stem family resulted from economic choices, most notably a preference for impartible land inheritance to avoid the impoverishing effects of a progressive subdivision of small landholdings. Impartible land inheritance was already a fact of Irish agrarian life before the Famine, although impartibility was exacerbated by it. The frequency of stem families was therefore limited by farm size, as larger farms could be subdivided among the various heirs without exhausting a family's resources.

To investigate the various issues around the emergence, or lack of emergence, of the stem family structure, we undertook a strategy which followed the Irish families of Admaston Township through the various census records for the years 1851 to 1881. Based on this investigation the conclusion reached was that the stem family household was much less prevalent in that community than in Ireland. Out of a total of 638 Irish household in Admaston, only about 3.3 per cent were of the stem variety, rather than the 10 to 15 per cent reported in comparable studies on Ireland itself. Therefore, the central question is why this discrepancy existed, given the fact that the Irish who came to Canada just after the Famine would have had the same "culture" as the compatriots they recently left behind in Ireland.

Aside from the specific matter of determining factors in the stem family itself, there are broader issues having to do with the causes of social organization and the various cultural, economic, historical, or other factors that are underlying or fundamental bases for the forms of social life itself. An investigation of the stem family, while interesting by itself, has wider implication for understanding the factors contributing to variations in the social life of a people.

In this wider sense, we are persuaded by the economic theory of social organization as a primary contributing factor in the forms of social life. For example, as the present study illustrates, one of the key differences between the Irish families of Admaston and those back home was that land was readily available for purchase in Canada, as sons could either inherit additional land from their fathers, or if necessary purchase it through wages earned by working for other farmers or in the lumber camps to buy land of their own. A related factor, as illustrated by Elliot's (2004) study of migrant Tipperary farmers in the Ottawa Valley, was that sons could also be set up with a stake of land by their fathers without having to wait in abeyance for the processes of inheritance to run their course.

Undoubtedly much land was transferred from generation to generation through inheritance, but it is also evident, as in the case of Elliot's study, that much land was also conveyed to adult sons while the father was still living. In such cases, the whole discussion of inheritance, impartible or not, becomes a somewhat irrelevant factor in the type of family structure the sons will eventually adopt. What is not clear, in these cases of what could be seen as "pre-inheritance gifts," is the extent to which fathers also provided the financial resources which allowed sons to purchase land on their own, so that sons would not need to find jobs in order to buy their own land. In any event, the stem family system was affected by the availability of good, productive land, no matter how it was distributed – both for the Irish in Canada and those back in Ireland.

Demographic factors contribute to the statistical prevalence of the stem family household; for instance, a son needs to marry and have children in order for a stem household to exist, and it would cease to exist after the death of his parents. In cases where delayed marriage was the norm, as in Ireland, the duration of the stem household was possibly further limited. Another important demographic factor concerns the fact that the devolution of the family farm to one son or more was limited by the size of the landholding, and the fact that parents can live with only one son. In any case, the suggestion put forward here is that while demographic factors provide an important context for understanding the prevalence of stem families, these factors are nonetheless tied in one way or another to the central issue of the availability of land.

There are also several reasons for questioning the notion that Irish Canadians were in some way "inclined" to live in stem families, as proponents of the cultural theory would suggest. What the Irish in eastern Ontario were inclined to do was to continue with farming and their rural way of life. A reasonable economic strategy was that, as it was less expensive to acquire land from one's parents than to buy from neighbours or the Crown, one son remained on the homestead to await his father's retirement or death. As far as the parents were concerned, assigning the farm to this son in return for a promise of support in old age was a better economic strategy than saving up enough money to build a separate house in which to live as an elderly nuclear couple. The stem family was generated by these sorts of economic realities, or "inclinations," rather than by cultural attachments to one particular household structure or another. This conclusion is based on a longitudinal study of a broad range of household situations over several decades from 1851 to 1881. The contention here is that conclusions about various family forms need to be based on concrete statistical or empirical evidence, rather than on unproven notions of social theorists.

Conclusion

The stem family as a household type is commonly found in agrarian societies. As such, it is found across a variety of geographical, social, and cultural settings, and traverses various time periods. Its main characteristic is a composition of household members which comprises three generations, and, while varying somewhat in its specific details from one geographical locale to another, it tends to result in a delay in both the age of marriage for the farmer's sons, and the eventual devolution of the property to one (usually the eldest) son after his own marriage and the birth of his children.[3] The next step in this analysis is to examine the structure and composition of Irish households as these factors relate to the issue of family size.

Chapter Seven

The Irish Family and Household

The third theoretical focus of this book is on the size of Irish families and its wider implications on the internal social structure of farming communities. The research strategy adopted here begins with a hypothesis about the factors responsible for the size of a family, factors that then could be tested on a data set of empirical examples. The approach taken, typical in anthropology, is more inductive in its perspective (from the ground up) than deductive (top down).

Family Size as an Adaptive Response

This study of family size is focused on an attempt to better understand the historical adaptation of the Irish immigrants in eastern Ontario after the Great Famine, especially in terms of the role that family size played in farm productivity. In the present study, a specific empirical question concerning Irish family organization became generalized into a broader question of the role of family size in social and economic change. The assumption was that the adaptation of the Irish to rural Canada would shed light on how immigrants adapt to the farming conditions of the countries to which they migrate.

Upon reviewing the literature on this adaptation, general themes emerged. One of the most significant of these themes is that the size of farming families and their internal composition are related phenomena. As families increase in size, the argument goes, certain structural changes begin to take place, such as the adoption of a "vertical" three-generational composition, as in the various permutations of the stem family structure, or alternatively, the emergence of a more "lateral" extension of the family unit, as various aunts, uncles, and their offspring are incorporated into the expanding household.

Some of the studies also incorporate a historical perspective, suggesting that family size has declined generally across geographical and cultural boundaries "from between 4 and 6 [persons] in the mid-nineteenth century to between 2 and 3 today" (Bongaarts 2001: 278). Concomitant with this general decrease in family size has been a corresponding decline in the frequency of extended families, with nuclear families becoming more dominant over time. Various reasons could be stipulated to account for these changes. One of the most significant is migration from rural areas to urban centres, and the possible mechanization of farms as they adopt more labour-saving devices. In another version of this argument, it is suggested that "Irish immigrants had a greater tendency to choose to build simple family households than did citizens of their host societies"; simple households were utilized as a strategy of assimilation whereby adopting the nuclear family system facilitated more opportunities for upward mobility than did the more complex stem family household (Shimizu 2016: 224).

Scholarly work on changes in family size, seen from a global perspective, reveals that researchers are far from unanimous in explaining even the most fundamental determinants of this phenomenon. The literature has revealed a puzzling array of perspectives, many of which contradict one another. As an example, the reasons are obscure as to why, in one study focusing on a 1900 sample, France had the smallest household size (3.6 persons), whereas Canada had the largest (5.1 persons) (Bongaarts 2001: 264). It is also puzzling as to why certain countries and regions of the world have not followed the general pattern of a decline in family size.

Even though many countries have been undergoing a modernization of their rural economies, household size did not change in Turkey and rose in India and Iran during Bongaarts's 1900 sample period (2001: 277). After attempting various correlations, such as level of fertility, mean age at marriage, and level of marital disruption, these three factors accounted for only 59 per cent of the country variation in household size. No reasons were suggested as to the reasons for such a relatively low level of predictability resulting from such a large (43-country) sample size using almost every demographic and economic variable imaginable.

Approaches to Irish Family Size

It is probably best to avoid the terms *theory* or even *explanation* when discussing the subject of family size. A theory implies an interrelated set of propositions that can be tested empirically. In turn, an explanation suggests a cause-and-effect relationship involving dependent and independent variables. The term *approach* is instead used here because it encompasses, in a more appropriate manner, the state of knowledge currently available concerning the fundamental determinants of family size without suggesting a level of abstraction that is not empirically justified.

Family and population size are interrelated variables at a certain level of abstraction, but at what "level"? A country such as China, for example, has a very large population, comparatively speaking, yet the current trend is towards smaller and smaller families, albeit by government edict, now apparently rescinded. In a First Nation village in northern Ontario where I have conducted ethnographic research, the overall regional population is quite small, yet a family of six or seven individuals is quite common. So, one might conclude that there is no necessary empirical connection between family and population size, but in an abstract sociological sense such an imputed relationship can be compelling. What is needed to shed light on the matter are the sorts of studies conducted here that use concrete data to illustrate real life trends in family composition and size.

There has been a long history of attempts to explain why populations, and consequently families, are the size that they are at various points in history. If we take Malthus's original assumption concerning population growth and carrying capacity as an example, we could be led to the assumption that agricultural production, or even land supply, provided fixed barriers to the expansion of human populations. This assumption has been the subject of harsh criticism; a revisionist approach has emerged that leans more towards a flexible carrying capacity. The land-agriculture variable as an independent force needed to be modified in Malthus's agriculture-population equation to accommodate the empirical realities of rural social and economic life.

"Population," in other words, could no longer be correctly understood as a dependent variable that was "acted on" by the exigencies of agricultural life, but instead could be seen as exerting pressure itself as a demographic force on the economic structure. This neo-Malthusian argument played an increasingly important role in influencing the understanding of Irish society's dramatic population surge prior to the Famine, and its equally dramatic plunge after it.

Kenneth Connell's *The Population of Ireland* (1950) was at least partly instrumental in the reassessment of Ireland's population dynamics in terms of the country's agricultural capabilities before the Famine. Connell offered an impressive argument that the potato was responsible for determining the population increase in pre-Famine times, thus stressing the pervasive impact of Ireland's economic structure on existing population trends. His point was that cultivation of the potato was largely responsible for the inevitable increases in Ireland's population growth because it acted in such a way as to increase the carrying capacity of Irish agricultural lands.

As compelling as Connell's suggestion was in theoretical terms, he nonetheless was unable to provide much in the way of concrete empirical evidence to substantiate the connection between demographic and economic propensities. A more recent, alternative, approach to the neo-Malthusian argument stressed by Connell has reversed the direction of influence, such that population by itself has come to be seen as the prime controlling variable. Much of the intellectual impetus for this anti-Malthusian suggestion emanates from the controversial work of Alexander Chayanov. At the centre of the Chayanovian thesis is the idea that agricultural growth can be caused by population increases rather than the other way around. Thus, while the much-discussed influences of the consumer/worker ratio are usually focused on issues relating to the intensity of domestic production, a sometimes overlooked aspect of the Chayanov model is what it says about changes in population structure in general, and family organization in particular. It is in this regard that the Chayanov approach can provide illumination on the factors influencing family structure and size.

Chayanov stated that productivity in peasant societies is directly related to the composition of the farming household. The principle that he promotes is that the amount of work done by the working members of the household will be inversely related to the number of dependent consumers that workers are required to support. Put another way, the higher the ratio of dependent consumers (i.e., not directly employed in agriculture) to agricultural workers in a household, the harder the latter must labour to satisfy the consumptive needs of the whole. What Chayanov is essentially saying, then, is that family size and composition determine the level of economic productivity on peasant farms; or as family size increases, so does farm size.

There is little doubt that Chayanov's theoretical work has drawn such intellectual interest because it essentially reverses the Malthusian dictum that presumed fixed barriers, such as economic carrying capacity, controlled population (and family) growth. Chayanov offered a way out of this cause-and-effect cul de sac by combining family and economic structures in peasant communities in such a way as to provide some flexibility in the causal or control variable.

Family and population growth are constrained by environmental and economic controls, as Malthus stipulated, but these constraints are not immutable. As Chayanov's thesis implies, growth is only constrained by people's imagination and industry. Of course, for much of human history, family growth has not been the issue; the problem has been to provide enough food to keep everyone from starving. So, in a way, Chayanov's proposal makes more historical sense than the one proposed by Malthus because securing enough food to eat has probably been a more pressing human concern in the past; only recently have overpopulation and overconsumption become problems in their own right.[1]

Chayanov's work is particularly relevant to Irish history because he understood that peasant families who were unable to expand their landholdings could nonetheless increase productivity by planting more labour-intensive crops. This strategy allowed a peasant family to increase the size of its holdings by maximizing the labour contribution of everyone in the household; Chayanov's identification of this dynamic serves to effectively diminish the theoretical importance of Malthus's environment and economic constraints. Thus, Chayanov changed Malthus's closed ecological system into an open one, or at least one with more flexible boundaries.

The relevance of these ideas for an understanding of Irish history is apparent because, for the most part, Irish families had little or no additional land available to them. It is true that there were some efforts in Ireland aimed at increasing tillage production through various reclamation projects, such as draining swamps and planting on hillsides, but, as Joseph Lee (1969: 73) has argued, such efforts were insufficient to overcome "the chronic inefficiency of [Irish] agriculture."[2] There is also little doubt that the prolific Lumper potato allowed for increased yields, and as its widespread adoption provides evidence in support of the Chayanovian thesis that agronomic intensification is a viable strategy for sustaining family and population increases in the peasant economy.

The Malthusian spectre can never be entirely eliminated or avoided, however, especially when there is an overreliance on a single crop, such as the potato, in an attempt to sustain population increases. The "corrective effect" that Malthus warned about was certainly evident when the potato crop failed in many areas of Ireland during the late 1840s, regardless of any Chayanovian efforts at increasing productive intensity or improving agricultural efficiency. In Chayanov's defence, such "circumscribed" situations as the Irish Famine were not dealt with in his empirical description of Russian farms. Nonetheless, his theory does predict that the farming family would have to take certain steps to adapt to circumstances, such as adjusting its size, rather than the size of its landholdings, to a more efficient use of its resources.

The Economic Perspective

One might glean from Chayanov's theory that family and household size, from an economic perspective, is largely a function of productive intensity. In farming communities, a large available labour pool within the household is a cost-effective advantage; scarce resources do not need to be expended on hiring outside labour during peak times in the agricultural cycle. A hypothesis supporting this perspective would be that family size is positively correlated with the increased size of a farm's holdings. Large farms can produce more food than smaller ones, the reasoning goes, and therefore can effectively support larger families. In Ireland, however, large families could be supported on small plots of land, but the balance was a precarious one, especially when there was a lack of agricultural diversity. There were also potato blights in other parts of Europe in the late 1840s, but famine did not result, at least not on the scale experienced in Ireland; this is because exports of food products were stopped and other foods were available to feed the population. In Ireland, even during the height of the Famine, exports of food to England continued unabated because of the free trade policy between the two countries.

The results of our sample of Irish families in eastern Ontario would appear to support this general relationship between family and farm size, but the results are deceptive in certain ways. One of these has to do with the gross size of a farm – many acres might well consist of woodlots, swamps, and rocky ground, areas not suitable for agricultural production. A useful approach would be to examine just the productive areas of a farm, such as the acreage devoted to tillage. In the case of the Admaston Irish, farmers dramatically increased their productive capacity during the first two decades (1851–71) after initial settlement; acreage devoted to crop production increased by nearly five times, but overall population size doubled. The question that begs to be answered on the basis of these facts is, if farm size has such a causal effect on family size, then why was there not an equally dramatic population increase corresponding to the very large increase in crop production?

The economic argument which sees an increase in farm size as the cause of increases in family size does not provide an adequate answer to our question; the presumed spur to population growth was present in Admaston in terms of an ability to increase productive capacity, but the expected corresponding result in terms of population gains did not occur. If we can accept the economic argument in modern times, to wit, that families will become more nuclear and less extended as societies urbanize and industrialize, then one also wonders why such a trend was already occurring in such a significant fashion in the rural farming community of Admaston in the 1860s.

This case is even more interesting because the Irish were known for large, extended (stem) families in their native country. However, it did not take them long to quickly dispense with this family form in their adopted country of Canada. In addition, if family size and composition were strictly a cultural matter, as some researchers suggest, then we would need to know more about how and why such a rapid change in social organization could occur. No factor that could be reasonably seen to account for this transformation has been identified. As with many proposed explanations used to account for family form and structure, the economic perspective is too one-dimensional and does not allow for a combination of interdependent factors that could produce the result for which explanations are sought.

Household and Family Size

Examining population structure from a demographic perspective one finds interesting relationships in discussions of household and family size in agrarian social systems. As discussed previously, the household is the usual social unit studied in census reports; this is because it is frequently difficult to recognize in census reports who are family members (that is, those who are referred to in anthropology as "consanguineal" relatives) and who are not. Until the proliferation of social service agencies and retirement homes in our modern age, there was a much greater propensity for people to look after each other in times of need. For example, a farmer's sister might have died in childbirth and so he and his wife were likely to raise some or all of the deceased mother's children, children who would then be listed in a household survey by surnames different than those of other members of the family.

One can also imagine other instances in which various unrelated persons would live in the same dwelling. A woman in her late teens or early twenties could be hired to help care for the young children of a large family before she marries. Young men might be hired to assist with farm labour at certain times, such as planting and harvesting seasons, in exchange for room and board. Elderly people who were lifelong friends of a family, although not necessarily related, could also help out with household chores in exchange for a place to live.

One of the main reasons for the demographic interest in the historical relationship between the size of households and the family members who are contained within them has to do with the idea that elasticity in the local labour market is due to fluctuations in household size, as household numbers rise and fall as the demand for local labour increases or decreases. Thus, from a demographic perspective, the size of a family is less an indicator of local economic conditions than of the fluctuating boundaries of household membership, as farm workers come and go throughout the agricultural cycles of ploughing, planting, tending, and reaping.

To further demonstrate the fluctuations in historical populations, I constructed a table that focuses on the mean family and household size for the Irish of Admaston Township; it also includes comparable figures for County Cavan, Killashandra Parish, in north-central Ireland (table 22). This table allows for a comparison of the Irish Canadian population of Admaston in the post-Famine years of 1861 and 1871, with corresponding figures for an Irish agricultural community in the pre-Famine years of 1821 and 1841.

Notwithstanding the differences in the overall number of households – Admaston had only 156 households in 1861 compared with 783 for Cavan in 1841 – there is a pronounced range of variation evident in the table. Cavan in 1821 has the smallest family size, at 5.13 persons, in the sample, while Cavan in 1841 had the largest, at 5.71 persons. Admaston in 1871 had the smallest household size, at 5.54 persons, whereas Cavan of 1841 had the largest, at 6.48 persons.

The most significant differences in the table are in the last column, "Family as a % of household size." The Admaston Irish, for both 1861 and 1871, clearly had a larger percentage of family members per household compared with their counterparts in Cavan, Ireland, by almost 10 per cent, on average. In pre-Famine times for the Irish of Cavan, Ireland, non-family members formed about 10 per cent of the household size, whereas in Admaston in the post-Famine period such individuals formed around 2 per cent of the household totals.

These differences can be accounted for in several ways. One of the more obvious explanations is that the Cavan Irish had a greater need for labour that their households could not provide from among their own members than did the Admaston Irish, who possibly could have afforded to hire outside labour. For Cavan, O'Neill (1984: 168) states that "the relationship between wealth and household size is clearly positive, reflecting the overall labor needs of the various farming groups." Nonetheless, if "labor needs" is the prime factor responsible for the difference between family and household size, it is interesting that there is so little empirical work investigating this phenomenon. The literature on agrarian societies has a conspicuous absence of socio-economic studies which analyse how variations in household size and composition factor into farming groups' levels of productivity.

Table 22 Mean family and household size: Cavan, Ireland, and Admaston, Ontario, 1821–71

Population	N=	Family size	Household size	Family as % of household
Cavan, 1821	857	5.13	5.69	90.2
Cavan, 1841	783	5.71	6.48	88.2
Admaston, 1861*	156	5.62	5.76	97.6
Admaston, 1871*	179	5.46	5.54	98.6

* Includes only Irish families.

Closer examination of the non-family household members of the Irish of Admaston Township in 1861, for example, reveals that there were 21 individuals listed in the census reports whose surnames differed from that of the household head. This total is composed of five males listed as labourers, two males as servants, and five women as servants/housekeepers. The remaining nine individuals are young children, presumably adopted or in some form of foster care.

Most of the men and women listed as labourers or servants were in their late teens or early twenties, along with a few elderly individuals. In all, taking together the men and women listed as performing household labour services such as child care or farmwork, there were 12 persons in such a category out of a total of Irish population of 898 in 1861. In other words, only 1.3 per cent of the Irish Admaston population were engaged in some form of full-time household labour as non-family members. One can then readily conclude from this percentage that a very small floating labour market existed in Admaston and that, by and large, family members, unlike their counterparts in Ireland, were able to manage their own labour requirements.

On the subject of outside household labour requirements, some of the possible reasons for the differences between Admaston and Cavan would lie in the area of labour-saving aids. For example, Cavan farmers generally used shovels to turn over the soil by hand when planting potatoes, while in Admaston oxen and horses were utilized to plough fields. Especially during planting and harvesting, large farms in Ireland could meet labour needs by providing living quarters for tenants. In exchange for rent, or at least a reduction in rent, the tenant farmers contributed their labour; the intensive tillage system in Ireland permitted large amounts of capital to be removed from the agricultural system, especially in the form of rents, so that the only productive factor that the farming population had any control over was people's labour. The severe capital shortage in

Ireland, where draft animals were uneconomical, meant that grain tillage required greater labour inputs than in other parts of Europe, especially on the smaller farms. All of these factors are important considerations when comparing the labour requirements of the Admaston Irish with those of their Irish countrymen back in their home country (O'Neill 1984: 22–3).

Farm Size and Household Size

One of the primary goals of the present study is to examine the post-Famine adaptation of Irish immigrants to Canada, with a view to understanding this experience in terms of significant themes and issues. For example, the conventional wisdom concerning agrarian societies holds to the maxim that "many hands make light work." A larger farm family size, the logical argument would have us believe, allows a household to be more productive than a smaller one: greater amounts of land can be cultivated, leading to higher crop yields and greater prosperity for the household members. In other words, there is a built-in incentive in agricultural communities to produce large families because of the increased productive capacity. It is all a matter of an economy of scale, one could argue. But is this ancient logic true? Are larger families more productive than smaller ones, on a unit-by-unit basis?

The scientific community has apparently bought into this convenient logic. There are several studies on the history of the family that have addressed the imputed causal relationship between farm size and marital fertility. As one such study explains:

> In many contemporary Third-World settings, a correlation has been found between the amount of land farm couples operate and the number of children they have. Accordingly, controversies have arisen in the literature which question whether the relationship is causal or spurious, and if causal, which variable is the cause and which the effect, [and] how strongly the cause operates. (Clay and Johnson 1992: 503–4)

This fundamental association between the size of available landholdings and the cumulative birthrate of farm families is generally explained in terms of a hypothesis:

> A farm family with access to larger amounts of arable land can raise its income by profitably employing more of its members in the family enterprise ... this income should increase the demand for children by making children more affordable and more profitable [as a source of family labour]. (ibid.: 492)

Look at the logic involved here. A family purchases more land, which in turn allows them to feed more members, which in turn allows the family to produce more food, which in turn allows the family to purchase more land, and we are back at the beginning. There is an obvious tautology hidden in this sequence of ideas – the very explanation underlying the reason for large farm families is hidden in the very details explaining why such families exist in the first place, that is, they exist because large families can support large families. One needs to examine empirical evidence to sort out the factors contributing to larger families, and not resort to faulty logical premises or syllogisms.

One way of putting this ancient logic to the test is to compare farm families on an increasing scale of productive capacity, which is to say, by comparing the size of a farm family with the size of the landholding on which it is situated. The Admaston Irish population, through the enumeration of census reports, has statistical data both on the size of farm families and on the size of their farms. Therefore, one is able to compare the manner in which changes in one variable is associated with changes in another, leaving aside for the time being which variable is the independent one (the causal one) and which was is the dependent one (the effect).

The first step in the analysis is to examine the farm size of the Admaston Irish population, the results of which are presented in table 23. Based on the Canadian (technically, Canada West) census data for Admaston Township, the mean household sizes for the three decades from 1851 to 1871 were compared with farm sizes, according to various categories of farm acreage. For the 1851 sample 59 households were included for analysis, of which most (83 per cent) comprised 100 acres. The reason for this distribution was that originally, say around 1850, the initial allotment given to new farmers under the pre-emption incentive program was probably 100 acres. The ten households at this time with 150- or 200-acre farms might well have settled in the area earlier than most other immigrants, and thus had an opportunity to purchase more land beyond the initial allotment.

By 1861 the distribution of farm size was more spread out than in the earlier decades, with four farms under the usual 100 acres and several over 300 acres; most, however, remained in the 100- to 199-acre category. This tendency for a more varied distribution of farm size continued into the 1871 decade with 13 farms now under 100 acres and three over 300 acres. Farms in the middle category (200–99-acre range) nearly doubled from 24 in 1861 to 45 in 1871.

Farms in the under 100-acre category form an interesting anomaly, as there were none in 1851, four in 1861, and thirteen in 1871. If my assumption is correct, and 100 acres was indeed the usual allotment in the

Table 23 Farm size compared to mean household size: Admaston, Ontario, 1851–71

			Household size			
Farm size (acres)	N=	1851	N=	1861	N=	1871
0–99	–	–	4	4.50	13	4.31
100–199	52	5.87	117	5.74	109	5.53
200–299	7	7.86	24	6.16	45	6.62
300+	–	–	2	9.00	3	9.00
Totals*	59		147		170	

* Household totals may vary from table to table because not all households were engaged in farming or because of missing data in the census reports.

pre-emption program, then there appears to be a certain "devolution" taking place in farm size, one that seemed to have increased as time went on. The most probable explanation would be that, in the later decades, farms were subdivided to provide for older sons entering marriage age. Lacking land transfer deeds or wills there is no way of determining the validity of this assumption; however, there is a method that could work just as well. Since the occurrences of these smaller farms are relatively few, one could comb through the census records for clues to possible transfers.

The procedure, then, is to formulate a hypothesis and then check it against the available data to determine its validity. In this case the hypothesis is that cases which contravene the general rule of increasing farm size with a corresponding increase in family (household) size are a result of a subdivision of the family estate, with the probability that farm size will decrease when a farmer's sons either inherit or purchase a portion of the family farm.

Taking the 1861 census records into consideration, the four cases of farm properties under 100 acres would appear to contravene the stated hypothesis because there are no farms listed in the 1851 census of less than 100 acres. It is interesting that three of the four cases are actually very close to, yet below, the 99-acre limit. For example, three of the farms are between 95 and 98 acres in size. None of the farmers holding these properties are listed in the Admaston census for 1851, so one can assume that they were not the holders of these properties originally, that is, between 1851 and 1861, they purchased 100-acre farms and then sectioned or partitioned off five to three acres for whatever purpose. A reasonable conjecture would be that several acres were allocated for a road allotment, or designated for public use, such as property sold or donated for a school or church. In any event these three cases do not fulfil the requirements for our hypothesis.

In the third case, James McGee's farm property is listed at 50 acres, but he was not enumerated in Admaston during 1851; one wonders how such a small property could have emerged when there were no properties in the 1851 census less than 100 acres. Again, resorting to a reasonable conjecture, it is probable that one of the larger (i.e., over 150 acres) properties was subdivided, and 50 acres were sold to Mr McGee. (Such a subdivision could even be checked with the land registry office for Renfrew County located in Pembroke, if one were so inclined.) Incidentally, Mr McGee was still resident on this 50-acre property in 1871. Looking ahead to the 1881 census, James, then 72 years of age, was no longer listed as the head of the household; that designation had fallen to his son, Thomas (age 28 and unmarried).

The 1871 census reveals 13 cases of property less than 100 acres, 11 cases with the deletion of James McGee and one of the farmers with 98 acres listed in 1861. Of these, the case of Patrick Sheahan and his mother is interesting to consider. In the 1851 census Patrick Sheahan is listed as owning 100 acres (lot 29, concession 9), but by 1871 he is listed as owning only 50 acres (lot 30, concession 9). Furthermore, his mother, the widow Mrs Sheahan, is listed in 1871 as the owner of 50 acres, also on lot 30, concession 9.

Revisiting the 1851 census it is apparent the original Patrick Sheahan had died, leaving 50 acres of his 100-acre property to his son, also Patrick (age 13 in 1851), and the other 50 acres to his wife. However, how does one reconcile the differences in the 1851 property designation (lot 29, concession 9) and the subsequent property of 1871 designated as lot 30, concession 9 (properties situated side by side, one would presume), later inhabited by his widowed wife and son? Again, a search of the land registry records would be necessary to sort this out. In addition, the 1881 census lists a Patrick Sheahan, age 47, with wife Joanna and four children, without a property designation. Also listed are Jeremiah Sheahan (age 30), wife Mary and two children, without a property designation. Further genealogical detective work might well reveal that Mrs Sheahan was originally, before marriage, a member of the Murphy family. There must have been many marriages in those days which interconnected families in a multiplicity of ways.

Curiously, John Murphy (age 60) is also listed as living on this property (lot 30, concession 9) in 1871, also on a 50-acre property with his wife Margret [spelling as in original]. In the same census year there is another John Murphy, age 53, living on lot 10, concession 9, along with six children. In the 1861 census there are also two John Murphys listed.

One (age 48) was living with his wife Margret and five children on 100 acres listed only as concession 9. The other one, John Murphy (age 40) on concession 10, was living with his wife Mary and five children. The 1881 census lists a John Murphy, age 60, with his wife Mary and four children (without any property designation given).

A further case is that of Patrick O'Gorman, age 65 in 1871 and living on 50 acres (lot 7, concession 24). In the previous decade he was living with only his wife, but on 100 acres (also lot 7). Also listed in the 1871 census is John O'Gorman, age 36, inhabiting 50 acres also on lot 7, concession 24; however, I cannot find a record of him in the previous 1861 census. In this case can one be justified in assuming that Patrick O'Gorman subdivided his original 100-acre property into two 50-acre sections, living on one of these himself and perhaps giving or selling the other to a son or another relative not previously listed in the records.

What, then, can one conclude concerning our original hypothesis about the smaller (less than 100-acre) properties in relation to the census records of 1861 and 1871? Certainly, one cannot arrive at a definite conclusion without further research; however, one can put forward several observations. There are no doubt properties consisting of 100 acres or more in 1851 that were further subdivided into smaller units in later years. But, without the ability to question the people involved in the transactions, we cannot determine if these subdivisions were the result of inheritance or some other practical matter.

In terms of the larger theoretical problem that is the subject of this investigation concerning the determinants of family and farm size, the 1861 sample in table 23 does depict a steady increase in household size, with a corresponding increase in farm size. In fact, household size doubled from 4.50 household members, on average, for farms with fewer than 100 acres to 9.00 members for farms with greater than 300 acres. Similarly, for the 1871 census year, there was an increase from 4.31 household members for the farms with fewer than 100 acres to 9.00 members for the ones with greater than 300 acres. Note that there are also very similar household averages for each category of farm size for the corresponding 1861 and 1871 household data – household size decreased slightly for the two categories of farm size smaller than 200 acres from 1861 to 1871, increased slightly for the 200–99-acre category, and stayed the same at nine household members for farms with more than 300 acres. Similarly, while the data set for 1851 is much smaller than for the following decades, there is a corresponding increase in household size as farm size increases, with a mean household size of 5.87 members for farms in the 100–199 range, and 7.86 household members in the 200–299-acre range.

Table 23 also reveals a major difference between the census years of 1861 and 1871 in that in the former sample of 1871 there were three times more households in the 0–99-acre category than in the previous census year of 1861, and nearly double the number of households in the 200–99-acre category, whereas those households of 100–99 acres actually decreased by 6.8 per cent (from 177 to 109). Without further research one can only speculate on the reasons for these shifts in the internal dynamics of Admaston farming household size. A reasonable hypothesis, however, would be that the partition of farms in the 100-acre category are a result of farmers' sons coming of age, which would account for both the increase in farms with fewer than 100 acres and the decrease in those of 100–99 acres. It is also reasonable to assume that the doubling in the number of farming households in the 200–99-acre category resulted from an expansion of farm properties. Notice, for example, that although the overall Irish population of Admaston increased by 10.4 per cent during the decade (from 898 to 991 individuals), there was a corresponding increase in the number of farming households by 15.6 per cent (from 147 households in 1861 to 170 in 1871). Thus, the internal social dynamic at work among the farming Irish is that the number of households increased faster than the population growth, resulting in households smaller in size.

Farm Size as a Variable Factor

The lesson here is that farm size by itself is too much of a variable to be of much use in comparative terms without examining also the internal composition of farm properties. As noted previously, Irish farms in Admaston Township were divided into three major categories as set out in the enumeration forms as administered by the census takers – tillage acreage on which crops are grown, acreage devoted to pasture, and woodlot acreage. In the 1851 census acreage devoted to crops and pasture, grouped together in the category of "under cultivation," comprised an average of 14.6 per cent of farm property. By 1861, crops and pasture encompassed 21.9 per cent of the average farm property, a proportion which increased again to 45.3 per cent in 1871. If we use "acreage under cultivation" as a measure of farm productivity, then this productivity increased by over three times in the two decades from 1851 to 1871. If we focus just on the acreage devoted to crop production, which is probably a truer measure of farm productivity than also including the size of a farm's pasture, this acreage increased from 7.4 per cent in 1851 to 36.3 per cent in 1871, an increase of nearly five times the acreage.

The point in reviewing these figures is that if there is a positive correlation between farm size and family size, this is not confirmed by the data presented here on Irish farms. Whichever measure one wishes to utilize, farm size in terms of total acreage increased from a total of 6,600.0 acres in 1851, to 22,916.8 acres in 1871, an increase of roughly 3.5 times. Other farm categories, such as crop productivity, increased between three and five times. Family (or more specifically, household) size did not keep pace with these increases in farm size as measured by total farm size or acreage devoted to crop production; family size only roughly doubled during this 20-year period. In other words, our conclusion here is that there is not a one-to-one correspondence between family size and farm size.

Clearly, then, in the Irish Canadian case, productive intensity seen in terms of either increased total farm size or increased tillage acreage, cannot be the causal factor in the determination of family size. Farm size by itself, as the cause of determining the size of a family, is far too imprecise a variable. As the Irish Canadian data of Admaston Township suggest, a large farm of, say, 400 acres may be composed primarily of woodlot, and therefore of limited productive capacity, whereas a farm of half this size may be composed almost entirely of acreage devoted to tillage and crop production.

In fact, the relationship between family and farm size might be reversed, as O'Neill (1984: 92) suggested for Cavan, Ireland, in the 1840s, when he indicated that "very large farm size often indicates poor or marginal land, such as rough mountain pasture which had no other use than grazing." Thus, the mere size of a farm tells us little about the its ability to support a family of any particular size; further data are required for an intensive analysis of such factors as the quality of a farm's soil, the uses to which farm acreage is put (i.e., pasture or tillage), decisions concerning crops grown or livestock raised, and a family's labour supply and requirements.

In terms of the household numbers, as documented for the Irish of Admaston Township and illustrated in tables 21, 22, and 23, the increase can probably be attributed to the partitioning of farms of aging parents so that newly married sons could have individual farms of their own. While more specific research is obviously still needed to verify this hypothesis, the practice of setting up sons with small farms from the partition of the parental estate would mark a significant departure from the practice in Ireland for the similar time period, where aging parents were apt to hang on to their farms for as long as possible, then only giving them up to the (usually) eldest son when the parents died or retired from farm life.

A delayed devolution of property in Ireland would result in a vertical extension of family size (i.e., the stem family), because three generations – the aging parents, a married son, his wife, and his children – would occupy the same household. This practice of impartible inheritance was apparently not practised as extensively among the Canadian Irish; because of the availability of land in the new country farms were many times larger on average in Canada than they were in Ireland.

Conclusion

The research strategy adopted in this chapter on family size comprised three different steps. First, this study of Irish families has been restricted to a single community; it does not attempt to generalize across many, possibly diverse, populations. This restriction allows for a more controlled comparison of changes that are apt to occur in one locale, thus reducing the possible number of variables on which any conclusions would be based.

Second, attempts here to compare factors responsible for variations in family size have been aided by the fact that comparable data are available from Ireland itself, thus allowing for the possibility of determining which factors are more or less cultural or economic; this data allowed for the possibility of examining factors pertinent to family size in the context of population expansion, rather than depopulation. Third, the approach taken has extended across a limited number of decades rather than over several centuries, as has been the case with several previous studies of family size. This more limited approach nonetheless has still allowed for a study of variations in family and household size, in a diachronic manner – as opposed to the synchronic manner characteristic of many anthropological studies using the "ethnographic present" approach. Thus, it is concluded here that a more controlled, longitudinal perspective, one focused within a single geographical area, is preferable, in an epistemological sense, to the wide-ranging perspectives of studies that randomly traverse cultural, geographical, and temporal boundaries.

Chapter Eight

Conclusion

This chapter draws together the main theoretical themes of the book: Chayanov's theory of domestic production, the debate about Irish stem families, and the possible determinants of family size. However, as a prelude to a discussion of these matters it is appropriate also to comment on whatever lessons might have been learned during the course of this study on the relationship between anthropology and history.

Lessons about Anthropology and History

It has been noted previously that anthropology and history have had a long period of commingling. I use this term with some trepidation since it is difficult to characterize the relationship between the activities of anthropologists and those of historians. Certainly, there is some overlap, but I am not convinced that scholars in either discipline feel comfortable with the conceptual universe of the other, even though they share the same subject matter – the study of the past.

The old adage that anthropology is history or it is nothing is rarely, if ever, heard in the halls of academia anymore. As an informal survey I asked the younger members of our department to identify the source of this famous quote; none of them could even remember hearing it, never mind identify who said it. One of them, who in fact teaches a course on the history of anthropological thought, guessed that the quote might be attributed to either Boas or Malinowski, because they were both "historical figures," thus missing the point of my query altogether.

In Canada there was a brief period, in the 1970s, when studies of the fur trade and First Nations were popular; among the most noteworthy were Charles Bishop's *The Northern Ojibwa and the Fur Trade* (1974) and Arthur Ray's *Indians and the Fur Trade* (1974). Drawing on the archives of the Hudson's Bay Company, these studies primarily focused on economic interactions between the Indigenous peoples of northern Canada and British merchants; they pointed out that, by 1780, the Hudson's Bay Company was forced to establish interior posts because of increased competition emanating from the south. The ideas and research emanating from these studies led to an increased concern with demographic change among the First Nations. A lively debate ensued in the literature during the 1980s concerning the extent to which trapping territories were an Indigenous institution (see Bishop and Morantz 1986).

Another notable contribution was made by by Bruce Trigger (*Natives and Newcomers*, 1985, and *The Children of Aataentsic*, 1987) in his studies of the Wendat (Huron); these were based on the 73 volumes of the *Jesuit Relations*, a series of records compiled between about 1710 and 1750 (Thwaites 1896–1901). The *Jesuit Relations* documented the attempts of Jesuit missionaries to convert the Wendat to Christianity and the consequent antagonisms between the two parties.

Whether using the accounts of fur traders or those of Christian missionaries, such attempts to document the lifeways of Indigenous peoples were fraught with problems of interpretation. Part of the problem is the obvious difficulty of cultural translation. Events are filtered first through the frequently ethnocentric accounts of the Europeans, and then, of course, there are inherent difficulties in attempting to record and interpret the social and cultural habits of any population living in the distant past. In fact, Trigger (1986: 67), commenting in an essay on cultural relativism, explained, "I found that trying to understand the mentality of seventeenth-century Jesuit missionaries required almost as great an act of anthropological imagination as did understanding the perceptions of the Hurons of that period."

As far as my own attempts to study the Irish adaptation to Canada based on extant census files, there are several research points worth indicating. On the plus side, the census material, both the documentation of families and agricultural characteristics, provides a plethora of data. On the negative side, we have only what is passed down; aside from our own interpretations, we are not able to gather any more data than are available in the stark, bare statistics of the census accounts.

Of course, there is no reason for complaint here, as one values what remains of the past. Archival records are often ephemeral. The virtually complete 1890 American census was destroyed by fire; much of the archival material of Ireland was also lost to fire during the revolutionary war of the early 1920s. In any event, we crave for more. Having conducted community studies of contemporary First Nations people in northern Ontario, and of Irish farmers in Donegal, I would give practically anything to be able to interview the Irish farmers of Renfrew County about their choices, ideas, and actions. But, alas, their voices are lost in time.

Chayanov's Theory of Domestic Production

This study of the post-Famine Irish immigrants of the Ottawa Valley has provided an excellent opportunity to examine several significant theoretical issues regarding the general matter of domestic productive intensity in agrarian societies and its relationship to farm size. First, this study demonstrates the continued vitality of the Chayanov model to generate theoretical debate concerning a variety of farming types, ranging from those of Russian peasants and New Guinea yam growers to those of the post-Famine Irish immigrants in North America. The present study, however, has highlighted several areas regarding the applicability of the Chayanov model, especially in terms of farmers' decision-making and their ability to assume risk, depending on variables in a low-versus-high consumer-worker ratio in a household. This issue could be made the more explicit subject of a wider ethnographic analysis; it appears likely that the choices and options open to farmers are considerably different for households with high- consumer-worker ratios than for those in the lower- ratio category. The conclusion, then, is that while Chayanov's theory opens avenues of fruitful enquiry it does not clarify some of the most significant theoretical issues in terms of the internal dynamics of domestic production.

Second, this study explores the relationship between risk and choice, and the internal dynamics and composition of households derived from Chayanov's model; this model suggests that lower consumer/worker-ratio households can take more risks in allocating productive labour. This is particularly demonstrated in the case of a household choosing to clear more land for possible future cultivated use, or, alternatively, choosing other options by which the members dedicate their productive efforts to maximizing crop production on acreage already under cultivation.

There is a theoretical and empirical point here worthy of further study as it relates to a clarification of the applicability of the Chayanov curve. Chayanov's model implies that productive intensity of all households is based solely on the internal composition of the household; however, the present study has demonstrated that certain farmers are more highly motivated to increase their agricultural production, for whatever reasons, than are others. These unexplored "motivating factors" need to be considered alongside Chayanov's theory since it is apparent that farmers' productive intensity is based not only on the need to provide for the consumptive demands of his household, but also on other, less obvious, factors. This is not to suggest that Chayanov's assertions are necessarily wrong, but that they are incomplete. A study of different ethnographic settings may well reveal what these motivating factors are; they could be something along the lines of Nietzche's "will to power," Weber's Protestant ethic and capitalism, or McClelland's (1961) "need for achievement." To mix our metaphors, in the instance of Chayaov's proposals, one theoretical size does not fit all ethnographic examples.

Third, the present study suggests that there has evidently been an overemphasis in the literature on farm productivity, as well as on such matters as cultivated areas, crop size and yields, and the intensity of labour devoted to these factors. This study of Irish Canadian farming households suggests that the total compilation of farm assets should be considered as an integral part of farm productivity. In this case, uncleared woodlots are valuable assets, and would have to be replaced at considerable cost if depleted. In other words, there are dynamics and interrelationships involving the family farm as a total system that make an emphasis on one farm asset to the neglect of others a serious epistemological error in assessing the relationship between domestic productive intensity and farm size.

Understanding the Intensity of Agricultural Production

Chayanov's theory of domestic production makes a valuable contribution to the understanding of agrarian societies because of its focus on the internal dynamics of variation from farm to farm to explain why some farms outproduce others. It is in this context that the post-Famine adaptation of Irish immigrants to Canada is studied. Chayanov's stated assumption is that production in pre-capitalist agrarian societies is directly related to the composition of the farming household itself, rather than to monolithic forces external to the farmers' social organization. This focus prompts the researcher to look inward in a sense, to the individuals and how they performed, and to the forces which framed their choices and decisions.

According to Chayanov, the amount of work done by the working members of a household will be inversely related to the number of dependent consumers they must support. In other words, the higher the ratio of non-working children to workers in a household, the harder the other working members must labour to satisfy the consumptive needs of the whole. There is a certain seductive appeal to Chayanov's notion that family size and composition determines the level of economic activity– it appeals to our common sense and seems straightforward – but there are subtleties with this approach that take time to uncover. These subtleties have been the subject of an ongoing debate which has encompassed several academic disciplines.

In anthropology, Marshall Sahlins, widely known for his theory of "specific evolution" (the development through time of specific societies, as opposed to "general" evolution, which comprises changes that influence all societies to one degree or another), was largely responsible for demonstrating the relevance of Chayanov's approach to ethnological analysis. Sahlins used ethnographic data collected previously by Melanesian ethnographers during fieldwork in (mainly) Tonga and New Guinea. His work suffered from several difficulties. Some of these stemmed from the fact that the original data had been collected for other purposes, rather than for the explicit purpose of determining the intensity of Melanesian domestic production. He also used a very small sample size, which can accentuate unduly certain trends, while minimizing others. Most of his analysis rested on sample sizes amounting to no more than a dozen cases. There were also difficulties in comparing the Melanesian societies themselves, which differed in terms of their socio-political complexity; these differences inhibited the validly of any conclusions drawn. For example, in some of the Melanesian societies, yam growers worked primarily for themselves, while in others the agricultural workers were motivated by provisioning the stores of important political leaders in a redistributive economy. An additional problem with Sahlin's studies was the lack of a longitudinal or historical dimension that could illustrate how variations in household size could lead to a corresponding change in domestic production.

Nonetheless, Sahlin's research did illustrate the applicability of ethnographic data to the sorts of economic analysis proposed by Chayanov, such as demonstrating that the empirical differences in domestic productive intensity among a variety of cultural examples was a widespread phenomenon. The present study of Irish farmers therefore proceeds from, and hopefully builds upon, this early attempt to understand domestic production. However, it also departs from Sahlin's approach in several significant ways. First, the focus here is on one people or "culture": the Irish, albeit in different settings, Ireland and Canada. Second, a longitudinal approach is offered, one which follows changes in the Irish agricultural economy over several decades. This approach, as opposed to a more "synchronic" one, allows for comparisons that can be made over time.

Increased Agricultural Production

While many of the findings of this study are inherently interesting, the most significant one concerns the startling increase in Irish farmers' agricultural production over several decades, from the time of their arrival after the Famine. Let us look at a bare bones statistical summary of what has been discovered in the Admaston census files, and then the specific data reorganized along certain themes.

First, the Irish population in 1851 comprised 410 persons, which then increased by just over two times to 898 persons in 1861, after which the population increased much less (by 10.4 per cent) to 991 persons. Overall there was a general decline in household size, with a corresponding decline over this 20-year period in the number of consumers per household. Thus, following Chayanov's theory, one would expect that agricultural production would follow the same trajectory, which is to say, that this production would also double in a corresponding manner and thereafter stabilize. Given the general decline in the consumer to worker ratio over this period (table 10 for example shows a c/w decline of about 10 per cent from 2.99 in 1851 to 2.69 in 1871), agricultural production could be expected to decline accordingly by the same measure.

In fact, this expectation is far from what actually happened, as agricultural production increased almost in an exponential manner. As table 10 illustrates, both the overall acres cultivated and the acres cultivated per worker increased by about 70 per cent (or over three times) over the two decades between 1851 and 1871. Looking more specifically at other measures of agrarian performance, crop production (as shown in figure 3) increased by five times; livestock (table 6) also increased, with sheep increasing by three times and horses by four times (oxen were the only decrease among the livestock, by three times). Then, as shown by a measure of household surplus production above consumer needs (table 14), Irish farmers increased their "surplus capacity" by 4.5 times from 1851 to 1871.

Increasing Socio-economic Differentiation

The remaining question is: Was this increased agricultural production evenly distributed among the Irish population of Admaston? Ideally, if the statistical data were available, one could construct a "Lorenze Curve." This is a graphic device used by economists to illustrate the cumulative percentage of income distribution in an economy. For example, in a completely egalitarian society 50 per cent of the population would own 50 per cent of the wealth, and so on, up and down the scale. Perhaps in the future, were more data made available, such an approach could be possible. However, for the present situation, with the data available from the census reports, a more modest representation has been formulated.

For each of the three census reports a representative sample of 30 Irish households was selected and organized into various categories, such as the average acreage cultivated per worker or the ratio of consumers to workers (tables 11, 12, and 13). These data then formed the foundation for three graphs (figures 4, 5, and 6) illustrating domestic variations in labour intensity. A key calculation on each graph, represented by "k", was the average labour required to maintain one person at normal consumption. Each of the 30 households selected for each of the three sample years were then plotted on each graph.

The results were then summarized in table 14 The number of households working above the normal labour capacity, or above the line of the graphs representing the expected worker labour intensity, increased steadily from 6/30 households (or 20 per cent) for 1851, to 10/30 (33 per cent) in 1861, to 13/30 (43 per cent) in 1871. The conclusion that could be reached from these results is that there was emerging among the Irish farmers of Admaston an ever-increasing class of workers whose labour intensity was well above the normal consumption requirements of their dependants. In other words, this evidence clearly illustrates an ever-increasing socio-economic differentiation among the Irish farmers. How is this trend to be interpreted given the various theoretical positions discussed thus far? Economically and socially speaking, what direction was the Irish population of Admaston headed? Were the Irish farmers becoming incipient capitalists, or simply strengthening their current mode of commodity production?

Capitalist Production versus Commodity Production

Surplus agricultural production among the Irish farmers of Admaston Township can be accounted for in two ways; as a form of incipient capitalist economy or as a strengthening of an existing economy based on commodity production. This distinction is largely based on Marxist theory.

In *capitalist production*, commodities are produced for their exchange value to generate profits and accumulate capital. *Capital*, one of the major factors involved in production, consists of property from which an income is derived, usually in the form of money. A subsidiary term, *capital good*, refers to a material economic good (something satisfying a human desire), other than land (because it is not created by humans), which is used to produce wealth. *Exchange value* refers to the production of commodities for what can be exchanged for them in a market to generate a profit (as opposed to *use value*, discussed below).

In southern Ontario during the mid-nineteenth century, the commodities that had the highest market value were wheat, oats, and horses. McCallum (1980: 9–14, 22–4) noted that southern Ontario was a major exporter of wheat beginning in the 1840s. New settlers, he noted, "adapted a system in which three or four acres were devoted to family needs and the rest of the land was taken up in wheat" (1980: 9). Due to the poor transportation facilities in southern Ontario, "until 1850 wheat was the only agricultural commodity that could be exported in any quantity" (ibid.: 10). New land yielded 30 or 40 bushels of wheat per acre, and the average was as high as 25 to 35 bushels (see Jones 1946: 356).

For the most part Ontario wheat was exported to Britain, as the American market remained closed because of tariff restrictions imposed in 1824. In 1850 Ontario exported about six million bushels of wheat amounting to about 80 bushels per farm, with record wheat prices. However, over the next two decades Ontario experienced a rapid decline in the wheat staple trade. In the last three years of the 1850s, low prices for wheat resulted owing to the end of the Crimean War and poor crops. Wheat prices and shipments recovered in 1866, but the recovery was short-lived and the wheat trade never again regained is former prominence in the Ontario economy.

The main reasons for the decline in wheat production were the twin pressures of diminishing soil fertility and western competition. By 1851 the average for the province had fallen to 16 bushels per acre, and by 1866 barley had largely replaced wheat in central Ontario. As McCallum (1980: 22) states, "by the 1870's Ontario's wheat trade had run its course." This is the wider context, then, in which to view the production of wheat in Admaston Township.

Admaston's wheat production in 1851 (table 2) of 15.7 bushels per acre was comparable to the 16.1 bushels per acre for the rest of the province in that year (Jones 1946: 86), but nowhere near the 30 or 40 bushels per acre grown on Ontario farms in earlier decades. From 1851 to 1861 wheat production in Admaston dropped slightly to 12.4 bushels per acre, but the overall production increased by almost six times (2,782 bushels grown in 1851 to 16,015 bushels in 1861). Over the next decade, from 1861 to 1871, there was a dramatic decline in wheat production to 6.4 bushels per acre and a corresponding decline in overall production by 3.6 times (to 4,448 bushels). Since this general decline in wheat production in the rest of the province was principally due to declining soil fertility, one could assume that the dramatic decline in Admaston's wheat production was also due to declining soil fertility.

The conclusion to be drawn from these various trends is that the rise in wheat production in Ontario as a staple crop used for export occurred largely in a period during the initial habitation of the Irish in Admaston Township just after the Famine. By the time farmers had cleared sufficient fields and were able to devote their energy to wheat production in the 1860s, the export market had largely ceased to exist. A rapidly declining market for wheat, in combination with a corresponding decline in soil fertility across the province, would lead one to the conclusion that growing wheat in Admaston for capital accumulation was not a viable option.

The demise of the wheat export market in Ontario (farmers continued to grow wheat for their own household consumption) left a vacuum that was eventually filled by barley. As McCallum (1980: 49) explained, "By 1870, exports of barley and oats from Ontario ports amounted to $4.7 million ... Barley remained the major crop of eastern Ontario and after 1865 the entire region bordering Lake Ontario until the McKinley tariff of 1890." An increasing production of barley as a staple crop was also facilitated by an internal demand spurred on by a burgeoning urban population in Ontario. The growth of populations in Toronto, Hamilton, and Kingston led farmers to raise more barley to supply the breweries and distilleries. There can be no doubt, however, that this increase in barley production hardly compared with the wheat boom of the previous decades.

The agricultural census records for the decades between 1851 and 1871 demonstrate that barley was hardly grown at all in Admaston. In 1851 only 277 bushels were produced in the entire township, and this figure dropped even lower with 83 bushels produced in 1871, with just 5 households out of 154 growing barley. Probably the distance from the Ottawa Valley to southern Ontario's breweries and an inability to compete with farmers who lived closer to urban centres were contributing factors.

Oats were grown in increasing quantities by the 1860s, and since oats were raised to feed working livestock, such as horses, probably the two should be discussed together. Quantities of oats raised in Admaston increased dramatically from 4,360 bushels in 1851 to 24,260 in 1861, an increase in production of five times (table 3). Correspondingly, the number of horses possessed by Admaston farmers increased from 53 in 1851 to 287 in 1861, also a five-fold increase (table 6).

It has previously been noted that oxen were preferred for ploughing the rough ground of the early farms of the 1850s, but thereafter horses were used because they could do the job much faster. Horses could also be used to pull carriages, and in a more stylish manner than oxen, for shopping trips into the village of Renfrew; they thus played a role in breaking up the monotony and isolation of farm life.

As far as commodity production of Renfrew County is concerned, what are we to make of Jones (1946: 116–17) suggestion that farms of the lower Ottawa Valley had secured a virtual monopoly on the supply of oats, horses, and hay for the lumber industry? Even McCallum (1980: 11) suggests that "the lumber industry of the Ottawa Valley ... provided the dominant market for farmers of the region [who] faced no serious competition."

If we again examine Admaston farms having horses (table 6) there is a remarkable consistency through the decades of the number of horses owned. For example, the number of horses owned per farm was 1.1 in 1851, 1.9 in 1861 and 1.6 in 1871. We can readily conclude from these small figures that horses were not raised for sale to the lumber camps, and that the oats raised by Admaston farmers were raised solely for the consumption of the farmers' horses. All of this is understandable in any event, given that in Admaston Township is one of the most southerly of the townships in Renfrew County. Townships farther up the Ottawa River, nearer Petawawa and Pembroke, would have been practically next door to the lumber camps, and because of their fortuitous location they would have had a more competitive advantage over centres farther down the river, such as Admaston.

Given the above, it becomes increasingly evident that the surplus production by Admaston's farmers is not explained by the emergence of an incipient capitalist economy. Rather, the explanation for such surpluses is to be found in the internal dynamics of Admaston's agricultural production. In other words, a *use value* approach (alternatively referred to as *simple commodity production*) provides the most plausible explanation for an increase in the intensity of agrarian production in the township. In this form of production, a commodity is produced for its use value, which is to say its benefit is from having or using it, or from it being sold or exchanged, with the proceeds then used for obtaining other use-value commodities that the farmer needs. In the case of the Admaston farmers, in order to purchase horses, which are relatively expensive but speed up agricultural production, they needed to raise the necessary money by producing a surplus of another farm product, such as grain crops. This process is then continued, so that other livestock, such as sheep, who have value in the sale of wool, can be purchased. The point in these various transactions is not to generate profits or accumulate wealth for the farmer in monetary terms, but to increase the overall value of the farm, and perhaps in turn to finance a transition from crop to livestock production.

Chayanov's theory of domestic production, with its emphasis on changes in the consumer/worker ratio, sometimes yields unforeseen results. In the case of the Irish farmers of Admaston Township, an examination of changes in agricultural intensity has uncovered an agrarian community which was experiencing a subtle process of socio-economic differentiation among its members. Starting in 1851, a relatively small number of farmers (20 per cent) were working above a level of what has been termed the "surplus labour capacity." By 1861, this surplus capacity rose to 33 per cent, then, by 1871, to 43 per cent. Using Chayanov's methodology, this present study could discover somewhat hidden processes of social and economic change in the Irish community.

One of these processes, not immediately evident, concerns the reasonable supposition about subsistence agriculture that farmers will work towards reducing risk and uncertainty. In the context of the Chayanov model the expectation is that the consumer/worker ratio will influence decision-making to the extent that farmers with many mouths to feed will attempt to ensure a sizeable crop, and therefore are not able to assume greater risk. Such farmers are also in a less favourable position than those with a lower consumer/worker ratio to expand on existing arable farm land, or to experiment with new crops that could possibly produce higher yields, because there is a more immediate demand on their labour to meet the household's consumptive needs.

Farmers with a lower c/w ratio, on the other hand, are less constrained by these parameters and have a greater potential for productivity gains. This variability in the c/w ratio is probably a core factor in the relatively high productivity of the 1871 Irish Canadian households in Renfrew County, which, when compared to their 1861 counterparts, had a narrower range of c/w ratios, and at the lower end of the scale. Overall, the 1871 farmers were in a more favourable position to assume possible risk than those of a decade earlier. Here again, variability in the c/w ratio of domestic productive intensity illustrates its explanatory potential. In the form of a proposition derived from the present study, the rule is that *assumable risk per farmer varies inversely with increases in the consumer/worker ratio*.

It has furthermore been noted that the "Chayanov's model, by itself, is not concerned with the fact of differentiation within the domestic units of production. By treating the family as an autonomous, homogeneous unit, the model [has] considerable theoretical interest as it relates intimately to the nature of the productive system" (McGough 1984: 193). Thus, Chayanov's model, as a mode of analysis in agrarian societies, sometimes reveals processes in the wider society itself that are not immediately evident using conventional economic approaches. The model is also a valuable tool in examining a wide range of ethnographic cases in historical anthropology, and this cross-cultural utility may well be its most enduring benefit.

In summary, the statistical evidence presented in this study suggests that there was much variability among Irish immigrant farmers. Some were apparently content to meet their consumptive obligations and not much more, while others were motivated to achieve a level of production far above the norm. The Irish immigrant population, as such, was far from homogeneous in worker intensity, and probably in other measures as well. This distinction between the go-getters, on the one hand, and those content with the economic status quo, on the other, is discernible with an analysis of domestic productivity. It is also evident that different farmers practised different production strategies and, as indicated above, held different aspirations for their holdings. Indeed, a study of aspirations and production strategies is possible through an examination of farmers' production choices.

The Irish Stem Family

The second major theoretical focus of this book has been on the prevalence of a household type called the stem family, a type of family commonly found in agrarian societies. To reiterate, the stem family is generally a three-generational household, while varying somewhat in its specific details from one geographic locale to another. Stem families tend to result in a delay in both the age of marriage for farmers' sons and the devolution of the property to one (usually the eldest) of the sons after he marries and has children.

The usual developmental cycle of households is seen to account for the relatively low incidence (10–15 per cent) of stem families in comparison with other forms, such as nuclear families. The reason for focusing on the stem family here is to ascertain if there has been a continuation of this family type as the Irish migrated and settled in eastern Canada. The extensive body of literature on Irish families (e.g., Connell 1962: Fitzpatrick 1983; Gibbon and Curtin 1978; Harris 1988; and Varley 1983) has noted a fairly high incidence of the stem variety in Ireland, so it is a matter of theoretical importance to find out if the stem family structure was continued after settlement in Canada, and, if so, to what degree.

In this burgeoning body of literature various theories have been proposed to account for stem families. For example, an "evolutionary" explanation would see stem families as a transitional type between a larger patrilateral extended household, or the "patriarchal family," and the smaller nuclear family. A "cultural" theory sees the stem family as resulting from the "weight" of Ireland's past traditions; in other words, this form of habitation, one that groups close male relatives together, is seen as part of a pattern that over time became part of the Irish people's "learned behaviour." A third theory sees the stem family as a mode of economic survival, with a cross-generational continuity of households, in which farmland and resources stay within the family group, albeit a restricted one.

It would be difficult to effectively test all of these various theories; however, the present study of Irish households departs from previous ones in several significant ways. First, it engages in a temporal-longitudinal approach, covering several decades of data on family types in the post-Famine period from 1851 to 1881. Second, the debate is taken out of Ireland itself, in this case the Ottawa Valley region of Canada, to ascertain which variables might be the same, or different, in accounting for the frequency of Irish stem families. In all, I am not aware of another study that takes this approach in adopting a research strategy of a longitudinal, long-term historical focus and applying it to the ethnographic area of Canada.

The results of the historical-ethnographic research on Irish Canadians presented in this book would likely lead one to agree with Birdwell-Pheasant's assertion that the stem family "is an adaptive pattern that can emerge whenever and wherever economic and demographic circumstances are right and the cultural setting is congenial" (1992: 230). It is evident, however, that for the post-Famine Irish of Renfrew County, the economic, demographic, and cultural conditions were not sufficiently conducive for the stem family to emerge as an adaptive setting for the post-Famine immigrants. In fact, economic circumstances could also be seen to explain both the emergence of, and the absence of, such family types, thus negating most of the explanatory power of such an approach. The debate concerning the Irish stem family, then, might be fruitfully examined in a much broader adaptive and geographical context than has been the case in the past, with most previous studies restricted to Ireland alone. Even within Ireland, a fruitful area of study could focus on the geographic variations of stem families – it is entirely unclear if they were more prevalent in Kerry, say, than in Donegal or Antrim.

A broadening of the conceptual and empirical basis of the stem family debate would be valuable. Even if one were to restrict the empirical focus of this controversy to Ireland itself, it is evident that there is much variation in the social and economic contexts within which stem families are embedded, suggesting that the search for a single explanatory variable is ultimately a sterile epistemological quest. Extending this focus historically through time and to other nations and geographical domains is surely apt to frustrate any explanatory endeavours.

Economic, demographic, social, and probably religious factors are important explanatory variables in the stem family debate, but are not exclusively responsible for the socio-cultural incidences of certain family types. An extended perspective – one which incorporates both the quantifiable data of empirical studies and the more subtle qualitative aspects of individual decision-making – would provide us with a more comprehensive basis than now exists for understanding the stem family situation. In terms of an overall conclusion, the data presented in this study lead one to argue that the Irish family organization would appear to be much more fluid that the Ireland studies alone suggest.

The Determinants of Family Size

While examining the relationship between farm and family size, it is important to keep in mind that the differences between Ireland and eastern Canada in the mid-nineteenth century were pronounced. Irish farmers in Ontario were not nearly as constrained as they were in Ireland. In Renfrew County a farm size of several hundred acres was relatively common; meanwhile the size of an average farm in Ireland was fewer than 25 acres. In addition, land in Canada during the 1860s could still be bought from the Crown at reasonable prices, or from other farmers who might be moving out of the area.

A reasonable conclusion, based on the fact that the economic circumstances were significantly different between the two countries during the several decades immediately after the Famine, would be that the internal socio-economic conditions or dynamics as they relate to family size and composition among the Irish are of a more subtle nature than is commonly explained in the literature in which one variable – demographic, cultural, or whatever else comes to mind – is utilized to explain a complex question.

While some may be disappointed to discover, after reading this book, that I can offer no definitive answer to the question about what determines family size, other than to say that each family's circumstance reveals the choices that the members of families make. Possibly the question is the wrong one to ask, because it leads one to expect a single, unfettered solution. Rather, the stem family can be seen as determined by external variables, as well as at its most basic level, as a basic survival tactic. In Ireland impartible inheritance helped prevent ruination of a family's landholding by circumventing continued subdivision to the point at which no one could make a living; the family farm usually devolved to the eldest son, leaving others to emigrate or join the ever-growing pool of available labour.

In the Irish Canadian case, farm size doubled or tripled in Admaston, suggesting that fathers were accumulating land, not so much to increase crop production for themselves or for immediate cultivation, but to facilitate partible inheritance to their sons. In such cases, it might well be the youngest son who eventually inherits the family farm, rather than the eldest, because, as Elliot (2004: 199) astutely suggests, the others might already have been given assistance in purchasing land of their own. Yet, land availability becomes explanatory of the prevalence of one family type or another only if it can be established that there existed various alternatives in household arrangements.

Further research on this topic might explore the alternatives open to the aging parents, for example, of living with a married son and his family. It is also possible that some elderly couples had adult children residing nearby, though not in the same household. Propinquity of such households suggests that an elderly couple's residence was close enough to their children's farms so that aid in various forms could be easily given. In other words, the census forms may show separate residences for the elderly couple and their adult children, when for all practical purposes they are close enough to be considered as living in a single "household."

Such subtleties of social organization are not likely to be uncovered in the large-scale comparisons that transcend nations, regions, and cultures. One might be led to conclude that certain factors, such as farm size, fertility patterns, and so on, might be more important as determining factors than is the case. Human beings can make their own decisions, within certain parameters of course, but they are not immune to the exigencies of social and economic forces or the cultural materialist transformations at work in any particular time period. In this regard one is reminded of Marx's famous pronouncement: "Men make their own history, but they do not make it just as they please; they do not make it under circumstances chosen by themselves, but under given circumstances directly encountered and inherited from the past" (Marx 1978 [1852]: 9).

Summary

This study of the Irish in Canada leads me to suggest that the practicalities of everyday life probably have more of an effect on the contours of social organization than many social scientists are apt to admit. The

Irish Canadian farmers and their families of Renfrew County were not ruled by a mysterious force that inclined them to live in stem families as in Ireland. What they were inclined to do in their new country was to continue farming, and as land even on the new frontiers was less expensive to obtain from parents than from neighbours or the Crown, one son likely remained on the homestead to await his father's retirement or death. In any event, assigning the farm to this son in return for support in old age was less expensive than hoarding money to build a separate household in which to live as a solitary elderly couple.

These are the sorts of "inclinations" or realities that tend to generate certain family forms, rather than any kind of attachment – cultural, economic, or otherwise – to a particular household structure. I will admit to admiring theoretical orientations as much as anyone else, but which comes first – the pressures of social organization, or attempts by ordinary people to survive in a difficult world? In this regard, I am sympathetic to Marvin Harris's cultural-materialist approach. As Barrett (2009: 91) summarizes, "Human activity organized to satisfy the material conditions of life is affected and limited by our biological make-up, the level of technology, and the nature of the environment, which in turn generate ideological and social organizational responses."[1]

The answer to the question of what determines the size of a family is not to be found in the large-scale statistical generalization of political economy. The reason why so little success has been achieved in attempts to isolate the empirical factors responsible for family size is that the units of comparison are essentially incommensurable entities. This is not to suggest that "science" does not have a role to play in understanding the characteristics of family life, its organization, and its composition. The issue here is one of perspective and interpretation. Much depends upon the viewer's vantage point. Are family forms seen to be a result of the practical decisions made on a day-to-day basis, or as the result of the large-scale machinations of historical movements guided by some invisible, and essentially inscrutable, force?

The conclusion arrived at here is that the determinants of family size are embedded in the specific social and economic aspects of each individual society. It would be inappropriate to adopt a social evolutionary approach such that relatively large kin-based families are less modern or "developed" than their smaller nuclear counterparts. Both family forms, nuclear and extended, are found across the world's cultural boundaries and time periods. There is an ethnocentric bent to the notion that family organization, characterized by sizes and types, is moving historically towards any one specific end result or another. As far as the world's families are concerned, there is no scientific basis for assuming teleological ends other than those that fulfil the practical purposes of its members.

The view emanating from the research conducted for this book is one of cultural relativism such that one's opinion as to whether a family is large or small depends on your individual perspective. A family of six persons, say, might be considered large from our perspective today, but this might not necessarily be the case in rural Ontario in the nineteenth century (in my own family of Irish immigrants, that of Catherine and Edward Hedican of Admaston Township, there were thirteen children). As far as the Irish families of Renfrew County, Ontario, are concerned, they did not exhibit any degree of uniformity to a set pattern or norm that a researcher could assert was "typical" or was the result of one particular causal determinant or another.

The point here is not that the study of family size is neither interesting nor sociologically relevant but that concern should be taken to avoid invidious comparison of sociological traits simply for the sake of matching one variable with another. The goal of such research should be to illustrate the range of social, cultural, and economic variation and thereby serve to celebrate the diversity of human family life. As Clifford Geertz (1973: 14) has written in *The Interpretation of Cultures*, culture "is not a power, something to which social events, behaviours, institutions, or processes can be causally attributed; it is a context, something within which they can be intelligibly – that is, thickly – described." As such, the elusive quest for generalizations concerning the determinants of family size and composition might well be found within cases, those "thickly" described, rather than across them.[2]

Social Class versus Social Differentiation

Throughout this study the term "social differentiation" has been used instead of "social class." Anthropologists have preferred to use "differentiation" rather than "class" for several reasons. One of these concerns the historical development of the discipline, a discipline whose research focused in its early stages primarily on hunter and gatherer populations. The main questions concerned whether such societies were primarily egalitarian, such that everyone in the society had an equal access to resources, or whether such societies were in a pre-class stage. Another reason is the operationalization of class analysis in ethnographic studies. For example, Sidky (2004: 420) has defined class as "one of several social strata whose members share similar

Conclusion 193

socioeconomic characteristics and positions, usually defined in terms of a differential access to the means of production."

The idea of linking "several social strata" to "access to the means of production" does not appear to be particularly relevant to the Irish farmers of Admaston Township; all of these farmers had an equal access to the land and productive technology in their locale, depending up their inclination to expend resources to attain their economic ends. Our study has shown that, over the decades between 1851 and 1881, there were farmers who increased their agricultural performance in comparison to their cohorts. Accounting for the reasons behind this differential performance is, of course, a difficult matter now, because we are not able to interview the farmers and ask them why they made the decisions that they did. However, we do have the results of their decisions, so if the reader is willing to engage in some extrapolation between their decision-making and the ultimate consequences of those decisions, we could posit the following trends.

Take, for example, the empirical data presented in table 23. Between 1861 and 1871 the Irish population of Admaston Township increased by 10.4 per cent (from 898 to 991 persons), yet the number of individual farms increased by 15.6 per cent (147 to 170). In other words, the number of farms increased faster that the population growth over this time. There are a few other pertinent facts relating to table 23. For example, between 1861 and 1871 the number of small farms (>100 acres) increased by three times (4 to 13), the number of medium size farms (100 to >200) decreased marginally, and the larger farms (>200 acres) nearly doubled (from 26 to 48). In other words, there were two processes at work over this period – farms were either downsized or expanded. Data presented in other tables are also pertinent to this trend. For example, in table 14, we see that the number of households whose members were working above the normal labour capacity increased from 33 per cent in 1861 to 43 per cent in 1871. In addition, as shown in table 22, family size decreased from 5.62 members in 1861 to 5.46 members in 1871.

So, to sum up, between 1861 and 1871 the overall population increased by about 10 per cent but the number of farms increased at a greater rate (at 15 per cent). Farm size increased in both the small and large categories, while family size decreased marginally. The number of households with members working above the norm increased by 10 per cent (from 33 to 43 per cent). The conclusion then is that there are two processes at work: (1) an increase in the number of small farms along with an increase in the number of farms overall indicates that some farmers are working harder to provide farms for the younger generation, and (2) some farmers are working harder to increase the size of their own farms, possibly with a view to the future in which these larger farms might be partitioned into smaller ones for the upcoming generation. Of course, one can never be certain of the motives involved, because we only have the historical facts to go on, but the assumptions made here are reasonable given the empirical data derived from the historical records (in particular, the various data contained in the Canadian census records of 1851–81).

We might now ask about the wider historical scenario involved in patterns of Irish immigration to Canada. There can be no doubt that the Great Famine was the defining moment of Irish history. No other person or series of historical events – the Viking raids (800), the Battle of Clontarf (1014), Cromwell's massacre at Drogheda and land-confiscations (1649–52), the Act of Union (1801), the Fenian Rising (1867), the Easter Rising (1916), the Civil War (1922–3), the "Troubles" in Northern Ireland (1968–98), the Good Friday Agreement (1998) – comes close to having the dramatic social, demographic, and economic impact of the Famine on the Irish population. As Donnelly and Miller (1998: xi) summarize:

> The economic power and the cultural hegemony of the Protestant upper class had vanished, while famine mortality and massive emigration had decimated the ranks of the predominantly Irish-speaking cottiers and labourers who had often resisted – sometimes violently – the process of socio-economic and cultural change.

The Famine was also the most significant line of historical demarcation for Irish emigration to Canada. As Whelan (1998: 144) states, "in the pre-famine period almost half a million Protestants emigrated from Ireland, especially from the midlands and south Leinster. Canada, and Ontario in particular, was the destination, and protracted, intense chain migration occurred." The question, then, is if the Protestant upper-class vanished because of the Famine, why did so many Protestants end up in Canada? This is an important question because a popular opinion is that the pre-Famine immigrants to Canada were wealthy Protestants, while those Irish arriving during or right after the Famine were poverty-stricken Catholics.

Donald Akenson, the pre-eminent historical source on the Irish in Ontario, has argued strongly that the Protestant (predominantly Anglican) emigrants to Canada in the pre-Famine period were not the wealthy class of landlords who subsequently vanished from Ireland's countryside. "Another of the fundamental misconceptions concerning the Old World background," Akenson (1984: 266) summarizes, "is that the Anglicans in Ireland were an upper-class Ascendency." Akenson suggests, in fact, that the greater number of Anglicans were of more modest economic status, such as teachers and skilled artisans, or were small farmers and domestic servants of the lower classes. "The real force of emigration [among Protestants] was the ambitious small farmer, artisan, or clerk" (ibid.) and not those from the upper class.

On the other hand, how about the so-called impoverished Irish Catholic immigrants; were there misconceptions concerning this group as well? According to Green's (2001: 225) summary of Irish emigration, by February 1847, "people everywhere were now seized by a panic to get out of Ireland ... The poor cottiers went first, and then in the early weeks of 1847 the small farmers began to forsake the country in droves ... more than 100,000 emigrants sailed for Canada in 1847, of whom it was estimated that at least a fifth perished of privation and disease." As far as the religious affiliation of these Irish emigrants is concerned, few exact figures were recorded; even broad estimates are lacking. James Donnelly (2001: 181–2) provides the following comments on the social profile of Irish emigrants: "We are better informed about the emigrants of the early 1850s than about those of the late 1840s. It would appear that in the years 1851–5 between 80–90 per cent of all Irish emigrants consisted of common or farm labourers and servants ... they were more likely to be Catholic, Irish-speaking, and illiterate."

Unfortunately, figures for Catholic versus Protestant emigrants are not provided, so one is only left with inferences; since the greatest numbers of emigrants were from the cottier, labourer, and servant classes, and since it is assumed that the Catholics formed the majority of these, then the assumption follows that the most destitute of the emigrants were Catholic. I do not have figures to dispute this assumption, yet the Catholics must have had some resources at their disposal to make the voyage to Canada. In addition, the assumption that emigrants sailed to Canada rather than the United States only because they were more destitute and could not afford the higher fare might not necessarily be correct. It could be that certain Irish sailed to Canada because they had relatives already living there, or that Canada provided greater opportunities because of the lower cost of farmland.

These points concerning the presumed impecunious nature of Irish Catholic emigrants to Canada are raised because of the startling agricultural success of the Irish Catholic farmers during the first decade after the initial Famine immigration period. Akenson (1984: 246–53), for example, has examined the Upper Canada (Leeds township in western Ontario) census reports for 1861 and presented the following summary of farm data based on 319 farmsteads:

	Irish-born Catholics	Irish-born Protestants	Non-Irish
Avg. cash value of farm	$1,476.20	$1,381.27	$1,026.03
Avg. cash value of implements	$65.95	$64.03	$65.46
Avg. cash value of livestock	$265.80	$265.35	$296.69
Avg. total farm enterprise	$1,807.95	$1,710.65	$1,388.18

Akenson, therefore, arrived at the following conclusions:

1 Among the immigrants the Irish-born were more successful than the non-Irish, and
2 Among the Irish immigrants, the Roman Catholics rated higher on all indices of success than did the Irish-born Protestants (1984: 247–8).

These unexpected results Akenson describes as "disquieting, or at least surprising ... this ethno-economic stratification is so perverse as to demand scores of questions" (1984: 247–8). And later, he concludes that it is "undeniable that the Catholic Irish immigrants did better than the Protestant Irish" (1984: 262). He does not accept the suggestion that Leeds Township is a mere random variation or that these results can "be wished out of existence" (1984: 249).

One explanation offered was that "the mode of agriculture that developed locally in this period ... was particularly suited to the propensities and abilities of the Irish-born" (Akenson 1984: 250); however, this reasoning can be discounted because Irish farmers in Canada were successful mixed-farm operators (raising livestock and running dairies), which was very much unlike the "spade-and-Lumper" husbandry practised back in Ireland.

Another pertinent point is that by the 1850s and early 1860s the days of free land were pretty much over in Canada West. One can assume, then, that Irish Catholics arriving in this period would by necessity have brought enough resources with them from Ireland to set up farms, thus, largely discounting the commonly held depiction of the impoverished Irish Catholic immigrant. How the Irish Catholics attained the cash needed to purchase their Canadian farms – either by selling farm holdings in Ireland, borrowing from friends and relatives who were established here, or working at various jobs after arrival – is largely irrelevant. The statistics clearly show that the Irish Catholics were more prosperous than their Protestant and non-Irish counterparts by 1860, or soon enough after the Famine.

There is no reason to delve into the statistical data on farm values any further. Suffice to say that the commonly held perception that the Irish immigrant population can be neatly divided into two classes – wealthy Protestant on the one hand, and impoverished Catholic on the other– needs revisiting and should become the subject of further research. Why this apparent misconception persists is a moot point, but there would appear to be a certain bias against the Irish Catholic population in the historical record. As Akenson (1984: 254) explains, there is a "kind of racist thinking ... once applied to the Irish to explain why they could not possibly be good farmers in the New World ... such prejudice is unacceptable [as is] the general repulsiveness of racialist explanations of human behaviour."

Concluding Comments

The intention of this book has never been to provide what might be called definitive answers to some of the outstanding questions or problems faced by anthropologists and historians in their acquisition of knowledge. The purpose, rather, has been to demonstrate that anthropological methodology, epistemology, and analysis are relevant to discussions of historical discourse. The choice to focus on the Irish of Renfrew County after the Famine was made mostly on the basis of my own personal interest in my family's Canadian origins, rather than on any burning desire to promote one theoretical approach or another.

This is not to say, however, that a focus on the history of the Irish adaptation in eastern Canada is not without scholarly merit. In fact, as the discussions in this book are meant to demonstrate, there are a variety of theoretical issues of wide significance – about the intensity of agricultural production, the nature of stem families, or the determinants of family size – which are informed by a focus on the Irish in Canada, and which are relevant to a range of academic disciplines such as social anthropology, history, rural sociology, ethno-history, and agricultural economics.

One may argue with some of the conclusions that I've reached on the various topics discussed herein (and I seriously hope that someone does!), but there can be no argument, I suggest, with the need for further anthropological studies of the historical transitions of human societies and cultures, or with the relevance of anthropological perspectives for engaging in a diversity of interesting historical contexts. I would not go so far as to say that anthropology is history or it is nothing, but it is evident that anthropologists should take the advice of their earlier predecessors and begin earnestly to expand the relevance of their discipline not only across cultural domains but across temporal frontiers as well.

Notes

1 Introduction

1 Duncan, for example, on the basis of rather slim historical evidence, maintained that "certain trends that were to become pronounced during and after the famine immigration were already evident, particularly a preference for urban life ... The widely accepted belief that the famine immigrants arrived in the port cities and never left them is quite inaccurate as far as Canada is concerned, whatever happened in the United States. As rapidly as the immigrants were moved out they began to flow back to the cities ... the immigrants have unmistakably shown a strong tendency to become urban. Thus, the typical immigrant in 1847 journeyed from rural Ireland to a port city to rural Canada and back to the city again" (ibid.: 19, 23).

   The contrary view, as stated by Akenson (1988: 17), is that "the statistically established fact is that in Canada they [Irish immigrants] were a rural people." These "statistically established facts" have been garnered by Darroch and Ornstein (1980), who studied a sample of households in the 1871 Canadian census which involved over 10,000 cases. Their conclusions were that the Irish were more likely to support themselves by farming than by any other occupation, and that most persons of Irish origin in Canada lived in small towns and in the countryside.

2 By 1901 Irish Catholics in Ontario, according to a study conducted by Peter Baskerville (2001), were just as likely to own their own homes as were the Scottish Presbyterians. In addition, Irish Catholics were more likely to achieve wealth and status in the province than were French-speaking Catholics. In urban centres the wealth differences between Irish Catholics and Irish Protestants was relatively insignificant.

3 Admaston/Bromley was incorporated in 2000 when Admaston and Bromley Townships were amalgamated. Thus, the last independent population figure for Admaston was 1,648 people in 1996 (see www.countyofrenfrew.

on.ca, retrieved on 25 April 2016). Further historical information on Admaston Township can be found in an article in the *Ottawa Citizen* (30 October 1937) on district place names in the Ottawa area.

4 The Griffith's Valuation (1847–64) was the first full-scale valuation of property in Ireland. It was overseen by Richard Griffith and published between 1847 and 1864. It is therefore considered by Irish historians as one of the most important surviving nineteenth-century genealogical sources (see http://www.askaboutireland.ie/griffith-valuation).

5 A "cottier," or "cotter," is a term for a tenant renting land from a farmer or landlord; a cottier usually occupied a cottage and cultivated small plots of land, such as an acre or two. During the Industrial Revolution in both Scotland and Ireland, many landlords realized that more money could be made by raising sheep than by cultivating crops. These landlords consequently raised rents in an attempt to dissuade cottiers from continuing their tenancy. In some cases, tenant farmers were forcibly evicted on spurious grounds, leading to a mass exodus of cottiers to industrial cities. After the Famine in Ireland the cottier class virtually disappeared (see Hickey and Doherty 1980: 98–9). For further information on Irish tenants and landlords in Ireland and Canada, see Wilson (1994, 2009).

6 I am particularly indebted to Carol McCuaig (a.k.a. Carol Bennett), Renfrew author and historian, for our numerous conversations and walking trips around Admaston Township. Much of the information here on personal lives was provided by her. This material has also been augmented by several of her own books, such as *The Kerry Chain: The Limerick Link* (McCuaig 2003), *Renfrew County People and Places* (Bennett 1989), *Founding Families of Admaston, Horton and Renfrew Village* (Bennett 1992), *Valley Irish* (Bennett and McCuaig 1983), *Renfrew County: People and Places* (McCuaig and Bennett 1989), and *People of St. Patrick's: Mount St. Patrick Parish, 1843–1993* (McCuaig 1993). In addition, several other volumes has been particularly useful in tracing the various families who emigrated to Renfrew County, such as *Tracing Your Kerry Ancestors* (O'Connor 2001) and *Tracing Your Irish Ancestors* (Grenham 1999), especially the sections on Kerry (pp. 276–81) and West Limerick (pp. 301–3).

I am also thankful to Carol for the times we spent tramping the old trails of Admaston, where she would stop occasionally and point out a depression in the ground and say, "Here was so and so's house, and the barn was over there." The fields are now all vacant, with flowing grass, but there was a time when many Irish families lived side by side throughout Renfrew County, no doubt sharing in their present struggles and reminiscing about their life back in Ireland. If you listen carefully, you can almost hear their voices still, carried along in the winds of time.

7 The significance of assisted emigration, whether privately through individual landlords, or through government programs, is a matter of some scholarly debate among Irish historians. In reference specifically to the Famine era, Anbinder (2001) suggests that emigration assistance from governments, religious and charitable organizations, or landlords resulted in only about 6 or 8 per cent of Irish emigrants in this period. Similarly, Kinealy (1994: 304) wrote that "landlord assisted emigration accounted for only about 5 per cent of the total." See also Norton's (2006: 303–9) discussion of assisted emigration, in which he suggests that many thousands of Irish, at least over 50,000 persons, were assisted by landlords to leave Ireland, figures which also correspond to MacDonagh's (1957) earlier estimates for the seven years between 1846 and 1852. Norton also cautions that it is difficult to make a clear distinction between "assisted emigration" and "compensation for surrender of land," and that "modern historians have probably understated the numbers in receipt of assistance *specifically* to emigrate" (2006: 368). Moran (1994) provides further clarification of the assisted emigration phenomenon, with specific details relating to Canada.
8 Concerning the chain migration phenomenon, Mannion (1974: 13, 16–21), cautions that political boundaries in both Canada and Ireland might lead to inaccurate conclusions; for instance, some residents might actually have lived closer to, or farther from, each other than one might assume, especially when the boundaries cut across a certain community or parish.
9 This letter is provided courtesy of Carol McCuaig, Renfrew, Ontario.
10 Will provided courtesy of Carol McCuaig, Renfrew, Ontario.
11 Determining a person's age from a census report is often a hit-and-miss affair. A census report designated for 1851, for example, might still be in the process of collection in 1852. In the absence of a parish birth record or birth certificate, census material cannot be counted upon for determining a person's age, let alone even an accurate spelling of their name. In the 1851 census Edward Hedican is listed as "Edmond Hardican" and in the later 1881 census of Renfrew North (Clare, Head, and Maria Townships) he is listed as "Edward Hennigan," with an age listed for him of 50, meaning that he would be born in 1831; however, in the 1851 census he is listed as 25 years old, meaning that he was born in 1826,. Apparently, one just gave their name and that of their family verbally to the census takers, who wrote down what they heard, or thought they heard.
12 The Walling's Map of 1863 was a subscription service in which people were charged a small fee for having their name indicated on a map. This map turns out to be of immense interest to anyone involved in historical research. For example, Edward Hedican is listed in the 1861 census as owning the 100-acre lot on concession 9, lot 11, in Admaston; one might therefore reasonably assume that he and his family lived there as well.

However, the Walling's Map shows them living on concession 7, lot 18, but whether or not Edward also owned this lot is not clear; he possibly might have been just renting a house on this property. In any event both properties are only seven lots apart, along what was then termed the "French Lake Road."

13 Purchasing land under a pre-emption process was a common practice in colonial times. Largely the program was an incentive to encourage settlement of new territories by offering land for sale at a minimal price if the tenant agreed to make improvements, such as building fences, houses, and barns, all of which had to be registered. This stipulation of registering improvements was evidently an attempt to discourage land speculators.

14 Such an example is described by Sheriff Ruttan in 1849: "With the exception of three or four pounds of green tea a year for a family, which costs us three bushels of wheat per pound, we raised everything we ate. We manufactured our own clothes ... [and] ... until within the last thirty years, one hundred bushels of wheat, at 2s. 6d. per bushel, was quite suffices to give in exchange for all the articles of foreign manufacture consumed by a large family" (James 1914: 569). Such a case could hardly be described as producing a surplus for profit in a capitalist economy.

2 Theoretical Perspectives on Farm and Family

1 The view that the social world is patterned and orderly assumes that laws are discoverable in the natural and social worlds. Emile Durkheim clearly stated the case for a positivistic science of society in *The Rules of Sociological Method*: "The first and most fundamental rule is: *Consider social facts as things*" (1938: 14). He explains further, "social phenomena are things and ought to be treated as things ... it is unnecessary to philosophize on their nature ... It is sufficient to note that they are the unique data of the sociologist ... to treat phenomena as things is to treat them as data, and these constitute the point of departure in science" (1938: 27).

2 In regard to the present study of Irish farms, there has been a lively debate for many years concerning if anthropology is, or should, be a science. Nonetheless, the various characteristics of Irish farms and families presented in this study will be considered in Durkheim's sense as "data," or part of a concrete reality, and not in some phenomenological sense whose very existence outside of the mind of the beholder is subject to debate. Of course, there have also been strong backlashes in anthropology to science, especially by the postmodernist and interpretive anthropologists who contend that science per se is an obsolete mode of enquiry. Some of this persuasion even goes so far as seeing science as immoral because it dehumanizes people by objectifying them. However, you cannot make

an opposing viewpoint go away just by criticizing it or accusing its practitioners of moral deficiencies; you must also demonstrate that this viewpoint is incorrect because it is at odds with the facts.

3 An examination of the issue of land inheritance further back in time than the nineteenth century leads to a far different picture. Upon reading Charles-Edwards's *Early Irish and Welsh Kinship* one finds an informative section on inheritance (1993: 61–73). The conclusion reached in this work is that "the evidence, then, supports the following picture of normal inheritance. Sons divide the inherited land of the father equally; he can dispose of a proportion of his acquisitions freely, but the rest can be used by the kindred to 'fill up' the shares of less fortunate kinsmen" (1993: 70). It is apparent that during this time period (dates are not specified) a more equitable distribution of a father's estate was the norm, and that the later principle of single inheritance was therefore not necessarily a "traditional" pattern of Irish land dispersal, as some might claim.

4 Of course Ireland is famous for the demographic idiosyncrasy of a very high proportion of bachelors in its population. As Connell explains, "in no other country whose statistics are available is the average age at marriage so high; in none is there so large a proportion of life-long bachelors and spinsters. The farmer, single on the average until he is 38, is the Irishman latest to marry, and of farmers between 65 and 74 one in four is still a bachelor" (1962: 502). See also Connell (1950) for information on further aspects of the Irish population, 1750–1845.

5 I am reminded at this point of Eliot Leyton's comment, made during the course of his fieldwork in an Ulster Irish village, that "the system of inheritance is open to manipulation and alteration" (1975: 79).

6 One can find similar analyses pointing to the demographic constraints on the statistical prevalence of the stem family among Basque households (Douglass 1988) and among households of central Italy (Kertzer 1989).

7 The biological aspects of family size has been the subject of a variety of other studies found in journals focusing on demography (Preston 1976), physical anthropology (Gagnon and Heyer 2000), and population studies (Wells 1992).

8 The subject of religion as a causal factor in Irish fertility patterns has been the subject of studies of Roman Catholic fertility patterns in Northern and Southern Ireland (Coward 1980), minority group status and fertility among the Irish (Kennedy 1973), and what O'Grada (1991) refers to as the "fertility transition" in Ireland between 1880 and 1911.

9 For further research into the farm size-family size hypothesis, see also studies by Hedican (2006) and Laidig, Schutjer, and Stokes's (1981) study of antebellum Pennsylvania, in which the relationship between agricultural variation and human fertility is discussed, and Cain's (1985) on the population effects of landholdings and fertility.

10 The methodology of "controlled comparison" in anthropology has a lengthy history and was developed to prevent many of the often-erroneous comparisons found in some other disciplines and in anthropology's past. As Sidky (2004: 46) explains, "Controlled comparisons involve the comparison of particular cases/societies that share certain factors in common (for example subsistence, economy, group size, sociopolitical organization, religious beliefs, and ecological setting). Selecting societies that have many things in common makes it easier to detect the factors that are constant between them. This is because the factors that are constant between them can be ruled out, or 'controlled,' as explanations for what is different between the two societies." Similarly, Salzman (2012: 68) suggests that "Controlled comparisons are made between societies or cultures that have many similarities, such that the differences that do exist can be seen to be related to other differences present. The similarities can be considered 'control factors,' in that similarities cannot be used to explain differences, which must be explained by, or at least related to, other differences." The classic papers by Fred Eggan (1954) and S.F. Nadel (1952) are the origins of this methodology in anthropology.

3 The Agricultural Conditions of Renfrew County

1 Further information on the soil conditions and general agricultural characteristics of Ontario and Renfrew County can be found in the following government reports: Nowland (1975); Webber and Hoffman (1967); Gillespie, Wickland and Matthews (1974); and Canada (1964). For an assessment of the soil conditions of southern Ontario that is closer to the time period discussed in this book, see Morwick (1932). Matthew and Gentilcore (1993) in the *Historical Atlas of Canada: The Land Transformed, 1800–1891* provide additional relevant information on the soil conditions of eastern Ontario. The reader might also profitably consult the *Census of Canada, Agricultural Profile of Ontario* (Canada 1996).
2 Crop heat units (CHUs) are based on a similar principle to growing degree days (GDDs), which are used to estimate the growth and development of plants during the growing season. Plant development is very dependent on the temperature and the daily accumulation of heat. Even though the amount of heat required to move a plant to the next development stage remains constant from year to year, the actual amount of time can vary considerably from year to year because of weather conditions. CHUs are calculated on a daily basis, using maximum and minimum temperatures. Warm-season crops do not develop at all when daytime temperatures fall below 10 degrees C, and develop fastest at about 30 degrees C. Plant development varies according to the CHUs; for example, corn development is

driven primarily by temperature, yet day length has little effect on the rate at which soybeans grow (Brown and Bootsma 1993). For examples of the calculations of CMUs see the following OMAFRA (Ontario Ministry of Agriculture, Food and Rural Affairs) website http://www.omafra.gov.on.ca/english/crops/pub811/10using.htm#chu.

3 See http://www.agr.gc.ca/eng/science-and-innovation/agricultural-practices/climate/future-outlook/climate-change-scenarios/length-of-growing-season-in-ontario/?id=1363033977515.

4 Land Use and the Allocation of Resources

1 The calculations of wood consumption in Admaston Township presented in this chapter are based on my ethnographic experiences in the 1970–80 period while I was living in a wood-heated log cabin in the Lake Nipigon area of northern Ontario among the Anishinaabe or northern Ojibwa, as described in my books *The Ogoki River Guides* (Hedican 1986) and *Up in Nipigon Country* (Hedican 2001); they are also based on my three summers (1969–72) of tree planting in the Thunder Bay area of northwestern Ontario. These experiences have given me an accurate knowledge of reforestation rates and the number of trees per acre that would be needed to heat a dwelling of the type that the eastern Ontario Irish farmers would have lived in during the nineteenth century.

The resulting calculations are based on what is usually termed a standard, or "bush," cord of wood, measured at 128 cubic feet, or a pile 4'×4'×8' in size. Of course, different trees have different heating capabilities (for example, hardwoods versus soft wood), so the calculations here are about as accurate as one could expect on average. Given all of these considerations, I estimate that, based on size data presented in the census material, the average Irish Canadian farmhouse during the historical period described in this book would consume roughly about two to three cords of wood during the winter months, and one cord or less in the warmer summer weather. Thus, an average household would use about 20 to 25 cords of wood annually for cooking and heating. With an estimate of approximately 10 to 15 bush cords of useable wood per acre of woodlot, an average household then would require about two acres of wood per year.

5 Measuring Agricultural Performance

1 There were English clerics who demonstrated a distinct lack of Christian charity by suggesting that Ireland's calamity was a form of divine retribution for its Roman Catholic citizens' having fallen into idolatry. The Reverend Hugh McNeill, for example, in a sermon at St Jude's Cathedral

in Liverpool in 1847, called the potato blight a "rod" from God: "That it is a sin against God's holy law to encourage the fables, deceits, false doctrines, and idolatrous worship of Romanism, no enlightened Christian – no consistent member of the church of England can deny" (qtd in Gallagher 1982: 84). The hypocrisy of such pronouncements was that the ultimate cause of the Famine, either directly or indirectly, was the Englishmen's bigotry towards the Irish in the first place, coupled with the hundreds of years of political and economic oppression that preceded it.

Of course, the most immediate cause of the Famine was the widespread failure of the potato crop due to spread of the fungus *Phytophthora infestans*. Other European countries also had their potato crops ruined by the blight; however, famine did not result because the people in these nations had other food sources to rely on, or had the financial means to import food to supplement existing supplies. One must dig deeper into the historical developments that led to the mass starvation in Ireland. One could start by pointing to Cromwell's invasion of Ireland (1649–50) and the large-scale land confiscations that occurred a few years later (in 1652–3). This followed from the forced removal of the Irish Catholic landowners, who were largely replaced by absentee landowners from England. Later on, the Act of Union in 1801 dissolved the Irish parliament. Under the terms of the Union, the destiny of Ireland would no longer be decided by the people of Ireland but by the members of parliament from Britain. The free-trade policy between Ireland and Britain that resulted from the Act of Union allowed for the export of food (grain, cattle, pigs, and sheep) from Ireland; even at the height of the Famine, British prime minister, Sir Robert Peel, decided against a prohibition of food exports from Ireland. The resentment of the Irish towards the English handling of the Famine left deep wounds. Furthermore, the Famine was at the root of a bitter hostility between the poor Irish tenant farmers and their landlords; this acrimony precipitated large-scale agrarian conflicts in later decades, conflicts which continued the Whiteboy disturbances of earlier times.

6 Population and Family in Transition

1 The statistical preponderance of "patri-stem" over "matri-stem" families in Admaston is probably a result of inheritance and other legal provisions. The support of elderly parents, for example, could only be ensured by making their maintenance a condition of the devolution of the farm property. Land was transmitted to males, in most circumstances, and so it follows that parents would co-reside with an inheriting son, rather than a non-inheriting daughter whose inheritance generally took the form of money, furniture, and livestock. Elliot (2004: 199) explains further: "the sometimes elaborate provisions made for widows in wills and maintenance

agreements when they were not given lifetime control over the homestead were also a direct result of the practice of transmitting land to male children. By making various arrangements for support, elderly people were able to live in their own homes independently until they died. When formerly landowning farmers or their widows did live with children, however, they normally lived with sons rather than daughters."

2 In the event that the reader is thinking "why doesn't the author follow up on these apparently excellent suggestions for further research?," I would point out that the present study was been carried on for a period of over 15 years, and it would take another 5 or 10 years of further research to pursue all of the avenues suggested here. In any event, no study is ever complete: interpretations and times change as new knowledge is gathered and assessed, so it is best that a younger generation of researchers travel down these untrodden paths, if they are so inclined.

3 Much of the literature cited in this book echoes the assumption that parental property usually devolved to the eldest son. In this regard, note Verdon's (1979) observation that internationally there would appear to be no consensus as to which son should inherit in a stem family culture. Furthermore, in a study of Irish Protestant families in eastern Ontario Elliot found that "the homestead almost always went to the youngest or second youngest, who had less time to wait ... [as] ... older sons were normally provided for as they became able" (2004: 198). Thus, the inheritance pattern that Elliot describes may well eventually end in some form of a stem family, but the pattern described is at odds with the tenor of the existing literature on the subject, in that it is normally the eldest son, not the youngest, who secures the prize.

7 The Irish Family and Household

1 Cross-cultural perspectives of Chayanov's theory have been discussed in a variety of publications, such as by M. Chibnik (1984), E.P. Durrenberger (1980, 1982, 1984), and R. Roberts and T. Mutersbaugh (1996).

2 The debate concerning Irish agricultural efficiency in the nineteenth century has been stimulated primarily by the controversial research of R.D. Crotty in his seminal work *Irish Agricultural Production: Its Volume and Structure* (1966). See also Joseph Lee (1989: 112–13, 360–1) for further discussions concerning problems in Irish agriculture.

8 Conclusion

1 Marvin Harris is an anthropologist noted for several highly scholarly texts, such as *The Rise of Anthropological Theory* (1968), as well as a number of

popular books such as *Cows, Pigs, Wars, and Witches: The Riddles of Culture* (1975). Cultural materialism focuses on the material conditions of life, such as the need to secure food and shelter. In other words, before there can be philosophy or poetry, people must protect themselves from the elements and find food to survive. The other accoutrements of culture are built up from these human needs.

2 There is no doubt that Geertz's "interpretive" view of culture has been the subject of controversy, especially for those who would claim that his theoretical proposals are basically "unscientific." Geertz, though, never claimed to be unscientific in his approach. As Geertz (1983: 4) explained, "the shapes of knowledge are always ineluctably local, indivisible from their instruments and encasements." As far as theory is concerned, he offered this somewhat inscrutable comment: "the essential task of theory building ... [is] not to generalize across cases but to generalize within them" (1973: 26). Furthermore, Geertz offered this rebuttal to the charge that his approach was anti-scientific: "I do not believe that anthropology is not or cannot be a science, that ethnographies are novels, poems, dreams, or visions, that the reliability of anthropological knowledge is of secondary interest, or that the value of anthropological works inhere solely in their persuasiveness" (1990: 274). For a more extended discussion of the interpretive controversy in anthropology, and the wider epistemological implications of anthropological knowledge and how it is derived, see Hedican (1994).

References

Akenson, D.H. 1982. "Ontario: Whatever Happened to the Irish?" In *Canadian Papers in Rural History*, vol. 3, pp. 204–6, D.H. Akenson, ed. Gananoque, ON: Langdale Press.
– 1984. *The Irish in Ontario: A Study in Rural History*. Montreal: McGill-Queen's University Press.
– 1988. "Data: What Is Known about the Irish in North America." In *The Untold Story: The Irish in Canada*, pp. 15–25, R. O'Driscoll and L. Reynolds, eds. Toronto: Celtic Arts of Canada.
– 1991. *Small Differences: Irish Catholics and Irish Protestants, 1815–1922: An International Perspective*. Dublin: Gill and Macmillan.
– 2005. *An Irish History of Civilization*, vol. 2. Montreal: McGill-Queen's University Press.
Anbinder, T. 2001. "Lord Palmerston and the Irish Famine Emigration." *Historical Journal* 44 (2): 441–69. https://doi.org/10.1017/s0018246x01001844.
Ankli, R.E., and K.J. Duncan. 1984. "Farm Making Options in Early Ontario." *Canadian Papers in Rural History*, vol. 4, pp. 33–9, D.H. Akenson, ed. Gananoque, ON: Langdale Press.
Anthony, D.W. 2007. *The Horse, the Wheel, and Language. How Bronze-Age Riders from the Eurasian Steppes Shaped the Modern World*. Princeton, NJ: Princeton University Press.
Arensberg, C.M. 1968 [1937]. *The Irish Countrymen: An Anthropological Study*. New York: The American Museum of Natural History.
Arensberg, C.M., and S.T. Kimball. 1940. *Family and Community in Ireland*. Cambridge, MA.: Harvard University Press.
Ashland Daily Press (Wisconsin, USA). 1893. "Ed Hedican Shot: A Desperate Gambler Held for Trying to Shoot an Officer." 30 March.
Bachnik, J.M. 1983. "Recruitment Strategies for Household Succession: Rethinking Japanese Household Organization." *Man* 18 (1): 160–82. https://doi.org/10.2307/2801769.

Barrett, S.R. 2009. *Anthropology: A Guide to Theory and Method.* Toronto: University of Toronto Press.

Baskerville, P. 2001. "Did Religion Matter? Religion and Wealth in Urban Canada at the Turn of the Twentieth Century: An Exploratory Study." *Social History* 34 (67): 61–95.

Bates, D.G. 1998. *Human Adaptive Strategies: Ecology, Culture, and Politics.* Boston: Allyn and Bacon.

Bennett, C. 1989. *Renfrew County People & Places.* Renfrew, ON: Juniper Books.

Bennett, C., and D.W. McCuaig. 1983. *Valley Irish.* Renfrew, ON: Juniper Books.

– 1992. *Founding Families of Admaston, Horton and Renfrew Village.* Renfrew, ON: Juniper Books.

– 2011. *Peter Robinson's Settlers.* Milton, ON: Global Heritage Press.

Bennett, J.W. 1982. *Of Time and the Enterprise: North American Family Farm Management in the Context of Resource Marginality.* Minneapolis: University of Minnesota Press.

Bhimull, C.D., E. Murphy, and M.E. Patteson. 2011. "A Prefatory Piece." In *Anthrohistory: Unsettling Knowledge, Questioning Discipline*, pp. 3–10, E. Murphy et al., eds. Ann Arbor: University of Michigan Press.

Birdwell-Pheasant, D. 1992. "The Early Twentieth-Century Irish Stem Family: A Case from County Kerry." In *Approaching the Past: Historical Anthropology through Irish Case Studies*, pp. 205–35, M. Silverman and P.H. Gulliver, eds. New York: Columbia University Press.

Bishop, C.A. 1974. *The Northern Ojibwa and the Fur Trade.* Toronto: Holt, Rinehart and Winston.

Bishop, C.A., and T. Morantz, eds. 1986. "Who Owns the Beaver? Northern Algonquin Land Tenure Reconsidered." *Anthropologica* 18 (1–2).

Bongaarts, J. 2001. "Household Size and Composition in the Developing World of the 1990s." *Population Studies* 55 (3): 263–79. https://doi.org/10.1080/00324720127697.

Boserup. E. 1965. *The Conditions of Agricultural Growth: The Economics of Agrarian Change under Population Pressure.* Chicago: Aldine.

Bourgholtzer, F. 1999. "Aleksandr Chayanov and Russian Berlin." *Journal of Peasant Studies* 26 (4): 13–164. https://doi.org/10.1080/03066159908438717.

Breen, R. 1984. "Population Trends in Late Nineteenth and Early Twentieth Century Ireland: A Local Study." *The Economic and Social Review* 15 (2): 95–108.

Brody, H. 1973. *Inishkillane: Change and Decline in the West of Ireland.* Harmondsworth, England: Penguin Books.

Brown, D.M., and A. Bootsma. 1993. *Crop Heat Units for Corn and Other Warm-Season Crops in Ontario.* Toronto: Ontario Ministry of Agriculture and Food, Factsheet Number 93–119.

Burch, T.K. 1967. "The Size and Structure of Families: A Comparative Analysis of Census Data." *American Sociological Review* 32 (3): 347–63. https://doi.org/10.2307/2091083.
– 1972. "Some Demographic Determinants of Average Household Size." In *Household and Family in Past Time*, pp. 91–102, P. Laslett and P. Wall, eds. Cambridge: Cambridge University Press.
Cain, M. 1985. "On the Relationship between Landholding and Fertility." *Population Studies* 39 (1): 5–15. https://doi.org/10.1080/0032472031000141246.
Canada. 1851, 1861, 1871, 1881. *Census of Canada, Renfrew County, Admaston Township, Ontario*. Ottawa: Government of Canada.
– 1964. *Soil Map of Renfrew County, Ontario*. Ottawa: Soil Research Institute, Agriculture Canada.
– 1996. *Census of Canada, Agricultural Profile of Ontario*. Ottawa: Statistics Canada.
– 2008. *2006 Census of Canada*. Ottawa: Statistics Canada.
– 2014. *Length of Growing Season in Ontario*. Ottawa: Agriculture and Agri-Food Canada. http://www.agr.gc.ca/eng/science-and-innovation/agricultural-practices/climate/future-outlook/climate-change-scenarios/length-of-growing-season-in-ontario/?id=1363033977515 (retrieved June 15, 2016).
Charles-Edwards, T.M. 1993. *Early Irish and Welsh Kinship*. Oxford: Oxford University Press.
Chayanov, A.V. 1966. *The Theory of Peasant Economy*. Homewood, IL: Richard D. Irwin.
Chibnik, M. 1984. "A Cross-Cultural Examination of Chayanov's Theory." *Current Anthropology* 25 (3): 335–40. https://doi.org/10.1086/203141.
Clark, S., and J.S. Donnelly, eds. 1983. *Irish Peasants: Violence and Political Unrest, 1780–1914*. Madison: University of Wisconsin Press.
Clay, D.C., and N.E. Johnson. 1992. "Size of Farm or Size of Family: Which Comes First?" *Population Studies* 46(3): 491–505. https://doi.org/10.1080/0032472031000146476.
Cohen, B.S. 1987. "History and Anthropology: The State of Play." In *An Anthropologist among the Historians and other Essays*, pp. 18–49, B.S. Cohen, ed. Oxford: Oxford University Press.
Cohen, D.W. 2009. "Unsettled Stories and Inadequate Metaphors: The Movement to Historical Anthropology." In *CLIO/ANTHROPOS: Exploring the Boundaries between History and Anthropology*, pp. 273–94, A. Willford and E. Tagliacozzo, eds. Stanford, CA: Stanford University Press.
Connell, K.H. 1950. *The Population of Ireland, 1750–1845*. Oxford: Oxford University Press.

– 1962. "Peasant Marriage in Ireland: Its Structure and Development since the Famine." *Economic and History Review* 14 (3): 502–23. https://doi.org/10.2307/2591890.

Coogan. T.P. 2002. *Wherever Green Is Worn: The Story of the Irish Diaspora*. New York: Palgrave Macmillan.

Coward, J. 1980. "Recent Characteristics of Roman Catholic Fertility in Northern and Southern Ireland." *Population Studies* 34 (1): 31–44. https://doi.org/10.2307/2173693.

Crawford, E.M. ed. 1989. *Famine: The Irish Experience, 900–1900*. Edinburgh: John Donald.

– 1997. *The Hungry Stream: Essays on Emigration and Famine*. Dublin: Institute of Irish Studies.

Crotty, R.D. 1966. *Irish Agricultural Production: Its Volume and Structure*. Cork: Cork University Press.

Cummings, H. 2000. *The Economic Impacts of Agriculture on the Economy of Lanark and Renfrew Counties*. Toronto: Ontario Ministry of Agriculture, Food, and Rural Affairs.

Currie, P. 1995. "Toronto Orangeism and the Irish Question, 1911–1916." *Ontario History* 87 (4): 397–409.

Curtin, G. 2000. *A Pauper Warren: West Limerick 1845–49*. Ballyhill, Co. Limerick: Sliabh Luachra Books.

Curtis, E. 1950. *A History of Ireland*. London: Methuen.

Darroch, A.G., and M.D. Ornstein. 1980. "Ethnicity and Occupation Structure in Canada in 1871: The Vertical Mosaic in Historical Perspective." *Canadian Historical Review* 61 (3): 305–33. https://doi.org/10.3138/chr-061-03-02.

Diamond, J. 1994 [1987]. "The Worst Mistake in the History of the Human Race." In *Applying Cultural Anthropology*, pp. 105–8, A. Podelerfsky and P.J. Brown, eds. Mountain View, CA: Mayfield Publishing.

– 1999. *Guns, Germs, and Steel: The Fate of Human Societies*. New York: W.W. Norton.

Dimatteo, L. 1996. "The Wealth of the Irish in Nineteenth-Century Ontario." *Social Science History* 20 (2): 209–34. https://doi.org/10.2307/1171237.

Dirks, N. 2002. "Annals of the Archive: Ethnographic Notes of the Sources of History." In *From the Margins: Historical Anthropology and Its Future*, pp. 47–65, B. Axel, ed. Durham, NC: Duke University.

Donnelly, J.S. 2001. *The Great Irish Potato Famine*. Gloucester: Sutton.

Donnelly, J.S., and K.A. Miller, eds. 1998. *Irish Popular Culture, 1650–1850*. Dublin: Irish Academic Press.

Douglass, W.A. 1988. "The Basque Stem Family Household: Myth or Reality?" *Journal of Family History* 13 (1): 75–89. https://doi.org/10.1177/036319908801300105.

Dressler, W., and K. Oths. 2008. "Reflections on Teaching SCRM: Survey Research Methods in Anthropology." *Practicing Anthropology* 30 (1): 40–1. https://doi.org/10.17730/praa.30.1.7331n0gu840t4265.

Duncan, K. 1965. "Irish Famine Immigration and the Social Structure of Canada West." *The Canadian Review of Sociology and Anthropology* 2 (1): 19–40. https://doi.org/10.1111/j.1755-618x.1965.tb01327.x.

Durkheim, E. 1938. *The Rules of Sociological Method*. Chicago: University of Chicago Press.

Durrenberger, E.P. 1980. "Chayanov's Economic Analysis in Anthropology." *Journal of Anthropological Research* 36 (2): 133–48. https://doi.org/10.1086/jar.36.2.3629473.

– 1982. "Chayanov and Marx." *Peasant Studies* 11 (1): 1–29.

– 1984. "Introduction: Chayanov and Agricultural Policy." In *Chayanov, Peasants, and Economic Anthropology*, pp. 1–25, E.P. Durrenberger, ed. New York: Academic Press.

Durrenberger, E.P., and N. Tannenbaum. 1979. "A Reassessment of Chayanov and His Critics." *Peasant Studies* 8 (1): 48–63.

Editorial Comment. 1984. *History and Anthropology* 1 (1): i.

Eggan, F. 1954. "Social Anthropology and the Method of Controlled Comparison." *American Anthropologist* 56 (5): 743–63. https://doi.org/10.1525/aa.1954.56.5.02a00020.

Elliot, B.S. 2004. *Irish Migrants in the Canadas: A New Approach*, 2nd ed. Montreal: McGill-Queen's University Press.

Environment Canada. 1980. *Agriculture Capability by Province-Census Division Breakdown, Quebec/Ontario*. Ottawa: Canada Land Data Systems Division, Land Data and Evaluation Branch, Land Directorate.

Etheridge, W.C. 1928. *Field Crops*. Boston: Ginn and Co.

Evans, M. 1974. "A Note on the Measurement of Sahlin's Social Profile of Domestic Production." *American Ethnologist* 2 (2): 269–79. https://doi.org/10.1525/ae.1975.2.2.02a00150.

Evans-Pritchard, E.E. 1961. *Anthropology and History*. Manchester: Manchester University Press.

– 1981. *A History of Anthropological Thought*. New York: Basic Books.

Fitzpatrick, D. 1983. "Irish Farming Families before the First World War." *Comparative Studies in Society and History* 5: 339–74.

Foster. B.L. 1978. "Socioeconomic Consequences of Stem Family Composition in a Thai Village." *Ethnology* 17 (2): 139–57. https://doi.org/10.2307/3773140.

Fried, M. 1967. *The Evolution of Political Society*. New York: Random House.

Gagnon, A., and E. Heyer. 2000. "Fragmentation of Quebec Population Genetic Pool: Evidence from the Genetic Contribution of Founders per Region in the 17th and 18th Centuries." *American*

Journal of Physical Anthropology 114 (1): 30–41. https://doi.org/10.1002/1096-8644(200101)114:1%3C30::aid-ajpa1003%3E3.0.co;2-l.
– 2001. "Intergenerational Correlation of Effective Family Size in Early Quebec (Canada)." *American Journal of Human Biology* 13 (5): 645–59. https://doi.org/10.1002/ajhb.1103.
Gallagher, T. 1982. *Paddy's Lament, Ireland 1846–1847*. New York: Harcourt Brace.
Geertz, C. 1973. *The Interpretation of Cultures*. New York: Basic Books.
– 1983. *Local Knowledge: Further Essays in Interpretive Anthropology*. New York: Basic Books.
– 1990. "Comment: Is Anthropology Art or Science?" *Current Anthropology* 31 (3): 274.
Gibbon, P., and C. Curtin. 1978. "The Stem Family in Ireland." *Comparative Studies in Society and History* 20 (3): 429–54. https://doi.org/10.1017/s0010417500009075.
– 1983. "Irish Farm Families: Facts and Fantasies." *Comparative Studies in Society and History* 25: 375–80.
Gillespie, J.E., R.E. Wickland, and B.C. Matthews. 1964. *Soil Survey of Renfrew County*. Toronto: Ontario Department of Agriculture.
Goldschmidt, W., and E.J. Kunkel. 1971. "The Structure of the Peasant Family." *American Anthropologist* 73: 1058–70.
Green, E.E.R. 2001. "The Great Famine: 1845–50." In *The Course of Irish History*, pp. 218–27, T.W. Moody and F.X. Martin, eds. Lanham, MD: Roberts Rinehart Publishers.
Grenham, J. 1999. *Tracing Your Irish Ancestors*, 2nd ed. Dublin: Gill & Macmillan.
Griffith's Valuation. 1847–1864. http://www.askaboutireland.ie/griffith-valuation/
Guillet, E.C. 1963. *The Pioneer Farmer and Backwoodsman*, vol. 1. Toronto: University of Toronto Press.
Guinnane, T. 1991. "Rethinking the Western Europe Marriage Pattern: The Decision to Marry in Ireland at the Turn of the Twentieth Century." *Journal of Family History* 16 (1): 47–64. https://doi.org/10.1177/036319909101600104.
Gulliver, P.H., and M. Silverman. 1995. *Merchants and Shopkeepers: A Historical Anthropology of an Irish Market Town, 1200–1991*. Toronto: University of Toronto Press.
Hammel, E.A. 2005. "Chayanov Revisited: A Model for the Economics of Complex Kin Units." *Proceedings of the National Academy of Sciences* 102 (19): 7043–6. https://doi.org/10.1073/pnas.0501987102.
Handelman, D. 2005. "Microhistorical Anthropology: Toward a Prospective Perspective." In *Critical Junctions: Anthropology and History beyond the*

Cultural Turn, pp. 29–52, D. Kalb and H. Tak, eds. New York: Berghahn Books.

Hannan, D. 1982. "Peasant Models and the Understanding of Social and Cultural Change in Rural Ireland." In *Ireland: Land, Politics, and People*, pp. 141–65, P.J. Drury, ed. Cambridge: Cambridge University Press.

Harris, C. 2008. *The Reluctant Land: Society, Space, and Environment in Canada before Confederation*. Vancouver: UBC Press.

– 1977. "The Simplification of Europe Overseas." *Annals of the Association of American Geographers* 67 (4): 469–83. https://doi.org/10.1111/j.1467-8306.1977.tb01156.x.

Harris, M. 1968. *The Rise of Anthropological Theory*. New York: Thomas Y. Crowell.

– 1975. *Cows, Pigs, Wars, and Witches: The Riddles of Culture*. New York: Random House.

Harris, M., and O. Johnson. 2000. *Cultural Anthropology*. Toronto: Allyn and Bacon.

Harris, R. 1988. "Theory and Evidence: The 'Irish Stem Family' and Field Data." *Man* 23 (3): 417–34. https://doi.org/10.2307/2803258.

Harrison, M. 1975. "Chayanov and the Economics of the Russian Peasantry." *Journal of Peasant Studies* 2 (4): 389–417. https://doi.org/10.1080/03066157508437947.

– 1977. "The Peasant Mode of Production in the Work of A.V. Chayanov." *Journal of Peasant Studies* 4 (4): 323–36. https://doi.org/10.1080/03066157708438028.

Hedican, E.J. 1986. *The Ogoki River Guides: Emergent Leadership among the Northern Ojibwa*. Waterloo, ON: Wilfrid Laurier University Press.

– 1994. "Epistemological Implications of Anthropological Field Work, with Notes from Northern Ontario." *Anthropologica* 36 (2): 205–24. https://doi.org/10.2307/25605771.

– 2001. *Up in Nipigon Country: Anthropology as a Personal Experience*. Halifax, NS: Fernwood Publishing.

– 2003. "Irish Farming Households in Eastern Canada: Domestic Production and Family Size." *Ethnology* 42 (1): 15–37. https://doi.org/10.2307/3773807.

– 2005. "The Ottawa Valley Irish after the Great Famine, 1851–1881: Rethinking the Stem Family Debate." *Northeast Anthropology* 69: 87–107.

– 2006. "What Determines Family Size? Irish Farming Families in Nineteenth-Century Ontario." *Journal of Family History* 31 (4): 315–34. https://doi.org/10.1177/0363199006291584.

– 2009. "Ways of Knowing in Anthropology: Alexandre Chayanov and the Perils of 'Dutiful Empiricism.'" *History and Anthropology* 20 (4): 419–33. https://doi.org/10.1080/02757200903219621.

- 2017. *The First Nations of Ontario: Social and Historical Transitions.* Toronto: Canadian Scholars Press.
Hickey, D.J., and J.E. Doherty. 1980. *A Dictionary of Irish History.* Dublin: Gill and Macmillan.
Hilts, S., and P. Mitchell. 1999. *The Woodlot Management Handbook.* Willowdale, ON: Firefly Books.
Hoffman, D.W., and H.F. Noble. 1975. *Acreage of Soil Capability Classes for Agriculture in Canada.* Toronto: Ontario Ministry of Agriculture and Food, Rural Development Branch.
Houston, C.J., and W.J. Smyth. 1978. "The Orange Order and the Expansion of the Frontier in Ontario, 1830–1900." *Journal of Historical Geography* 4 (3): 251–64. https://doi.org/10.1016/0305-7488(78)90264-5.
- 1980. *The Sash Canada Wore: A Historical Geography of the Orange Order in Canada.* Toronto: University of Toronto Press.
- 1988. "Orangemen in Canada." In *The Untold Story: The Irish in Canada,* pp. 743–52, R. O'Driscoll and L. Reynolds, eds. Toronto: Celtic Arts of Canada.
- 1990. *Irish Emigration and Canadian Settlement: Patterns, Links, and Letters.* Toronto: University of Toronto Press.
Humphries, S.C. 2011. "Between Disciplines, After Modernity." In *Anthrohistory: Unsettling Knowledge, Questioning Discipline,* pp. 252–6, E. Murphy et al., eds. Ann Arbor: University of Michigan Press.
James, C.C. 1914. *History of Farming in Ontario.* Toronto: Glasgow, Brook, and Co. (available through the Project Gutenberg EBook #30808 www.gutenberg.net)
Johannesen, A.B., and A. Skonhoft. 2011. "Livestock as Insurance and Social Status: Evidence from Reindeer Herding in Norway." *Environmental and Resource Economics* 48 (4): 679–94. https://doi.org/10.1007/s10640-010-9421-2.
Jones, R.L. 1946. *History of Agriculture in Ontario, 1613–1880.* Toronto: University of Toronto Press.
Kalb, D., and H. Tak, eds. 2005. *Critical Junctions: Anthropology and History beyond the Cultural Turn.* New York: Berghahn Books.
Kane, E. 1968. "Man and Kin in Donegal: A Study of Kinship Functions in a Rural Irish and Irish-American Community." *Ethnology* 7 (3): 245–58. https://doi.org/10.2307/3772890.
Kelly, K. 1971. "Wheat Farming in Simcoe County in the Mid-nineteenth Century." *Canadian Geographer* 15 (2): 95–112. https://doi.org/10.1111/j.1541-0064.1971.tb00146.x.
Keneally, T. 1998. *The Great Shame and the Triumph of the Irish in the English-Speaking World.* New York: Random House.
Kennedy, R.E. 1973. "Minority Group Status and Fertility: The Irish." *American Sociological Review* 38 (1): 85–96. https://doi.org/10.2307/2094333.

Keogh, W.G. 2009. "Contested Terrains: Ethnic and Gendered Spaces in the Harbour Grace Affray." *Canadian Historical Review* 90 (1): 29–70. https://doi.org/10.3138/chr.90.1.29.

Kertzer, D.I. 1989. "The Joint Family Household Revisited: Demographic Constraints and Household Complexity in the European Past." *Journal of Family History* 14 (1): 1–15. https://doi.org/10.1177/036319908901400101.

Kinealy, C. 1994. *The Great Calamity: The Irish Famine 1845–52*. Dublin: Gill and Macmillan.

Knight, F.H. 1965 [1921]. *Risk, Uncertainty and Profit*. New York: Houghton Mifflin.

Knodel, J. 1977. "Breast Feeding and Population Growth." *Science* 198 (4322): 1111–15. https://doi.org/10.1126/science.929189.

Knodel, J., and H. Kintner. 1977. "The Impact of Breast Feeding Patterns on the Biometric Analysis of Infant Mortality." *Demography* 14 (4): 391–408. https://doi.org/10.2307/2060586.

Kroeber, A. 1952. *The Nature of Culture*. Chicago: University of Chicago Press.

– 1963. *An Anthropologist Looks at History*. Berkeley: University of California Press.

Kuznets, S. 1978. "Size and Age Structure of Family Households: Explanatory Comparisons." *Population and Development Review* 4 (2): 187–223. https://doi.org/10.2307/1972278.

Labelle, K.M. 2013. *Dispersed But Not Destroyed: A History of the Seventeenth-Century Wendat People*. Vancouver: UBC Press.

Laidig, G.L., W.A. Schutjer, and C.S. Stokes. 1981. "Agricultural Variation and Human Fertility in Antebellum Pennsylvania." *Journal of Family History* 6 (2): 195–204. https://doi.org/10.1177/036319908100600205.

Laslett, P. 1972. "Introduction." In *Household and Family in Past Time*, pp. 1–89, P. Laslett and R. Wall, eds. Cambridge: Cambridge University Press.

Lee, J. 1969. "Irish Agriculture, 1815–1914." *Agriculture History Review* 17 (1): 64–76.

– 1989. *Ireland, 1912–1985: Politics and Society*. Cambridge: Cambridge University Press.

Lehmann, D. 1986. "Two Paths of Agrarian Capitalism, or a Critique of Chayanovian Marxism." *Comparative Studies in Society and History* 28 (4): 601–27. https://doi.org/10.1017/s0010417500014122.

Leyton, E. 1975. *The One Blood: Kinship and Class in an Irish Village*. St. John's, NL: Institute of Social and Economic Research, Memorial University of Newfoundland.

MacDonagh, O. 1957. "Irish Emigration to the United States of America and the British Colonies during the Famine." In *The Great Famine: Studies in Irish History 1845-1852*, pp. 319–88, R. D. Edwards and T. D. Williams, eds. Dublin: Gill and Macmillan.

MacKay, D. 1990. *Flight from Famine: The Coming of the Irish to Canada*. Toronto: McClelland & Stewart.
Mair, L. 1965. *An Introduction to Social Anthropology*. Oxford: Clarendon Press.
Maltby, A., and J. Malby. 1979. *Ireland in the Nineteenth Century: A Breviate of Official Publications*. Oxford: Pergamon Press.
Mannion, J.J. 1974. *Irish Settlements in Eastern Canada: A Study of Cultural Transfer and Adaptation*. Toronto: University of Toronto Press.
Marx, K. 1978 [1852]. *The Eighteenth Brumaire of Louis Bonaparte*. Peking: Foreign Language Press.
Matthew, G.J., and R.L. Gentilcore, eds. 1993. *Historical Atlas of Canada: The Land Transformed, 1800–1891*, vol. 2. Toronto: University of Toronto Press.
McCallum, J. 1980. *Unequal Beginnings: Agriculture and Economic Development in Quebec and Ontario until 1870*. Toronto: University of Toronto Press.
McClelland, D.C. 1961. *The Achieving Society*. Princeton, NJ: D. Van Nostrand Co.
McCuaig, C. 1993. *People of St. Patrick's: Mount St. Patrick Parish 1843–1993*. Renfrew, ON: Juniper Books.
– 2003. *The Kerry Chain: The Limerick Link*. Renfrew, ON: Juniper Books.
– 2006. "John Windle's Story." *Ballyguiltenane Rural Journal*. 28th Edition: 57–9.
McGuaig, D.W., and C. Bennett. 1989. *Renfrew County: People and Places*. Renfrew, ON: Juniper Books.
McGough, J.P. 1984. "The Domestic Mode of Production and Peasant Social Organization: The Chinese Case." In *Chayanov, Peasants, and Economic Anthropology*, pp. 183–201, E.P. Durrenberger, ed. New York: Academic Press.
McGowan, M.G. 1999. *The Waning of the Green: Catholics, the Irish, and Identity in Toronto, 1887–1922*. Montreal: McGill-Queen's University Press.
McInnis, M. 1992. *Perspectives on Ontario Agriculture, 1815–1930*. Gananoque, ON: Langdale Press.
McInnis, R.M. 1982. "A Reconsideration of the State of Agriculture in Lower Canada in the First Half of the Nineteenth Century." In *Canadian Papers in Rural History*, pp. 9–49, D. H. Akenson, ed. Gananoque, ON: Langdale Press.
McNeill, P. 2005. *Research Methods*. New York: Routledge.
Miller, B.D., P. Van Esterik, and J. Van Esterik. 2001. *Cultural Anthropology*. Toronto: Pearson Education.
Miller, K.A. 1985. *Emigrants and Exiles: Ireland and the Irish Exodus to North America*. New York: Oxford University Press.
Miller, O. 1962. *The Donnellys Must Die*. Toronto: Macmillan Co.
Mitchell, R.D. 1979. "Comment on Cole Harris: 'The Simplification of Europe Overseas.'" *Annals of the Association of American Geographers* 69 (3): 474–76. https://doi.org/10.1111/j.1467-8306.1979.tb01273.x.
Moodie, S. 1913 [1852]. *Roughing It in the Bush; Or, Forest Life in Canada*. Toronto: Bell & Cockburn.

Moody, T.W., and F.X. Martin, eds. 2001. *The Course of Irish History*. Lanham, MD.: Roberts Rinehart Publishers.

Moran, E. 2000. *Human Adaptability: An Introduction to Ecological Anthropology*. Boulder, CO: Westview.

Moran, G. 1994. "State Aided Emigration from Ireland to Canada in the 1880s." *The Canadian Journal of Irish Studies* 20 (2): 1–19. https://doi.org/10.2307/25512998.

– 2004. *Sending Out Ireland's Poor: Assisted Emigration to North America in the Nineteenth Century*. Dublin: Four Courts Press.

Morwick, F.F. 1932. *Soils of Southern Ontario*. Toronto: Ontario Department of Agriculture, Ontario Agricultural College.

Munson, M.K, and S.M. Jamieson, eds. 2013. *Before Ontario: The Archaeology of a Province*. Montreal: McGill-Queens University Press.

Murphy, E., et al., eds. 2011. *Anthrohistory: Unsettling Knowledge, Questioning Discipline*. Ann Arbor: University of Michigan Press.

Nadel, S.F. 1952. "Witchcraft in Four African Societies: An Essay in Comparison." *American Anthropologist* 54 (1): 18–29. https://doi.org/10.1525/aa.1952.54.1.02a00040.

Netting, Robert McC. 1989. "Smallholders, Householders, Freeholders: Why the Family Farm Works Well Worldwide." In *The Household Economy: Reconsidering the Domestic Mode of Production*, pp. 221–44, R.W. Wilk, ed. Boulder, CO: Westview Press.

Nicholson, M.W. 1985. "The Irish Experience in Ontario: Rural or Urban?" *Urban History Review* 14 (1): 37–45. https://doi.org/10.7202/1017880ar.

Norton, D. 2005. "On Landlord-Assisted Emigration from Some Irish Estates in the 1840s." *The Agricultural History Review* 53 (1): 24–40.

– 2006. *Landlords, Tenants, Famine: The Business of an Irish Land Agency in the 1840s*. Dublin: University College Dublin Press.

Nowland, J.L. 1975. *Agricultural Productivity of the Soils of Ontario and Quebec*. Ottawa: Department of Agriculture, Research Branch.

O'Connor, M.H. 2001. *Tracing Your Kerry Ancestors*, 3rd ed. Dublin: Flyleaf Press.

O'Driscoll, R., and L. Reynolds, eds. 1988. *The Untold Story: The Irish in Canada*. Toronto: Celtic Arts of Canada.

O'Grada, C. 1991. "New Evidence on the Fertility Transition in Ireland, 1880–1911." *Demography* 28 (4): 535–48. https://doi.org/10.2307/2061421.

O'Grada, C., and B. Walsh. 1995. "Fertility and Population in Ireland, North and South." *Population Studies* 49 (2): 259–79. https://doi.org/10.1080/0032472031000148506.

O'Hara, P. 1998. *Partners in Production? Women, Farm, and Family in Ireland*. New York: Berghahn.

O'Mahoney, C., and V. Thompson. 1994. *Poverty to Promise: The Monteagle Emigrants, 1838–1858*. Darlinghurst NSW, Australia: Crossing Press.

O'Neill, K. 1984. *Family and Farm in Pre-Famine Ireland: The Parish of Killashandra*. Madison: University of Wisconsin Press.

O' Sullivan, P. 2003. "Developing Irish Diaspora Studies: A Personal View." *New Hibernia Review* 7 (1): 130–48. https://doi.org/10.1353/nhr.2003.0031.

Ottawa Citizen. 1937. Origin of Place Names in District: Admaston. 30 Oct.

O'Tuathaigh, G. 1972. *Ireland before the Famine, 1798–1848*. Gill History of Ireland, vol. 9. Dublin: Gill & Macmillan.

Pollack, A. 1979. "Commentary – Europe Simplified." *Annals of the Association of American Geographers* 69 (3): 476–77. https://doi.org/10.1111/j.1467-8306.1979.tb01274.x.

Power, T.P. 1991. *The Irish in Atlantic Canada, 1780–1900*. Fredericton, NB: New Ireland Press.

Preston, S.H. 1976. "Family Sizes of Children and Family Sizes of Women." *Demography* 13 (1):105–14. https://doi.org/10.2307/2060423.

Ray, A.J. 1974. *Indians and the Fur Trade*. Toronto: University of Toronto Press.

Redclift, M.R. 2003. "Community and the Establishment of Social Order on the Canadian Frontier in the 1840s and 1850s: An English Immigrant's Account." *Family and Community History* 6 (2) 97–106. https://doi.org/10.1179/fch.2003.6.2.003.

Perry, R.J. 2003. *Five Key Concepts in Anthropological Thinking*. Upper Saddle River, NJ: Prentice-Hall.

Roberts, R., and T. Mutersbaugh. 1996. "On Rereading Chayanov: Understanding Agrarian Transitions in the Industrialized World." *Environment and Planning* 28: 1–12.

Rudolph, R.L. 1992. "The European Peasant Family and Economy: Central Themes and Issues." *Journal of Family History* 17 (2): 119–38. https://doi.org/10.1177/036319909201700202.

Russell, B.H. 2002. *Research Methods in Anthropology*. Walnut Creek, CA: Altamira Press.

Russell, P.A. 1982. "Upper Canada: A Poor Man's Country? Some Statistical Evidence." In *Canadian Papers in Rural History*, vol. 3, pp. 129–47. D.H. Akenson, ed. Gananoque, ON: Langdale Press.

– 2012. *How Agriculture Made Canada: Farming in the Nineteenth Century*. Montreal: McGill-Queen's University Press.

Ryan, P. 1991. "A Study of Irish Immigration to North Hastings County." *Ontario History* 83 (1): 23–37.

Sahlins, M. 1971. "The Intensity of Domestic Production in Primitive Societies: Social Inflections of the Chayanov Slope." In *Studies in Economic Anthropology*, pp. 30–51, G. Dalton, ed. Washington, DC: American Anthropological Association.

Salazar, C. 2003. "Demographic Growth and the 'Cultural Factor' in Ireland: Rethinking the Relationship between Structure and Event." *History and Anthropology* 14 (3): 271–81. https://doi.org/10.1080/0275720032000154561.

Salzman, P.C. 2012. *Classic Comparative Anthropology: Studies from the Tradition.* Long Grove, IL: Waveland Press.

Schneider, H.K. 1974. *Economic Man: The Anthropology of Economics.* Salem, WI: Sheffield Publishing.

Scott, W. 2000. "'An Unprecedented Influx': Nativism and Irish Famine Immigration to Canada. *American Review of Canadian Studies* 30 (4): 429–53. https://doi.org/10.1080/0272201000948106.

Segalen, M. 1986. *Historical Anthropology of the Family.* Cambridge: Cambridge University Press.

Shanin, T. 1990. *Defining Peasants: Essays Concerning Rural Societies.* Oxford: Blackwell.

Shimizu, Y. 2016. *Studies of Post-1841 Irish Family Structures.* Osaka: St Andrew's University Research Institute.

Shortall, S. 1993. "Canadian and Irish Farm Women: Some Similarities, Differences and Comments." *The Canadian Review of Sociology and Anthropology* 30 (2): 172–90. https://doi.org/10.1111/j.1755-618x.1993.tb00171.x.

Sidky, H. 2004. *Perspectives on Culture: A Critical Introduction to Theory in Cultural Anthropology.* Upper Saddle River, NJ: Pearson Prentice Hall.

Silverman, M., and P.H. Gulliver, eds. 1992. *Approaching the Past: Historical Anthropology through Irish Case Studies.* New York: Columbia University Press.

– 2005. "Historical Anthropology through Local-Level-Research." In *Critical Junctions: Anthropology and History beyond the Cultural Turn,* pp. 152–67, D. Kalb and H. Tak, eds. New York: Berghahn Books.

Sivakumar, S.S. 2001. "The Unfinished Narodnik Agenda: Chayanov, Marxism and Maginalism Revisited." *Journal of Peasant Studies* 29 (1): 31–60. https://doi.org/10.1080/714003931.

Skeoch, A.E. 1982. "Developments in Plowing Technology in Nineteenth-Century Canada." In *Canadian Papers in Rural History,* vol. 3, pp. 156–77, D.H., Akenson ed. Gananoque, ON: Langdale Press.

Skinner, G.W. 1993. "Conjugal Power in Tokugwa Japanese Families: A Matter of Life or Death." In *Sex and Gender Hierarchies,* pp. 236–70, B.D. Miller, ed. New York: Cambridge University Press.

Smith, A.E. 1979. "Chayanov, Sahlins, and the Labor-Consumer Balance." *Journal of Anthropological Research* 35 (4): 477–80. https://doi.org/10.1086/jar.35.4.3629542.

Stocking, G.W. 1968. *Race, Culture, and Evolution: Essays in the History of Anthropology.* New York: The Free Press.

– 1985. *Objects and Others: Essays on Museums and Material Culture*. History of Anthropology Series, vol. 3. Madison: University of Wisconsin Press.

Strickland, S. 1970. *Twenty-Seven Years in Canada West*, vol. 1. Edmonton: M.G. Hurtig.

Symes, D.G. 1972. "Farm Household and Farm Performance: A Study of Twentieth Century Changes in Ballyferriter, Southwest Ireland." *Ethnology* 11 (1): 25–38. https://doi.org/10.2307/3773158.

Tagliacozzo, E., and A. Willford. 2009. "History and Anthropology: Strange Bedfellows." In *CLIO/ANTHROPOS: Exploring the Boundaries between History and Anthropology*, pp. 1–26, A. Willford and E. Tagliacozzo, eds. Stanford, CA: Stanford University Press.

Tannenbaum, N. 1984a. "The Misuse of Chayanov: Chayanov's Rule and the Empirical Bias in Anthropology." *American Anthropologist* 86 (4): 927–42. https://doi.org/10.1525/aa.1984.86.4.02a00060.

– 1984b. "Chayanov and Economic Anthropology." In *Chayanov, Peasants, and Economic Anthropology*, pp. 27–38, E.P. Durrenberger, ed. San Fancisco, CA: Academic Press.

Thwaites, R.G., ed. "1896–1901." *The Jesuit Relations and Allied Documents*. Cleveland: Burrows Brothers.

Tilley, C. 1978. "Anthropology, History, and the *Annales*." *Review* 1 (3/4): 207–13.

Trigger, B.G. 1985. *Natives and Newcomers: Canada's "Heroic Age" Reconsidered*. Montreal: McGill-Queen's University Press.

– 1986. "Evolutionism, Relativism and Putting Native People into Historical Context." *Culture* 6 (2): 65–79.

– 1987. *The Children of Aataentsic. A History of the Huron People to 1660*. Montreal: McGill-Queen's University Press.

Tucker, G. 1931. "The Famine Immigration to Canada, 1847." *American Historical Review* 36 (3): 533–49. https://doi.org/10.2307/1837913.

United States Department of Agriculture. 2017–18. *World Agricultural Production*. https://www.fas.usda.gov/data/world-agricultural-production.

Vanhaute, E. 2004. "Structure and Strategy: Two Rural Communities in the Kempen Region of Belgium, 1850–1910." *History of the Family* 9 (2):193–220. https://doi.org/10.1016/j.hisfam.2004.01.004.

Varley, A. 1983. "The Stem Family in Ireland Reconsidered." *Comparative Studies in Society and History* 25: 381–95.

Vaughn, W.E., ed. 1989. *A New History of Ireland: Ireland under the Union*. Oxford: Clarendon Press.

Verdon, M. 1979. "The Stem Family: Towards a General Theory." *Journal of Interdisciplinary History* 10 (1): 87–105. https://doi.org/10.2307/203302.

Vincent, S. 2012. *Dimensions of Development: History, Community, and Change in Allpachico, Peru.* Toronto: University of Toronto Press.

Webber, L.R., and D.W. Hoffman. 1967. *Origin, Classification and Use of Ontario Soils.* Toronto: Ontario Department of Agriculture and Food.

Wells, R.W. 1992. "The Population of England's Colonies in America: Old English or New Americans?" *Population Studies* 46 (1): 85–102. https://doi.org/10.1080/0032472031000146026.

Wharton, C.R. 1971. "Risk, Uncertainty, and the Subsistence Farmer: Technological Innovation and Resistance to Change in the Context of Survival." In *Studies in Economic Anthropology*, pp. 152–78, G. Dalton, ed. Washington, DC: American Anthropological Association.

Whelan, K. 1998. "An Underground Gentry? Catholic Middlemen in Eighteenth-Century Ireland." In *Irish Popular Culture, 1650–1850*, pp. 118–72, J.S. Donnelley and K.A. Miller, eds. Dublin: Irish Academic Press.

Wilson, C.A. 1994. *A New Lease on Life: Landlords, Tenants, and Immigrants in Ireland and Canada.* Montreal: McGill-Queen's University Press.

– 2009. *Tenants in Time: Family Strategies, Land, and Liberalism in Upper Canada, 1799–1871.* Montreal: McGill-Queen's University Press.

Wilson, D.A. 1989. *The Irish in Canada.* Ottawa: Canadian Historical Association.

Wilson, D.A., ed. 2007. *The Orange Order in Canada.* Dublin: Four Courts Press.

Wilson, H.K., and W. M. Meyers. 1954. *Field Crop Production: Agronomic Principles and Practices.* Chicago: J.B. Lippincott Co.

Wilson, T.M., and H. Donnan. 2006. *The Anthropology of Ireland.* New York: Berg.

Wolf, E.R. 1955. "Types of Latin American Peasantry: A Preliminary Discussion." *American Anthropologist* 57 (3): 452–71. https://doi.org/10.1525/aa.1955.57.3.02a00050.

– 1966. *Peasants.* Englewood Cliffs, NJ: Prentice-Hall.

– 1982. *Europe and the People without History.* Berkeley: University of California Press.

Woodham-Smith, C. 1962. *The Great Hunger: Ireland 1845–1849.* New York: Old Town Books.

Index

Admaston Township: description of, 17–19; land use in 1851, 81; land use in 1861, 82; land use in 1871, 83–4; population structure of, 129–32; Irish population in, 133–5
agricultural production: theories of, 45–8; factors related to, 6, 180–1; variations in, 84–5; wheat, 85–7, 99; oats, 87–9, 99–100; potatoes, 89–91, 100; barley, peas, and hay, 91–3, 99; Admaston and all-Ontario compared, 98–101
Agriculture Canada, data on length of growing season in Ontario, 70–1
Akenson, D.H., 3, 10, 12, 13, 14, 15, 16, 62, 195–7, 199n1
Anbinder, T., 201n7
Ankli, R.E., 17
Anthony, D.W., 95
anthropology and history. *See* history and anthropology
Arensberg, C.M., 4, 41, 52–3, 136–8, 149
Ashland Daily Press (Wisconsin, USA; 30 March 1983), 28

Bachnik, J.M., 30
Barrett, S.R., 191

Baskerville, P., 199n2
Bates, D.G., 77
Bennett, C., 10, 21–2, 80, 96, 200n6
Bhimull, C.D., 40
Birdwell-Pheasant, D., 48, 50, 52, 147, 149, 188
Bishop, C.A., 176–7
Boas, Franz, on historical particularism, 35
Bongaarts, J., 56–7, 160
Bootsma, A., 205
Boserup. E., 108
Bourgholtzer, F., 47
Breen, R., 54, 146
Brody, H., 52–3
Brown, D.M., 205
Burch, T.K., 56

Cain, M., 203n9
Canadian Immigrant (13 July 1833), 63–4
capitalist production, discussion of, 182–3. *See also* commodity production; socio-economic differentiation; subsistence economy
Census of Canada, Agricultural Profile of Ontario, 1996, 75, 204n1

Census of Canada 1871, Renfrew County, 88, 101, 116, 145, 171, 173
Census of Canada 1881, Renfrew County, 27, 116, 145, 171, 172, 201n11
Census of Canada 1996, Renfrew County, 75
Census of Canada West 1851, Renfrew County, 23, 27, 81, 93, 116, 170, 173, 201
Census of Canada West 1861, Renfrew County, 26, 27, 116, 141, 170, 171, 172
chain migration, 21–2
Charles-Edwards, T.M., 203n3
Chayanov, A.V., 43, 108
Chayanov's theory of domestic production, 43, 46–8, 67, 108–9, 178–80, 185–6; operationalizing Chayanov's theory, 109–12; discussion of, 114–16, 125–6, 142–3, 162–3, 181; economic perspectives on, 164–5
Chibnik, M., 207n1
childhood dependency ratio, in Ireland and Admaston, 138–43
Clare Champion (Ireland), xiii
Clark, S., 10, 34
Clay, D.C., 58–9, 168
Cohen, D.W., 38–9
commodity production, definition of, 30–1, 32; versus capitalist production, 182–7; discussion of, 185–6. *See also* peasant economics; subsistence economy
conacre system, description of, 148
Connell, K.H., 49, 51–2, 156, 161–2, 187, 203n4
consumer, definition of, 111
Coogan, T.P., 11, 35
cottier (cotter), definition of, 200n5
Coward, J., 203n8

Crawford, E.M., 12
crop heat units (CHUs), 204–5n2. *See also* Bootsma, A.; Brown, D.M.
Crotty, R.D., 207n2
Cummings, H., 70–1, 73, 75–6
Currie, P., 14
Curtin, C., 48–9, 50–1, 53–5, 146, 149, 187
Curtin, G., 18, 26

Darroch, A.G., 15, 199n1
Diamond, J., 45, 85, 95
Dimatteo, L., 14
Dirks, N., 40
Doherty, J.E., 200n5
domestic mode of production. *See* subsistence economy
Donnan, H., 4
Donnelly, J.S., 10, 12, 13, 34, 194–5
Douglass, W.A., 48, 52, 203n6
Dressler, W., 115
Duncan, K.J., 13, 17, 199n1
Durkheim, E., 202n2
Durrenberger, E.P., 47, 125, 207n1

economic differentiation. *See* socio-economic differentiation
egalitarian society, discussion of, 122
Eggan, F., 204n10
Elliot, B.S., 3, 12, 22, 154–5, 157, 190, 206–7n1, 207n3
Environment Canada, soil classifications, 72
Etheridge, W.C., 89
ethnographic present, concept of, 40–2
Evans, M., 47
Evans-Pritchard, E.E., 36

family farm, adaptive strategies of, 77–8
family size: theories of, 44; comparative approaches,

53; historical approaches, 53–4; gendered approaches, 54–5; research approaches, 55–6; determinants, 56, 189–92; biological factors, 56–7; cultural factors, 57–8; economic factors, 58, 164–5; in 1996, 71; as an adaptive response, 159–60; as related to population size, 160–3; as an aspect of household size, 165–8; as a variable factor, 173–5

Fitzpatrick, D., 50, 53, 146, 187
Foster, B.L., 48
Fried, M., 32

Gagnon, A., 56, 59, 203n7
Gallagher, T., xi, 12, 13, 94, 100, 206n1
Geertz, C., 192, 208n2
Gentilcore, R.L., 204n1
Gibbon, P., 48–9, 50–1, 53–5, 57, 146, 149, 187
Gillespie, J.E., 204n1
Goldschmidt, W., 48
Green, E.E.R., 11, 195
Grenham, J., 200n6
Griffith's Valuation, 1847–1864, xiii, 18, 200n4
Guillet, E.C., 65, 66, 79
Guinnane, T., 49, 52
Gulliver, P.H., 4, 37–8, 39

Hammel, E.A., 48
Handelman, D., 39
Hannan, D., 49
Harris, C., 6, 9, 17, 150
Harris, M., 33, 191, 207–8n1
Harris, R., 48, 187
Harrison, M., 47
Hedican, E.J., 5, 43, 47–8, 52, 105, 203n9, 205n1, 208n2
Heritage Renfrew Archives, xiv

Heyer, E., 56, 57, 59, 203n7
Hickey, D.J., 200n5
Hilts, S., 105
Historical Atlas of Canada, 98, 100–3
History and Anthropology, "Editorial Comment," 37
history and anthropology: relationships between 35–8; historical ethnography 38; as anthrohistory 40; lesson about, 176–8
Hoffman, D.W., 72–3, 204n1
households, definition of, 29–30, 110; structure and composition, Ireland and Admaston compared, 143–8; as an aspect of farm size, 168–73
Houston, C.J., 4, 12, 13, 14
Humphries, S.C., 41

inheritance: issues of, 25–7, 48, 50–1, 149; and family structure, 154–5, 157
Irish emigration: to Canada 8–11; Irish diaspora, characteristics of, 11–12; statistics, 13–16, landlord assisted 20–1
Irish families, in Canada and Ireland, 148–52
Irish Heritage Day (17 March), 10
Irish persons, in Renfrew County, 19–29
Irish settlement: of Renfrew County, 16–7
Irish stem families. *See* stem families

James, C.C., 64, 202n14
Jamieson, S.M., 5
Johannesen, A.B., 96
Johnson, N.E., 58–9, 168
Johnson, O., 33
Jones, R.L., 63, 65–6, 79, 86, 88, 99–100, 127, 183, 185

Kalb, D., 39
Kane, E., 45, 53
Kelly, K., 86, 99
Keneally, T., xi
Kennedy, R.E., 203n8
Keogh, W.G., 14
Kertzer, D. I., 203n
Kimball, S.T., 4, 52, 136–8, 149
Kinealy, C., 201n7
Kintner, H., 142
Knight, F.H., 78
Knodel, J., 142
Kroeber, A., 35
Kuznets, S., 56

Labelle, K.M., 5
Laidig, G. L., 203n9
Laslett, P., 48, 52
Lee, J., 163, 207n
Lehmann, D., 47
Leyton, E., 203n5
livestock production, 95–8; Admaston and all-Ontario compared, 101–3

MacDonagh, O., 201n7
MacKay, D., 4, 12
Mair, L., 35, 36–7
Malby, A., 10
Malby, J., 10
Malthus, Thomas, theory of, 107–8, 161–3
Mannion, J.J., 3, 10, 12, 201n8
marriage age, in Ireland and Admaston, 135–8
Martin, F.X., 11
Matthew, G.J., 204n1
Matthews, B.C., 204n1
Marx, K., 190
McCallum, J., 6–7, 64–5, 66, 79, 86, 99, 127, 183–5
McClelland, D.C., 179

McCuaig, C., 20, 22, 24, 200n6, 201nn9–10
McCuaig, D.W., 200n6
McGough, J.P., 186
McGowan, M.G., 14
McInnis, M., 86, 126
McInnis, R.M., 126
McNeill, P., 115
Meyers, W.M., 85, 87, 93
Miller, B.D., 33
Miller, K.A., 13, 21, 194
Miller, O., 14
Mitchell, P., 105, 151
Moodie, S., 15
Moody, T.W., 11
Moran, E., 77, 201n7
Moran, G., 12, 20
Morantz, T., 177
Morwick, F.F., 204n1
Munson, M.K., 5
Murphy, E., 40
Mutersbaugh, T., 207n1

Nadel, S.F., 204n10
National Archives of Ireland, xiii
National Library of Ireland, xiii
Netting, R. McC., 30, 33
Nicholson, M.W., 14
Noble, H.F., 72–3
Norton, D., 20–1, 201n7
Nowland, J.L., 204n

O'Connor, M.H., 200n1
O'Driscoll, R., 10
O'Grada, C., 57–8, 203n8
O'Hara, P., 54
O'Mahoney, C., 20
O'Neill, K., 37, 90, 97–8, 100, 106, 125, 133, 135, 137, 139, 141–2, 149, 166, 174
Ontario Land Registry Office (Pembroke), xiii

opportunity cost, concept of, 29, 104
Ornstein, M.D., 15, 199n1
O'Sullivan, P., 35
Oths, K., 115
Ottawa Citizen (30 October 1937), 17, 200n3
O'Tuathaigh, G., 4, 11, 18, 137

patrilocal residence, definition of, 111
Patterson, M.E., 40
peasant economics, 31–4. *See also* subsistence economy
Perry, R.J., 32
Pollack, A., 151
positivism, definition of, 44
Power, T.P., 10
Preston, S.H., 203n7

Ray, A.J., 176
Redclift, M.R., 10
Reynolds, L., 10
Roberts, R., 207n1
Rudolph, R.L., 34
Russell, B.H. 115
Russell, P.A., 6, 8, 17, 33–4, 63, 65–6, 67, 79
Ryan, P., 10, 11

Sahlins, M., 45, 47–8, 116, 180
Salazar, C., 56–7, 59, 145
Salzman, P.C., 204n10
Schneider, H.K., 29, 30
Schutjer, W.A., 203n9
Scott, W., 14
Segalen, M., 48, 52
Shanin, T., 32
Shimizu, Y., 160
Shortall, S., 55
Sidky, H., 30, 36, 192–3, 204n10
Silverman, M., 4, 37–8, 39
Sivakumar, S.S., 47

Skeoch, A.E., 96
Skinner, G.W., 30
Skonhoft, A., 96
Smith, A.E., 47
Smyth, W.J., 4, 12, 13, 14
socio-economic differentiation: measurements of, 122–5; among Irish farmers, discussion of, 181–2; and social class, 192–7
soil conditions, of Renfrew County, 68–76, 151
Soil Map of Renfrew County, Ontario (1964), 204n1
stem family: theories about, 43–4, 152–4; characteristics of, 48–55, 145–6, 175; theoretical focus on, 187–9. *See also* households; Irish families
Stocking, G.W., 36
Stokes, C.S., 203n9
Strickland, S., 65
subsistence economy, definition of, 30–1. *See also* capitalist production; commodity production; peasant economics
systematic sampling, description of, 115–19
Symes, D.G., 45–6, 53

Tagliacozzo, E., 39
Tak, H., 39
Tannenbaum, N., 47
theoretical goals and objectives, 42–4
Thompson, V., 20
Thwaites, R.G., 177
Tilly, C., 38
Treaty of Niagara (1764), 5
Trigger, B.G., 177
Tucker, G., 13

Upper Canada (1850), characteristics of, 5–8

Van Esterik, J., 33
Van Esterik, P., 33
Vanhaute, E., 48
Varley, A., 51, 187
Vaughn, W.E., 12
Verdon, M., 48, 156, 207
Vincent, S., 32

Walling's Map of 1863, 201–2n12
Walsh, B., 57–8
Webber, L.R., 204n1
Weber, Max: concept of ideal types, 33; Protestant ethic and capitalism, 179

Wells, R.W., 203n7
Wharton, C.R., 78
Whelan, K., 194
Wickland, R.E., 204n1
Willford, A., 39
Wilson, C.A., 3, 200n5
Wilson, D.A., 10, 14
Wilson, H.K., 85, 87, 93
Wilson, T.M., 4
Wolf, E.R., 32–3, 34, 39
Woodham-Smith, C., xi
woodlot, importance to farm economics, 103–6
worker, definition of, 111

www.ingramcontent.com/pod-product-compliance
Lightning Source LLC
Chambersburg PA
CBHW022215090526
44584CB00012BB/562